CHOMP COMP
The Small Business Guide to Lower Workers' Comp Premiums

Barry S. Spurlock
Keith R. Wertz

Copyright ©2007 Barry S. Spurlock and Keith R. Wertz

Library of Congress Catalog Number: 200790744

ISBN: 0-9797127-2-6
ISBN13: 978-0-9797127-2-2

Published by Lighted Path Publishers, LLC, Louisville, KY

Printed in the United States of America
10 9 8 7 6 5 4 3 2 1

All rights reserved. No part of this publication may be reproduced, stored in a retrieval system or transmitted in any form or by any means, electronic, mechanical, photocopying, recording or otherwise, without the prior written permission of the publisher.

Lighted Path Publishers, LLC and the authors of this publication make available the information contained within this publication for informational purposes only. While it is the intent and belief that the information will be helpful, no warrantee, expressed or implied, is extended that the information contained herein is accurate or complete. As workers' compensation legislation, administrative rules and practices of insurance providers vary significantly, the information provided in this publication is general in nature, and may not apply to particular factual or legal circumstances. Furthermore, the information contained in this publication does not constitute legal or professional advice and should not be relied upon as such. Should you require legal advice, you are encouraged to consult competent, licensed legal counsel.

This book contains copyrighted material owned by the National Council on Compensation Insurance, Inc. (NCCI), which is used with NCCI's permission. NCCI's material may not be reproduced, in whole or in part without NCCI's express written consent.

Scripture taken from the HOLY BIBLE, NEW INTERNATIONAL VERSION®. Copyright © 1973, 1978, 1984 International Bible Society. Used by permission of Zondervan. All rights reserved.

The "NIV" and "New International Version" trademarks are registered in the United States Patent and Trademark Office by International Bible Society. Use of either trademark requires the permission of International Bible Society.

Scripture quotations marked NLT are taken from the Holy Bible, New Living Translation, copyright 1996, 2004. Used by permission of Tyndale House Publishers, Inc., Wheaton, Illinois 60189. All rights reserved.

Scripture taken from the New King James Version. Copyright © 1982 by Thomas Nelson, Inc. Used by permission. All rights reserved.

Contents

1 THE SMALL BUSINESS CHALLENGE
You're Not Alone 15
Maybe Size Does Matter 16
A Built-in Bias 18
It's Just Not Fair 21

2 THE ABC'S OF WORKERS' COMP
Knowledge is Power 23
A Compromise 24
Sources of Coverage 25
The Same But Different 27
A Foundation to Build Upon 30

3 ALL I KNOW IS THAT IT COSTS TOO MUCH
Insert Yourself into the Process.. 31
The Manual Premium 32
Experience Rating 36
Discounts, Credits and Debits 38

4 CLASSIFIED INFORMATION
Classified Information 41
Classifications and Ratings Bureaus 42
What's the Big Deal 44
An Honest Mistake 45
An Ounce of Prevention.. 46
Correcting the Mistake.. 47

5 JUMPING THROUGH HOOPS
Legislated Premium Discounts 49
Safety Management Program 50
Safety Committees.. 52
Safety Inspections 52
Investing in Safety 52
Drug Free Workplace Programs 53
But Wait There's More 53
Criteria Determined by the Insurance Company 54
Workplace Safety Premium Debits 54
Initiative Required 54

6 WHO'S WEARING THE SAFETY HAT?
Designating a Safety Coordinator 57
A Healthy Perspective 58
A Key Figure 59
An Effective Communicator 60
The Ideal Candidate 61

7 ACCIDENT PRONE
Unlucky at Life 63
The Errors of Our Ways 64
Identify the Repeaters 66
Focus on the Problem 67
Search for Common Ground 68
A Plan of Attack 71

8 ERECTING ROADBLOCKS
You're Not Immune 73
Injury Prevention 75
Due Diligence 76
Education 78
Communication 79
Early Return to Work 80
Difficult to Maneuver 81

9 TO CATCH A THIEF
A Thief by Any Other Name 83
No Small Business Immunity 84
Are Red Flags being Raised? 85
Injury Reporting 85
What Other Employees Say 86
Description of the Injury 86
Employment Status 87
Financial Pressures 87
Evasiveness 88
Personal Ties 88
Attitude 89
Seeking a Settlement 89
Medical Treatment 90
Unmasking the Thief 91

10 DON'T SHOULDER THE BURDEN YOURSELF

No one Man is an Island 93
A Firm Foundation 95
Assembling the Team 96
How it Works 96
Summary 100

11 A "HIGH" PRIORITY

A Pervasive Problem 101
Through the Eyes of Small Business Owners 103
Small Businesses are Targeted 104
The Solution 104
Overcoming Obstacles 106
Drug-Free Workplace Resources 107

12 LESS THAN FULL STRENGTH

The Choice is Yours 111
What's in it For Me? 112
Lowers Premiums 113
Discourages Fraud 113
Helps Healing 115
Improves Morale 115
Confronting the Myths 116
Modified Duty within Small Businesses 117

13 LET THE GAMES BEGIN

Competition Breeds Lower Premiums 121
Monopolistic States 122
Competition Among Agents and Brokers 122
Competition among Insurance Carriers 124
Comparing Apples to Apples 125
More than Premium 126
Ability 126
Liability 127
Stability 128
Dependability 129
Price 130

14 MARKETING 101

TIME FOR ANOTHER HAT 133
CREATING TOP OF MIND AWARENESS 134
REPETITION 135
VARIETY OF MEDIUMS 136
PERCEIVED IMPORTANCE 137
CREATING BUZZ 138
DEVELOPING A MARKETING STRATEGY 139

15 YOU DIDN'T HIRE GUINEA PIGS

TRULY PROACTIVE 141
THE TERM PROACTIVE AND ITS MISUSE 142
HOW DO YOU SELECT THE GUINEA PIG? 144
HOW TO BE PROACTIVE WITH SAFETY 145
BEING REACTIVE IS IMPORTANT TOO 146
THE BOTTOM LINE 147

16 THINK YOU'RE TOO SMALL FOR A WRITTEN PROGRAM?

THINK AGAIN! 149
WHY IS A FORMAL, WRITTEN PROGRAM SO IMPORTANT? 150
IMPORTANT CHARACTERISTICS OF A GOOD SAFETY PROGRAM 152
IN SUMMARY 155

17 LOOKING FOR TROUBLE

IDENTIFYING AND CONTROLLING HAZARDS 157
IDENTIFICATION OF HAZARDS 158
CHOMP COMP DEFINITION OF HAZARD 158
HAZARD IDENTIFICATION PROCESS 160
CONTROLLING HAZARDS 164
SUMMARY 168

18 MEASURING UP

AN HONEST PERSPECTIVE OF SAFETY PERFORMANCE 169
TRAILING INDICATORS VS. LEADING INDICATORS 170
THE PROBLEM WITH TRAILING INDICATORS 172
LEADING INDICATORS: YES IT IS FEASIBLE TO USE THEM! 177

19 SAFETY AND LOSS CONTROL TRAINING

MAXIMIZING VALUE 181
TRAINING VS. EDUCATION.. 183
THE NECESSITY OF GOOD TRAINING 184
WHAT IS GOOD TRAINING? 184
VERIFYING THE EFFECTIVENESS OF TRAINING 190
YOU DON'T HAVE TO BE PERFECT 190
METHODS OF DELIVERING TRAINING 191
TRAINING SUPERVISORS 192
TRAINING FUNDAMENTALS 193

20 ERGONOMICS

WHAT IS ERGONOMICS?.. 195
TWO SMALL BUSINESS MISCONCEPTIONS 196
WHAT ARE THE RISK FACTORS?... 199
LISTEN TO YOUR EMPLOYEES' BODY LANGUAGE................................... 201
HOW TO CONTROL RISK FACTORS 202
REGULATORY TRENDS 203

21 LONG-TERM HEALTH EFFECTS

ANSWERING TOUGH QUESTIONS 205
UNDERSTANDING EXPOSURE.. 207
TIME IS OF THE ESSENCE 208
ROUTES OF EXPOSURE.. 208
BREAKING IT DOWN: KEY TERMINOLOGY 209
KNOWING HOW MUCH IS TOO MUCH 213
CONTROLLING EXPOSURES 214
ROLE OF THE MSDS 215
RESOURCES 215
NATURAL DOESN'T NECESSARILY MEAN SAFE 216
OBVIOUS RED FLAGS 216

22 FIT FOR DUTY

FIT FOR DUTY.. 219
BUT WE'RE TOO SMALL.. 220
WHAT DO THE UNDERWRITERS THINK? 221
KNOW YOUR NETWORK 222
THE POWER TO CHOOSE 222
HEALTH & WELLNESS INITIATIVE IDEAS 223
MAKING THE IDEAS WORK.. 224

23 LEGAL PITFALLS

I Thought Workers' Comp Was Legal Protection 227
Who Made You The Judge? 228
Paramount Protection 230
Knowing When to Keep Your Pie Hole Shut 231
Third Party Liability 232
Disciplinary Action 233
Modified Duty ≠ Immunity 234
Screening Pre-Existing Conditions 234
Ensuring Attorney Suitability 235
Disclaimer 236

24 THERE'S NO SHAME IN ASKING FOR HELP

Looking Beyond Yourself 237
Insurance Loss Control Consultants 238
I'm From the Government and I'm Here to Help 241
OSHA Consultation Programs 241
College Interns 243
Private Sector Safety Consultants 244
You Gotta Ask 246

25 HELP IS AT YOUR FINGERTIPS

Help is at Your Fingertips 247
Your Insurance Company's Website 248
Your State's Workers' Compensation Website 249
OSHA's Website 249
Other Beneficial Web Resources 250

26 THE SECRET WEAPON

Unveiling the Secret Weapon 257
Proper Perspective 258
A Helping Hand 259
Tapping into Unlimited Power 260
Conclusion 265
Comments and Questions 265

About the Authors

Barry S. Spurlock

Barry has extensive experience as a safety professional working in manufacturing, insurance loss control and in academia. He holds a Bachelor's degree in Industrial Safety and Risk Management and a Master's degree in Loss Prevention and Safety Administration, both from Eastern Kentucky University. He currently works as a loss control consultant with Midwestern Insurance Alliance and as a principal consultant with his own firm, Spurlock & Higgins, LLC. In addition to his current consulting capacities, Barry has been an adjunct faculty for Indiana University since 2002, teaching various courses for students pursuing degrees in occupational safety management and safety science. Barry is an active member of the American Society of Safety Engineers and is a frequent speaker at regional, corporate, state and national safety conferences. He lives with his wife Candace and two children, Emma and Emory, in Louisville, KY.

Keith R. Wertz

Keith has 15 years of insurance loss control experience, and currently serves as the Loss Control Manager for Midwestern Insurance Alliance. In that capacity he directs and provides consultative loss control services to a clientele comprised largely of small businesses. He holds a Master's degree in Loss Prevention and Safety Administration from Eastern Kentucky University and is an active professional member of the American Society of Safety Engineers. Keith is the co-author of "Managing Workers' Compensation: A Guide to Injury Reduction and Effective Claim Management" and has been a repeat speaker at state safety conferences. He resides in Lexington, KY with his wife Deena and is a father of three, a grandfather of six, and serves as a deacon in his local church congregation.

Preface

Small businesses are the life-blood of the U.S. economy. A staggering 98% of all private-sector businesses in the United States are small businesses. 87% have fewer than 20 employees. With very few exceptions, these employers are required to provide their employees with workers' compensation coverage. For many, the cost of providing that coverage takes a significant bite out of their company's profits.

Through individual consultations, the authors of CHOMP COMP have had the distinct honor and privilege of working with hundreds of small business owners and managers to better manage their workers' compensation costs. Through those consultations and the relationships formed in the process, the authors of CHOMP COMP became convinced that it's not a lack of desire that keeps small businesses from controlling the cost of their workers' compensation premiums aggressively. Instead, it's a lack of knowledge.

Unfortunately, resources that are specifically targeted to assist small businesses reduce their workers' compensation costs are nearly non-existent. As a result, the overwhelming majority of small business employers learn how to control the cost of their workers' compensation premiums through years of trial and error. The result is that they pay for those years of errors through much higher than necessary workers' compensation premiums.

CHOMP COMP is written specifically to small businesses owners and managers and is intended to be used as a resource and guide for companies with fewer than 100 employees. It is not written for large corporations that have staff safety professionals, a risk manager or an occupational nurse. It is written with the full understanding that the individuals who will be reading this book wear many hats and, despite the significance of the topic, cannot devote a great deal of their time to it.

Although CHOMP COMP assumes that the small business owner or manager knows nothing about workers' compensation insurance, it does not delve into impractical timelines explaining the evolution of workers' compensation insurance. Nor does it list specific details about workers' compensation legislation that are bound to change in some jurisdictions within months of the book's publication. Instead, CHOMP COMP provides practical information to help small business employers and managers understand workers' compensation insurance and the factors that can influence premiums now an in the years to come. From there, it tackles those factors one after another.

The authors have taken great effort to present the material in an easy to-read format and have intentionally limited the length of the chapters to enable small business employers and managers to read and digest chapters in the spare 15 to 20 minutes they can carve out of their busy schedules. If you are a small business owner or manager, it is the hope, and indeed the prayer of the authors that this book will provide meaningful guidance in your efforts to take a bite out of your workers' compensation premium.

Acknowledgements and Dedication

Above all, we desire to thank our Lord and Savior Jesus Christ for His sacrifice and gift of eternal life. We acknowledge that every ounce of strength; every ability; and indeed every breath we take is all because of His grace and mercy. We pray that everything that is done through this book ultimately brings glory and honor to Him. We would like to thank everyone at Midwestern Insurance Alliance for their support, and particularly Norm, Marc and Kent Risen and Cathy New for the opportunity and privilege to work for such a first-rate organization.

To my devoted wife Deena, thank you for the faith that you place in me and for being the glue that bonds our home together. To my children Nick, Brittany and Nathan, nothing has given me greater joy than to see each of you accept God's gift of forgiveness and salvation through Jesus Christ. To Mark and Gloria Hester; and Perry and Kristie Dressler, thank you for your friendship and prayers, both are invaluable to me. Finally, to my co-author Barry, you are indeed a credit to the safety profession. I count it a privilege to call you a friend.
- Keith

To my loving wife Candace, words cannot express my undying love for you. I'm forever grateful for all your support and the numerous nights you've had an empty pillow beside you while I labored on this project. You are an amazing gift from God that I don't deserve. To Emma and Emory, thank you for being the wonderful children you are and for your sacrifice of quality time with dad. The two of you inspire me to be a better man. I am humbled and honored that God would entrust me to be your dad. To my parents, Bobby and Marilyn, thank you for all the sacrifices you made, always challenging me, instilling in me the value of hard work and most importantly for raising me in a Christian home. To Lindsay, Papaw, Granny and Aunt Sharon, thank you for your love, support and positive impact you've had on my life. I also want to thank Dr. Earl Blair of Indiana University for his friendship, mentorship and inspiration. Finally, and certainly not least, I want to thank my co-author, Keith, for his friendship, Christian fellowship, inspiration, support and understanding for all my shortcomings.
- Barry

CHAPTER 1

The Small Business Challenge

Although competing in the same marketplace, there are inherent differences between small businesses and their larger counterparts. Knowing these differences creates a well-informed consumer of workers' compensation insurance and alerts small business owners and managers of the need to take action.

You're Not Alone

It's probably safe to assume that most adult Americans have daydreamed about the prospect of going into business for themselves. It appears that more than ever before, many have taken the leap from fantasy to reality. Give some thought to the prevalence of small businesses within the United States, or even within the town in which you live. Simply attempt to count the small businesses (those that employ less than 100 employees) on your commute to or from work. For most of us, there are just too many to count. That is an incredible testament to the entrepreneurial spirit of the American people.

According to 2004 U.S. Census Bureau statistics, more than half of the people employed in the private sector are employed by businesses that have fewer than 100 employees. Even more revealing about the prevalence of small business is the fact that 98% of all private-sector business establishments in the U.S. employ fewer than 100 employees; 91% employing less than 20 workers. Incredibly, that's only 9% of private sector businesses that have 20 employees or more.

Despite the overwhelming prevalence of small businesses in the United States, success in a small business is not guaranteed. Many reliable statistics suggest that only half of small businesses remain in operation 5 years after their inception. However, an incredible number of small businesses not only survive, they thrive year after year.

Some of the reasons for the success of small businesses are the very characteristics that distinguish them from their larger counterparts. The ever-changing nature of business relationships, consumer needs, product marketing, delivery methods and virtually every other aspect of business is a reality that gives small businesses the advantage. The very nature of small businesses makes change quicker and easier than it is in larger companies. Simply put, it's much easier to turn around a small speedboat than it is to change the direction of a massive cruise ship. Furthermore, small businesses can typically be more responsive to customer needs and desires; can more aptly mirror the values of the local community; and can function more within the realm of customer loyalty.

Maybe Size Does Matter

Unfortunately, not all of the characteristics of small businesses are advantageous. In fact many of the very things that make small businesses unique also work to their detriment. Small businesses, with very few exceptions, must play by the same rules as the much larger companies. Small businesses must wade through the same governmental red-tape, adhere to the same restrictions, comply with the same laws as the larger companies, and they must do so with considerably fewer resources.

Regardless of whether or not there are blood-relatives working together, many small businesses function as a family. For that reason, there is typically an innate concern for protecting each employee from being injured at work. Despite that concern, small businesses typically do not employ individuals with specialized training and expertise in areas directly relating to injury prevention, claims management and insurance. In fact, few even have laypersons working within their ranks that are comfortable enough with their abilities to consider themselves competent in those disciplines. In short, large businesses frequently have the council of experts that small businesses lack. The result is that large businesses are in a better position to be more effective than small businesses at the things that influence workers' compensation premiums.

Not only do small businesses frequently lack the ability to hire individuals with specialized knowledge in safety, insurance and claims management, but much of time the owners and managers of small businesses are spread unbelievably thin. In fact, the owners and managers within small businesses typically perform such a wide range of duties that they often fail to afford due attention to addressing the aspects of business management that have the most profound impact upon workers' compensation premiums. Because small business owners are spread so thin, the squeaky wheel gets the grease. It's an unfortunate reality, until there's a workers' compensation claim, responsibilities such as sales, production, hiring, firing, billing, and appeasing customers, are the wheels that are squeaking much louder than the one labeled "workers' compensation."

Traditionally, small businesses have not been well served by the safety and health community. Most of the regulations to which all companies are obligated to comply have been written with the large employers, not small businesses, in mind. Likewise, the enforcement efforts have, by and large, sidestepped the small business community, and by default have sent the message that small businesses are on their own. Even some workers' compensation insurance companies focus their consultative loss control assistance on policyholders that pay the largest premiums.

A Built-in Bias

As presented so far, some of the very characteristics that set small businesses apart are the same characteristics that make it difficult for them to compete on a level playing field with their larger counterparts. To add insult to injury, some characteristics over which small business owners have little or no control also make it difficult for them to obtain reasonably priced workers' compensation coverage. In fact, workers' compensation insurance, in many ways, has a built-in bias against small businesses.

First, insurance carriers incorporate a premium discount when providing a quote for workers' compensation coverage. As the premium increases in size, so does the discount. This is done for at least two reasons.

One reason is that premiums paid by large companies are attractive to insurance carriers, thus making them more eager to offer a premium discount to attract their business. In this respect, insurance companies are no different than any other business. If you owned a doughnut shop and had one customer who ordered 1 doughnut to eat for breakfast and another who ordered 1,000 to feed the participants of a convention, you would be much more likely to provide a discount to the latter customer in an attempt to secure future large orders.

A second reason that workers' compensation carriers offer premium discounts to larger companies is that the administrative costs incurred by the insurance carrier do not increase proportionately with the number of employees. Although a company with 350 employees has 10 times the number of employees as a small business that only has 35 employees, the administrative costs incurred by the insurance company for the larger company are not ten times that of the smaller company. It doesn't take ten times longer to review the application, calculate a premium quote and to issue a policy for the larger company. Nor does it take ten times the resources for the insurance company to provide consultative loss control services to the 350-employee company.

Regardless of the reasoning, the fact still remains that small businesses are placed at a financial disadvantage because their premium is likely not sufficient to warrant a significant premium discount, if any at all.

Premium discounts are not the only disadvantage to small businesses that is built into workers' compensation insurance. Although each state has unique rules relating to workers' compensation, most jurisdictions only permit companies with a workers' compensation premium in excess of a specified threshold to be "experience-rated." For example, state workers' compensation rules may dictate that only companies with an annual premium of $5,000 or more for 3 consecutive years may be "experience-rated." The experience rating process is described in much greater detail in a later chapter of this book. For now, it will suffice to describe it as the process by which premiums are adjusted, based upon your company's past workers' compensation claims history. Put in practical terms, your small business may have gone 6 years without a workers' compensation claim and receive no automatic premium reduction as a result, simply because your company's insurance premium is too small. However, a larger company, even if only slightly over the "experience rating" threshold, may receive a substantial premium reduction for having the same workers' compensation claims record.

You may be screaming "foul" by now. But there is justification for excluding small businesses from the experience rating process. Think back to your high school or college years. Do you recall a statistical principal called Bernoulli's law, or the "law of large numbers?" The principal states that with a large enough number of trials, the experimental probability gets very close to the theoretical probability. On the surface this may appear to have absolutely nothing at all to do with workers' compensation premiums. However, consider the fact that workers' compensation premiums are based on the insurance company's prediction of what your company will cost them in claims during the policy year. One thing at which the insurance company looks to make that prediction is the number and cost of claims that your company submitted in the past. However, the law of large numbers implies that the more employees you have, the more accurate your company's past claims experience is going to be in predicting your future claims experience. Hence the fewer employees your company has, the less reliable your past claims will be in predicting the future. Since companies that have small premiums have relatively few employees, the past workers' compensation claims are less likely to be an accurate predictor of future claims. In that respect, insurance companies are taking more of a gamble when insuring small companies. To offset that gamble, they are more apt to charge full fare for the ride.

Regardless of whether your premium is sufficient to allow your company to be experience rated, the insurance company will also take into consideration the "loss ratio" for the company. If you hated math in high school and now own a small business, you're going to like it even less. Basic math is the enemy to small businesses when considering the concept of a loss ratio. Quite simply, the loss ratio of a company is the ratio between the amount of money that the insurance company is holding in reserve to pay for the claim (medical costs, wage-replacement and other benefits), and the amount of money that has been paid to the insurance company in workers' compensation insurance premiums.

Consider a small business with an annual workers' compensation premium of $4,500 in which an employee slipped and fell on the ice and broke his collarbone. In this example, the total incurred amount paid by the insurance company was $9,000. If that were the only workers' compensation claim that the small business submitted during that year, the loss ratio would be 200% ($9,000 divided by $4,500). That's not too attractive to an insurance company that requires no more than a 70% loss ratio just to break even. However, that same claim incurred by a company with a $90,000 premium would have a much less significant impact upon the loss ratio.

If you haven't already been thoroughly disgusted with the manner in which the system appears to penalize small businesses, consider the fact that some insurance companies who provide workers' compensation coverage have a self-imposed minimum premium threshold. For example, an insurance company may arbitrarily set their minimum premium threshold at $10,000. If you operate a small business and have an annual workers' compensation premium of $7,500, they will not insure your company. That automatically reduces the number of insurance companies from which you can seek quotes for coverage. Simply because of the size of your premium, you may not be able to find competitive workers' compensation coverage from any insurance company and thereby be relegated to your state's alternative.

It's Just Not Fair

Despite the overwhelming presence of small businesses in the United States, small business owners and the managers within them have an uphill battle to fight if they intend to come out on top.

First, as a person within a small business charged with the responsibility of securing workers' compensation coverage, you must recognize that there are inherent differences between your company and the medium and large sized companies. Some of these differences are to your advantage, such as the relative flexibility of small businesses. However other differences, such as not having specialized expertise on your staff to wade through the issues of insurance, injury prevention and claims management are to your detriment.

You must also be aware that your company is placed at a disadvantage to larger companies based almost exclusively on the amount of premium your company pays. It's somewhat of a catch 22 that the less you pay in premiums, the less favorably the workers' compensation system treats you when calculating your future premiums.

Seeking workers' compensation coverage for a small business is analogous to running in a marathon with hundreds of thousands of other business owners. Side-by-side you stand at the starting line beside owners of companies large and small, each waiting for the pop of the starting gun. However before the race, you and each small business owner running the race are required to place a ball and chain around your ankles. Don't be discouraged. You may not sprint into first place, but with persistence and a strategy to prevent and control loss, you can finish strong. In fact, you will finish ahead of your small business counterparts that leave workers' compensation and loss control to chance.

CHAPTER 2

The ABC's of Workers' Comp

What is workers' compensation? When is it required? What are the benefits? These are just a few of the questions that are answered in this brief chapter. Without unnecessarily delving into the history of workers' compensation, this chapter provides the foundational knowledge that is necessary to understand the remainder of the book.

Knowledge is Power

Simply put, knowledge is power. The more you know, the more you can influence the conditions that impact you and your company. This is true in virtually every aspect of business, and it is certainly true with respect to workers' compensation insurance. Far too many owners and managers of small businesses accept their limited knowledge of workers' compensation as sufficient for their needs. They rely upon professionals such as claims adjusters, insurance agents and others to walk them safely through the minefield of workers' compensation. However, people outside of your company must balance your interests with their own. The truth is, if you desire to reduce the cost of your workers' compensation premiums now and in the years to come (and who doesn't) a superficial knowledge of workers' compensation is insufficient. This book provides the foundational knowledge you will need to make a difference and take a bite out of your workers' compensation premiums.

No assumptions are made that you have any specific knowledge of workers' compensation or the actions that can be taken to control the cost of workers' compensation premiums. As such, the chapter begins with the basics. What is workers' compensation? When is it required? What are the benefits? This is the foundational knowledge that you will need to understand the remainder of this book. It does not provide a chronological history of workers' compensation or other information that you can live without. What is included in this chapter is quite simply required knowledge for any small business owner or manager.

A Compromise

Workers' compensation insurance was created as a compromise between employees and their employers. Through their workers' compensation provider, employers agreed to pay for work-related injuries, regardless of who was at fault. In return for that promise to pay, employees forfeited their right to sue their employer because they were injured at work. That basic premise remains today.

Although having assurance that medical bills and lost wages for work-related injuries will be paid is indeed beneficial to employees, workers' compensation is not considered by most to be an employee benefit. Instead, it is a legally mandated right. With a very limited number of exceptions for such things as business owners, independent contractors, farm workers and unpaid volunteers, employers are required to maintain workers' compensation coverage for their employees. In fact, many small business owners are surprised to learn that family members are not necessarily excluded from coverage simply because of they are kin. There are fines and other forms of punishment for businesses and business owners who do not provide coverage as required by law.

Although it is far from perfect, taking a few minutes to consider the alternative (i.e. no workers' compensation insurance) forces the sobering realization that you are far better-off with the current system than without it. If an employer were to be taken to court every time an employee was injured (or claimed to be injured) many small companies would be forced out of business. This would undoubtedly quench the entrepreneurial spirit of many would-be small business owners and stifle the U.S. economy.

Sources of Coverage

Although laws require that employers maintain workers' compensation insurance, there are several sources from which it can be obtained. These include state-operated insurance programs, private insurance companies, government-established funds, assigned-risk pools and self-insurance programs.

A handful of states operate as "monopolistic" states. This means that that state has created a virtual monopoly with respect to workers' compensation coverage. In these states, employers have no choice but to purchase their workers' compensation policy from the government-run workers' compensation fund.

In states that are not monopolistic, private insurance companies are the most common source from which workers' compensation coverage is obtained. Because private insurance companies are competing for business, this is frequently called the "competitive market." However, private insurance providers do not always compete for every company's business. In fact, there are some businesses that many private insurance companies choose not to insure. These include start-up businesses that have not yet proven their ability to prevent and control losses, businesses that have a poor workers' compensation claims history, and businesses in high hazard industries such as roofing and coal mining. Many multi-line insurance companies seek to package workers' compensation insurance with other forms of business insurance. There are also regional insurance providers who specialize in providing workers' compensation insurance alone. The later are referred to as mono-line workers' compensation carriers.

In addition to monopolistic systems and private insurance companies, some states operate government-established workers' compensation funds, but permit employers other options when selecting a workers' compensation provider. In these states, the government-established fund accepts those who are unable to obtain workers' compensation coverage in the competitive market, but also tries to attract more desirable businesses through competitive pricing.

In states that do not operate government-established funds, "assigned risk pools" are the where companies must go to obtain coverage if they cannot buy coverage in the competitive market. However, the assigned risk pool is generally the most costly source for workers' compensation coverage. If you absolutely must use the assigned risk pool, your company will be assigned to an insurance company that agrees to do business with the assigned risk pool. The reality is that the insurance companies to which these businesses are assigned are accepting the business grudgingly, which often is apparent in the quality of service provided.

Self-insuring for workers' compensation is an option for some employers. State laws in most states permit employers to self-insure, which involves paying for workers' compensation claims out-of-pocket. The laws that govern self-insurance however, include financial requirements established by state law that make self-insurance virtually impossible for many small businesses.

Lastly, group self-insurance is a source for workers' compensation coverage in many states. Group self-insurance is where two or more employers enter into agreements to pool their workers' compensation liabilities for the purpose of qualifying as a self-insurer. There are two types of group self-insurers, homogeneous self-insurers and heterogeneous self-insurers. Homogeneous self-insurers are employers engaged in the same type of business, such as a group of automotive dealers. Heterogeneous self-insurers (also called common self-insurers) are employers that may be dissimilar in their business activity. Although group self-insurance may be able to offer a slightly lower premium than a private insurance company, it is important to remember that every member in the group self-insurance arrangement is financially liable for its own claims, as well as workers' compensation claims of the other members of the group.

The Same But Different

The laws that govern workers' compensation are state laws. In fact, not only does each of the 50 states have its own unique workers' compensation laws, but so do the U.S. territories of Puerto Rico, Guam, the U.S. Virgin Islands, and American Samoa, not to mention federal workers' compensation laws that cover employees of the U.S. government. Although most of them are similar in many respects, the differences among the state workers' compensation laws make it very difficult to make almost any generalized statement about workers' compensation law that is universally applicable. However, there are a few generalizations that can be made about workers' compensation law.

One such generalization is that workers' compensation law provides for benefits to be paid regardless of fault. It makes no difference if an injury was the result of an employee's utter carelessness, or if the failure of the employer to provide proper training caused the injury. In short, there is no need for finger-pointing, because workers' compensation is no-fault insurance. Just because fault is not an issue in determining whether an injury is a workers ' compensation claim, that does not mean every injury that occurs while the employee is on-the-clock will be deemed to be compensable. Stipulations within state workers' compensation laws typically allow the insurance carrier to deny claims for work-related injuries that occur as a result of horseplay, intoxication, intentional acts and a very few other scenarios.

In addition to being no-fault insurance, workers' compensation insurance coverage is uniform within each state. Defined by state statute, benefits include medical treatment, rehabilitation, lost-wage replacement, permanent impairment payments and burial benefits. There are not policy options to choose from, nor does workers' compensation coverage differ from one insurance carrier to the next.

Additionally, most workers' compensation policies also include employers' liability coverage, which is insurance coverage that is intended to pay damages for law suits stemming from a workers' compensation claim. The general exception to packaging workers' compensation and employers' liability insurance together are the monopolistic states. If your business is in one of the handful of monopolistic states, you will likely need to purchase employers' liability insurance separately.

Yet another generalization that can be made concerning workers' compensation is that the medical expenses of the injured employee are paid by the workers' compensation provider without any deductible or co-pay required of the injured employee. Relative to medical expenses, many states use a fee schedule to determine the amount payable for compensable medical expenses. As such the workers' compensation provider frequently pays less for a compensable medical expense than an employer would pay if he were to pay for the same medical treatment out-of-pocket.

In addition to medical expenses, workers' compensation coverage pays benefits to employees who are disabled (temporarily or permanently unable to work) as a result of their work-related injury. Although the specific monetary amounts paid vary from one state to the next, these disability benefits are generally described as temporary total disability, temporary partial disability, permanent total disability, or permanent partial impairment.

Temporary Total Disability

Temporary Total Disability is paid for the time period an employee is completely unable to perform work because of an injury. It is commonly paid at the rate of two-thirds (2/3) of the employee's pre-injury average weekly wage, and is subject to a maximum period, which is defined differently by each state.

Temporary Partial Disability

Temporary Partial Disability is paid when the employee is partially unable to work. For example, an employee's injuries might limit the number of hours an employee is able to work, or might involve an employee who is temporarily assigned to a job that pays less than his pre-injury job. In states that have temporary partial disability benefits (some do not) the benefits are commonly paid at the rate of two-thirds (2/3) of the difference between the employee's pre-injury and post-injury average weekly wages, and are also subject to a maximum defined by each state.

Permanent Total Disability

In general terms, Permanent Total Disability awards are paid when it is known that the employee will never again be able to work as a result of his injury. However, frequently state workers' compensation laws takes into account an employee's age, education, training and experience in making the determination of whether he is capable of substantial gainful employment.

Permanent Partial Impairment

In addition to medical expenses and disability benefits, workers' compensation also pays benefits for permanent impairments resulting from a work-related injury. These are often called Permanent Partial Impairment benefits. Impairment means the partial or total loss of the function of a part of the body. In many states these benefits are paid according to a schedule. In other words, the state law governing workers' compensation ties a maximum dollar figure to the loss of a hand, foot, thumb, eye, etc. However, other states calculate these benefits based upon the injured employee's average weekly wage or degree of impairment.

Death Benefits

In the event of a compensable work-related fatality, workers' compensation benefits are paid to the surviving spouse and dependent children. Except in situations in which the deceased employee has no dependents, the benefit amount is determined by the loss of income being produced by the deceased worker. As such, not only the wage of the deceased employee, but also his age, and the age of his dependent children are taken into consideration in determining the benefit amount. In the absence of a spouse or dependent children, most state workers' compensation laws provide for defined burial benefits.

A Foundation to Build Upon

This chapter has provided the foundational knowledge of workers' compensation. However, it is strongly recommended that you not rely upon this information alone as your knowledge-base of workers' compensation insurance. Because workers' compensation statutes differ from one state to the next, it is important that you become familiar with your state's rules. Most states have handbooks for employers that provide detailed descriptions of worker' compensation rules and procedures within the respective state. Many of these handbooks are made available free of charge and are posted on the states' web-sites. The Internet addresses and contact information for each state's workers' compensation agency is provided in "Appendix A."

CHAPTER 3

All I Know is that It Costs Too Much

Although it is among the most costly expenses, many small business owners have an inadequate understanding of how workers' compensation premiums are calculated. Through both explanation and example, this chapter presents the process of calculating workers' compensation insurance premiums. The myth that workers' compensation premiums are a fixed and unalterable business expense is dispelled in this chapter, providing the small business owner with both hope and confidence that he can take a bite out his workers' compensation premiums.

Insert Yourself into the Process

Although the topic of calculating workers' compensation premiums is not likely one that will have you on the edge of your seat, it is a topic that is absolutely essential for owners and managers of small businesses to understand. After all, it is very likely that the reason that you are reading this book is that you want to have a significant impact upon your future workers' compensation premiums. In other words, you want to insert yourself into the premium calculation process. But, you cannot do that effectively until you first understand the process.

Through both explanation and example, this chapter will present a broad overview of calculating workers' compensation premiums. You will likely be introduced to some new terms such as "manual rate," "manual premium," "experience modifier," and "scheduled credits." If you have focused solely on the bottom-line in the past, you may find it beneficial to have a copy of your own company's workers' compensation policy or a recent quote from an insurance carrier in-hand when reading through this chapter.

The Manual Premium

The process for calculating a company's workers' compensation premium can be viewed as a three-step process. The first step that insurance underwriters go through is determining the "manual premium." Although the last two steps can make significant adjustments to the manual premium, it is important to remember that it is the manual premium that determines your premium more so than anything else. Calculating the manual premium is a relatively simple process. However, you must first be familiar with three terms, "classifications," "manual rate" and "estimated payroll."

Classifications

Classifications are the fundamental building block upon which workers' compensation premiums are built. In general terms, they are job descriptions and are usually determined, at least initially, by the insurance agent or insurance carrier. Each employee falls within a particular classification based the overall business activity, or (under special circumstances) based upon the type of work performed by an individual employee. As you may have guessed, there are many different classifications. Some are very similar to one another. For example, there is a classification for truck drivers who travel within a 200 mile radius and a different classification for truck drivers who travel long distances. There is a classification for employees who work on the retail floor of a building materials dealer and different classification for the employees who work in the "yard" of a building materials dealer, loading trucks and operating forklifts. However, there are a finite number of classifications. So there simply cannot be one that describes every individual's job duties exactly. Instead, employees are categorized into the classification that is the best fit. The following is an example of a classification.

CODE 3300 –
BED SPRING OR WIRE MATTRESS MANUFACTURING

Code 3300 is assigned to insureds engaged in the manufacture of metal bed springs or wire mattresses. Steel or iron wire, iron or steel angle, channel bar, strip and tubing stock, rivets, nuts and bolts, paint and lacquer are received from others. The operations involve the fabricating of the wire into spiral coils, curled mesh and diversely twisted links on power machines specifically fitted for such dies. The coils are then tempered and the stock is machined to form the frame. The springs are then fastened to the frames with hand pliers and riveted by hand or machine. This classification is also applied to insureds engaged in the manufacture of automobile cushions or seats, folding couches or daybeds, gliders or similar products composed of metal springs and attached to metal frames. The finished products are dipped in paint tubs or sprayed with lacquer by compressed air sprays and then baked.

Figure 3. 1

The classification used above is from the classification system that was developed by the National Council on Compensation Insurance (NCCI) which currently includes approximately 600 different job classifications.

Note that the classification in figure 3.1 has a numerical code associated with it. This is commonly called the "classification code." It is merely a number used in the insurance industry as a means of abbreviating the classification description. The most commonly used classification code in the NCCI system is 8810, as that is the classification code that represents clerical workers.

Although some states use their own classification system, three-fourths of the states rely upon the NCCI classification system. The book that contains the written description for each of the NCCI classification codes is called the "Scopes® of Basic Manual Classifications" (also known simply as the Scopes® Manual). If yours is a state that uses the NCCI system for classification codes, you will want to remember the name of that manual. It will come in handy later.

Manual Rates

For each classification, there is a corresponding rate that the insurance carrier charges for workers' compensation coverage. These rates are called the "manual rates," and are expressed in the amount charged for each $100 in payroll.

Quite a wide disparity exists between the manual rates of different classifications. For example, the manual rate for classification 5703 (Building Raising and Moving) might be $44.89 per $100 in payroll whereas the manual rate for the classification 8810 (Clerical) may be .37¢ per $100 in payroll. As you can see, the manual rates for the classifications that represent low hazard jobs, such as clerical work, are relatively inexpensive. Conversely, classifications that represent more hazardous work, such as building raising and moving have a much higher manual rate. This is the part of the process designed to charge employers in hazardous industries more for workers' compensation insurance than those in low hazard industries.

There can even be a considerable difference in the manual rate between classifications that are very similar in nature. For example classification 7729 (Long-haul Trucking) might be $12.25 per $100 in payroll and classification 7228 (Short-haul Trucking) might be $16.85 per $100 in payroll

Estimated Payroll

The last piece of the puzzle needed to calculate a manual premium is the estimated payroll. You, as the employer must provide the insurance company with the anticipated payroll for each of the classifications that are represented in your business. For example, imagine that your company is a small auto body repair shop with auto body technicians, outside salespeople and clerical employees. You would be asked to provide estimated annual payroll for the time frame of the upcoming workers' compensation policy. Your estimated payroll may look something like figure 3.2.

CLASSIFICATION CODE	PAYROLL
8393 AUTO BODY REPAIR	$644.487
8742 SALESPERSONS - OUTSIDE	$238,459
8810 CLERICAL OFFICE	$66,555

Figure 3. 2

From this point, arriving at the manual premium is little more than fifth-grade math. Simply multiply the manual rate with the corresponding estimated payroll and divide the product by 100. As illustrated below, your manual premium is the sum of the individual classification premiums. (Figure 3.3)

CLASSIFICATION CODE	MANUAL RATE	ESTIMATED PAYROLL	MANUAL PREMIUM
8393 AUTO BODY REPAIR	$2.60	$644.487	$16,757
8742 SALESPERSONS - OUTSIDE	$ .98	$238,459	$2,337
8810 CLERICAL OFFICE	$ .37	$66,555	$246
			$19,340

Figure 3. 3

Because insurance companies base workers' compensation premiums on anticipated payroll, an individual representing the insurance carrier must audit your actual payroll after the policy period has ended. This is done to determine how close your estimated payroll was to the actual payroll. If the payroll was overestimated, you will receive a refund to compensate for overpayment. Conversely, an underestimated payroll will generate an additional bill from the insurance carrier.

Experience Rating

'The first step in calculating the workers' compensation premium was to calculate the manual premium. As already explained, that process ensures that companies in high-hazard industries pay more for workers' compensation coverage than companies in low-hazard industries. The next step in the process is called "experience rating." This is the part of the process that ensures that companies with fewer injuries pay less than companies with more injuries.

Although it is often viewed as a reward and punishment system, the intent of experience rating is not to reward companies that have few injuries, nor to punish companies that have had many injuries. Instead, it is a process that uses the cost of past claims to predict what the claims will cost in the upcoming policy year. The logic behind this process is that past workers' compensation claims are the best available indicator for the insurance company to gauge future workers' compensation claims of a particular company.

Particularly for small businesses, it is important to note that not all companies are eligible to be experience rated. Each state has its own rules. These rules generally include a minimum premium threshold. For example, a state might require an employer to have a premium of at least $5,000 for three consecutive years (or $10,000 for one year) before it is eligible to be experience rated.

For companies that are eligible to be experience rated, the frequency (number) and severity (cost) of workers' compensation claims from three consecutive policy years are factored into a mathematical formula that yields an a number called an "experience modifier." Although the process for determining an experience modifier is quite complex, what is done with the experience modifier is relatively simple.

An average experience modifier is expressed as 1.00 and simply means that a company has average losses and will pay 100% of their manual premium after experience-rating. A higher than average experience modifier would be any number greater than 1.00. For example, a company with a 1.43 experience modifier will pay 143% of their manual premium. The 43% surcharge is prompted by the higher than average claims costs the company has experienced. However, the experience modifier is not always 1.00 or greater. It can also be lower than 1.00. If a company has an experience modifier of .73, they will pay only 73% of their manual premium after experience-rating. This effectively gives the company a 27% discount and reflects the company's lower than average past workers' compensation claims.

Figure 3.4 compares the impact of different experience modifiers for a company with a manual premium of $19,340. As that illustration shows, the experience modifier can have a significant impact on what you pay for workers' compensation insurance. The difference between the low experience modifier and the high experience modifier in that example is more than $13,500.

Manual Premium	Experience Modifier	Discount/Surcharge	Modified Premium
$19,340	.73	$5,222 Discount	$14,118
$19,340	1.00	No Change	$19,340
$19,340	1.43	$8,316 Surcharge	$27,656

Figure 3. 4

The experience modifier is not calculated by your insurance agent. In most circumstances, it is not even calculated by the workers' compensation insurance carrier. Instead, it is calculated by an independent entity. In fact, the same organization that is so widely used for its system of classification codes (NCCI) is also responsible for calculating the experience modifiers for all employers in many states. So regardless of who you choose for an insurance agent, or which insurance carrier provides workers' compensation coverage, the experience modifier is the same.

That does not mean that once you are assigned an experience modifier, that you are stuck with it for years. Each year, prior to the renewal of your company's workers' compensation policy, NCCI (or the rating organization in your state) will issue you a new experience modifier which was calculated using updated information about past workers' compensation claims.

Discounts, Credits and Debits

The third and final step in calculating the workers' compensation premium is the application of discounts, credits or debits. These are applied after the manual premium and modified premium have been calculated.

As mentioned in the initial chapter of this book, workers' compensation premiums have a built-in bias against small businesses. This built-in bias takes the form of a premium discount. In short premium discounts are volume discounts. The larger the modified premium – the larger the discount. Insurance companies offer premium discounts to companies with larger premiums because the overhead expenses for the insurance company do not increase proportionally with the premium.

In addition to premium discounts, several state workers' compensation laws provide legislated credits. These credits are applied whenever certain actions are taken by the employer. For example, at the writing of this book, legislation is Pennsylvania provides a 5% premium discount if the employer implements a certified workplace safety program. In New Hampshire, employers who are enrolled in a managed care program are entitled to receive a 10% premium reduction. Similarly, legislation in Massachusetts provides for a 15% reduction in premiums for employers who are in the assigned risk pool and hire a qualified loss management firm to help them contain costs. Colorado employers who implement the specified steps in the state's Cost Containment Certification Program and receive safety certification become eligible for dividends up to 10% and a 2.5% premium discount if they implement a designated medical provider program.

Last but not least, about half of the states permit insurance carriers to offer scheduled credits. These are percentage discounts applied to the modified premium for actions that the employer takes to reduce the probability and/or severity of injuries. The insurance carrier is limited to a defined list of criteria that can result in a scheduled credit. These may include the existence of a formal safety program, above-average employee selection criteria, employee training, an active drug-testing program, a modified duty program and even the workers' compensation carrier's perception of management's cooperation.

However, unlike the premium discounts and legislated discounts, the insurance carrier not only has the ability to credit (decrease) the premium based upon these characteristics, but also has the ability to debit (increase) the premium for the lack of such efforts. Much of the information that is used to determine whether or not to apply a credit or debit to the premium for these and other characteristics comes from the insurance company's loss control consultants who visit employers prior to the insurance carrier initially quoting a premium or prior to the insurance carrier renewing a policy. Even the observations made by the loss control representatives regarding the physical condition of the workplace and the actions of the employees during an on-site visit can influence the underwriter's decision to apply a credit or debit.

Regardless of the reason, any credit or debit that is applied to the modified premium can have a very significant impact on the net premium (the amount that the employer ultimately pays). Figure 3.5 depicts the application of each of the above-mentioned credits, yielding a final workers' compensation premium.

CLASSIFICATION CODE	MANUAL RATE	ESTIMATED PAYROLL	MANUAL PREMIUM
8393 AUTO BODY REPAIR	$2.60	$644.487	$16,757
8742 SALESPERSONS - OUTSIDE	$ .98	$238,459	$2,337
8810 CLERICAL OFFICE	$ .37	$66,555	$246
MANUAL PREMIUM			$19,340
EXPERIENCE MODIFIER (.72)			- $5,415
MODIFIED PREMIUM			$13,925
SCHEDULED CREDITS/DEBITS (.24 -)			-$3,342
PREMIUM DISCOUNT (.04 -)			- $557
ANNUAL NET PREMIUM			$10,026

Figure 3. 5

The illustration in figure 3.5 reveals a company that has made significant strides to address the cost of workers' compensation premiums. They have implemented safety initiatives that have earned them a 24% premium reduction and have kept the frequency and severity of workers' compensation claims low enough to score an experience modifier of .72. As such, the company is charged a net premium that is nearly 50% less expensive than the manual premium. You can have similar success, if you commit yourself to the implementing the strategies set forth in this book.

CHAPTER 4

Classified Information

No, the information in this chapter is not top-secret. But it's as vital to attacking the high cost of workers' compensation premiums as is a war strategy to the Pentagon. The classification of employees is the fundamental building block for calculating workers' compensation premiums. This chapter explains what they are; who assigns them; how to determine if they are correct; and what to do if they are thought to be wrong.

Classified Information

Chapter 3 introduced the concept of workers' compensation classifications and explained how those classifications are used to help determine a company's insurance premium. In that chapter, it was explained that each employee falls within a particular classification based upon the overall business activity, or (under special circumstances) upon the type of work performed by an individual employee. In that same chapter, classifications were described as the fundamental building block for the process of calculating companies' workers' compensation premiums. Therefore, it stands to reason that if the classification being used is incorrect, the premium that your company is being charged for workers' compensation insurance will be wrong as well.

Because the classification of employees is so fundamental to determining your workers' compensation premium, it is important for you to make sure that your employees are properly classified. In fact, you are encouraged to make that one of the very first steps in the process of taking a bite out of your workers' compensation premiums.

For companies who have misclassified employees, the bite can be significant. Some companies have been able to cut their premiums nearly in half simply by applying the knowledge that you will gain by reading this chapter. But even much more modest reductions in workers' compensation premiums may be worth waging an all out war (if necessary) to have your employees classified differently than they are currently.

Classifications and Ratings Bureaus

You may be familiar with Standard Industrial Classification (SIC) system or even the relatively new North American Industry Classification System (NAICS) that has effectively replaced the SIC codes to classify businesses for the census and other purposes. If you are not familiar with those classification systems, there is only one thing that you need to know about them for now. They have absolutely, positively nothing to do with workers' compensation classifications. The classification systems used for workers' compensation purposes were created by workers' compensation rating bureaus and bear little resemblance to other industry classification systems.

The majority of states use the National Council on Compensation Insurance (NCCI) as a rating bureau for workers' compensation. In those states NCCI establishes the classifications used for workers' compensation. In the remaining states, an independent rating bureau is used as opposed to NCCI.

Workers' compensation classification systems, such as the one maintained by NCCI, seek to classify businesses based upon the work performed by employees. The goal is to lump businesses with similar exposures together.

There are roughly 600 different workers' compensation classifications within the NCCI classification system. The classification systems in the non-NCCI states may have greater or fewer classifications, but one thing holds true for each classification system. There is <u>not</u> a perfect match for every business. Instead, the goal is to identify the classification that is the best match for your operation.

With a few exceptions, the classification system attempts to assign a single classification to every employee within a business as opposed to assigning different classifications based upon individual job duties. This single classification is called the "governing classification." It is generally the classification that best describes the business as a whole, and it is intended to encompass the wide range of jobs that are performed within that business. For example, a business that involves the manufacture of box springs and mattresses would likely be classified (in the NCCI classification system) as 2570 (box spring and mattress manufacturing). Even though the company very likely employs individuals, such as maintenance workers, shipping/receiving employees, supervisors, and others who are not physically involved in the manufacture of box springs and mattresses, they are all intended to be covered by that single classification.

As mentioned above, there are exceptions to having a single classification being used to encompass every employee in a business. Because they are common in so many businesses, clerical employees, drivers and outside salespeople are frequently classified separately. In insurance underwriting terms, these are called "standard exceptions." These classifications, (particularly the clerical classification) often have lower rates associated with them, as compared with the governing classification. Thus, the tendency is for employers to want to lump as many employees as possible into standard exception classifications. However, there are very well-defined rules regarding who can and who cannot be classified as "clerical." For example, to fall within the "clerical" classification the employee must be exclusively involved in office work such as bookkeeping, filing, and correspondence. Additionally, the employee must work in an area of the facility that is physically separated from the other business operations.

Another exception to having a single classification that covers all employees may exist when a single business includes more than one undertaking or enterprise that is included on the same workers' compensation policy. An example of this might be a convenience-store and a full-service car wash that are included on a single workers' compensation policy. However, there are some well-defined rules for this exception as well. For instance, to be considered a separate undertaking, the operation must be one that is not ordinarily within the scope of the principal operation. Using the above example, there may very well be justification for having the employees of the carwash classified under the car wash classification and having the employees of the convenience store classified under the retail store classification. But to do this, the secondary operation (in this case, the car wash) would have to be separated from the primary operation (the convenience store) by some type of physical barrier and must be able to exist as a stand-alone business if the convenience store ceased to exist.

Construction-related companies represent another significant exception. As opposed to having a governing classification, construction entities are permitted to divide the payroll of employees between various construction-related classifications, insofar as those classifications are listed on the policy. However, for this to happen the employer must keep accurate payroll records showing the amount of payroll in each classification.

What's the Big Deal

Having employees classified correctly is a big deal. These classifications distinguish high hazard industries from low hazard industries. And, these classifications serve as the basis for the manual rate. If you recall from Chapter 3, the classification and corresponding manual rate are the first factors used to calculate an insurance premium.

If your business is assigned to a high hazard classification you will be charged a higher manual rate than employers assigned to a lower-hazard classification. These manual rates vary quite widely from one classification to another, even when there is seemingly little difference between the classifications. The following is an example of just how dramatic the difference in manual rates can be between two very similar NCCI classifications.

CLASSIFICATION CODE	MANUAL RATE
6017 - Dam or Lock Construction – Concrete Work	$22.34
6018 - Dam or Lock Construction – Earth Moving	$3.83

Figure 4.2

Although it may seem logical to only be concerned with misclassified employees when the proper classification would generate a lower insurance premium for your company. The opposite should concern you as well. In fact, when employees are improperly placed into an unrealistically low risk classification, there can be a long-term negative impact on that company's premiums. This can happen when the losses incurred by a company are consistent with the true operations. When this happens, the experience modifier can jump well above 1.00, pushing the premium up. Then, when someone finally catches-on and the proper classification is applied, you may be hit with a higher manual rate and a high experience modifier both at the same time.

An Honest Mistake

The misclassification of employees is generally done in error. Despite the popular mantra that big business is evil, the misclassification of employees is generally not something that is done by insurance companies to generate an unjustifiably high premium. After all, even the largest insurance companies are staffed with humans -- and humans not only can, but do occasionally make mistakes.

Although a typographical error made by an insurance company employee in entering a classification code into a computer is a possible explanation for misclassifications, that is frequently not the reason. More often than not, misclassifications result from either an insufficient knowledge of your operation or an insufficient knowledge of the possible classifications.

Particularly for small businesses, the insurance agent is generally the one who initially determines what he believes to be the proper classification(s) for your employees. At a minimum, your insurance agent provides the insurance carrier with a description of your operation so that the insurance company can assign employees to the appropriate classification(s). If the information provided to the insurance carrier is inaccurate or provides an insufficiently detailed description of the operation, the chances that your employees will misclassified is great.

Even when the information provided to the insurance carrier is accurate and detailed, employees can still be misclassified. After all, there are hundreds of classifications, some with small and seemingly insignificant differences. The truth is that it is easier than one might think to place employees into the wrong classification. Furthermore, many businesses do not fit perfectly in any existing classification. In those cases the various individuals who have a role in determining the correct classification use their own judgment to determine which classification is the closest match.

Another explanation for misclassifications is that many (if not most) businesses go through operational changes over time. Even if those operational changes are relatively small, they may be significant enough to warrant reclassification. But if those changes are never brought to the attention of the agent, broker or insurance company, it is very likely that the original classification will continue to be used for years.

Although the misclassification of employees is generally done in error, it is occasionally done intentionally. When an employer intentionally bends the truth about the job functions of employees for the purpose of having them assigned to a lower-risk classification, the employer commits premium fraud.

An Ounce of Prevention

Ideally, your company's workers' compensation classification(s) will be correct from the start. To increase the likelihood that your company is correctly classified, make sure that your insurance agent or broker receives a thorough and accurate description of your operation. Regardless of how many times that your agent or broker has been to your facility, do not assume that he has a sound understanding of your operation from those visits. Request that all of the information you provide be forwarded to each prospective insurance carrier from which a quote is being solicited.

Beyond decreasing the likelihood that your employees will be misclassified, providing detailed information about your operation can also give the insurance company an increased sense of comfort with your operation as an insurance risk, which could prove beneficial in securing schedule credits and help shave a few dollars off of your premium.

Correcting the Mistake

Having your employees properly classified can not only impact your current and future workers' compensation premiums, identifying and correcting misclassifications could very well score you a refund for the amount that you overpaid as a result of the misclassification in the past. If you suspect that your company is misclassified and that the misclassification has you paying a higher rate, it is possible that you will not only be able to get the classification corrected for the current and future policy years, many states will also allow you to recover overcharges that resulted from misclassification for the past few years.

The first step is to contact your insurance agent or broker and make him aware of your concern. Ask your agent to provide you with a copy of the current classification description, as well other possible classifications.

If you feel that your classification is not correct, but you have no clue what other classifications might be more appropriate, the "Quick Search" feature on www.ncci.com is a good starting point (as long as your business is located in a state that uses NCCI classification system.) That search tool provides a list of classifications based upon the key word(s) that you enter. Unfortunately, it will not provide the full description of that classification. For that, you will need to refer to the Scopes® Manual). Your agent or broker likely has a copy of this manual.

Simply allowing the agent to work with the insurance company to address your concern may be all that is needed to correct a misclassification. But before making a classification change, the insurance company may direct a loss control consultant, premium auditor or other person to travel to your facility to see your operation first-hand. However, if you provide sufficient information, photographs, brochures, etc. there may be sufficient evidence for the insurance company to change the classification without an on-site visit.

If allowing the insurance agent to work with the insurance company proves unfruitful and you are still convinced that your employees are misclassified in a higher cost classification, your next contact should likely be the rating bureau in your state.

Your first step in dealing with the rating bureau is to simply speak with the customer service representatives. It is entirely possible that discussing your situation over the phone will provide some degree of satisfaction. In many cases it will provide you with a clearer understanding of why the current classification is believed to be correct. Conversely, it may arm you with specific information with which to challenge the current classification further.

If simply speaking with a customer service representative from the rating bureau does not adequately address your classification concern, request a copy of past inspections reports that the rating bureau has of your operation (if any exist). If there has been a past inspection of your operation, review the report and attempt to evidence mistakes or misnomers that could have resulted in a misclassification.

As a last resort, you may want to request an inspection from the rating bureau. However, be aware that the inspection may be relatively expensive, and is not guaranteed to produce the results you want.

If you go through all of that and still are not satisfied, the odds are against you. But that does not mean that you have exhausted all possible avenues. You can still appeal the decision of the rating bureau inspector to the rating bureau's appeals board or to the agency that oversees insurance in your state.

CHAPTER 5

Jumping Through Hoops

Some states have laws that provide for a premium discount for companies that implement safety programs, safety committees, or drug free workplace programs. If you're willing to jump through a few hoops, you could score big.

Legislated Premium Discounts

Workers' compensation insurance can be a quite costly. For many small businesses it is one of the most significant expenses. Quite literally, every dollar that is spent on workers' compensation insurance is one less dollar that can be invested into growing your company and investing in the employees that have helped elevate your company to its current level of success. For that reason, everything within your power should be done to take a bite out of your premiums… even if that involves jumping through a few hoops.

Like it or not, government entities that have been granted the power to create laws have grown accustom to the practice of tying incentives to specific desired behavior. Often the specific desired behavior is closely tied to the topic of safety. The manner in which federal highway funds are distributed may be the most well-known example. Although individual states are not stripped of their right to self-govern, the level of federal highway funding distributed to individual states is often tied to their compliance with federal guidelines regarding speed-limits, seatbelt laws and motorcycle helmet laws.

In a growing number of states, the same principle has been applied to individual businesses that are required to maintain workers' compensation insurance. Specific laws are written into state statutes that provide for a discount on your premium insofar as you implement safety programs, safety committees, or drug free workplace programs in accordance with the specific state requirements. Collectively these laws are referred to as "workplace safety premium credit laws."

Often these laws do not merely suggest, but require insurance carriers to provide a specific percentage discount on the workers' compensation premium to policyholders meeting the requirements. However, a few states give the insurers some latitude in determining which policyholders will receive specific workplace premium credits.

Safety Management Program

At the writing of this book more than a dozen states have laws that require insurance carriers to provide a premium credit to employers who implement or maintain an overall safety management program that conforms to the state's criteria. Although the requirements differ in each state, the following provides an example of what an employer may be required to implement to warrant a workplace safety premium discount.
- formal written safety policies
- safety committee
- routine workplace safety inspections
- documented safety meetings
- appropriate safety training
- effective accident investigations

Most workplace safety premium credits specify the percentage discount that must be applied if the criteria have been met. For example, within the District of Columbia, insurance carriers are required to grant a 5% premium discount if the insured has been certified by the Department of Employment Services as having a safe workplace program. However, a few laws place the amount of the discount on a sliding scale, based upon the frequency and severity of workers' compensation claims during the previous year. For example, (as illustrated in figure 5.1) Colorado law provides the following sliding scale for companies that do not qualify for experience and/or schedule rating, but have fulfilled the states requirements for a certified safety program:

Premium Dividend	Dividend Criteria
10%	If the insured business entity has been loss free for at least the last year immediately preceding the effective date of the premium dividend.
8%	If the insured business entity had one medical loss exceeding $250 in the last year immediately preceding the effective date of the premium dividend.
6%	If the insured business entity had two medical losses, each exceeding $250, in the last year immediately preceding the effective date of the premium dividend.
4%	If the insured business entity had three medical losses, each exceeding $250, in the last year immediately preceding the effective date of the premium dividend.
2%	If the insured business entity had three medical losses, each exceeding $250, and one claim for loss of time in the last year immediately preceding the effective date of the premium dividend.
0%	If the insured business entity had more than three medical losses and one claim for loss of time in the last year immediately preceding the effective date of the premium dividend.

Figure 5.1

It should be of particular interest to small businesses that some of the states that offer this type of workplace safety premium credit ensure that it is made available to small employers as well as large employers.

Some states view workplace safety premium credits as a right afforded to all employers who implement and maintain a safety program meeting the states' minimum requirements. However, others are less inclusive. Some states make the premium credit available only to businesses that meet a minimum premium threshold. Others limit the workplace safety premium credit to employers who are in the assigned risk pool, or who have been targeted because of a poor loss history.

Safety Committees

Having an active safety committee is one of the criteria that must be met to receive a workplace safety premium credit in a number of states. However, in at least one state (Pennsylvania) having an active is safety committee that meets the states requirements is the sole criteria for securing a credit.

Safety Inspections

A small handful of states provide a workplace safety premium credit to employers only following one or more inspections by qualified loss control professionals who evaluate the workplace hazards and safety management efforts while onsite. At the writing of this book, Delaware is one of the states that adheres to this practice. Although Delaware employers must ask for the inspection and must pay for it as well, it has the potential to generate a 19% premium discount.

Investing in Safety

At least one state, namely New York, offers the opportunity for employers to apply for a workplace safety premium credit for amounts invested in the creation of safer work environments. The credit equals up to five percent of the amount invested, up to 15% of the employer's annual earned premium for that year. Employers that apply for this credit are required to provide tangible evidence that the investment would result in a safer work environment.

Drug Free Workplace Programs

At the writing of this book, 10 states have legislation that provides for a premium discount for employers that implement and maintain an approved drug-free workplace program. In each case, the individual state defines what constitutes a qualifying (or approved) program. Common required elements of an approved drug-free workplace program include the following.
- Substance Abuse Policy (written)
- Annual Employee Substance Abuse Education
- Annual Supervisor Training
- Employee Drug Testing
- List of Locally Available Treatment and Counseling Sources

When it comes to premium credits for drug-free workplace programs, the magic number is "5." Almost every state that has legislation permitting (and in some cases requiring) insurance carriers to provide such a discount seem to fixate on 5% as the universally accepted amount for a premium credit. The lone dissenter at the writing of this book is Georgia, which requires insurers to grant a 7.5% premium credit to employers that have been certified by the state as having a drug-free workplace.

But Wait There's More

Closely related to the workplace safety premium credits discussed in this chapter are other credits offered to specific employers for performing specific desired behavior. Some states require insurance companies to provide a specific percentage discount to businesses that have enrolled in a managed care program or have designated a medical provider for the treatment of work-related injuries and illnesses. At least one state (Louisiana) provides for a 2% reduction in premium for targeted employers that send a designated representative to a cost containment meeting sponsored by the state. Another state (Minnesota) permits insurance carriers to discount the insurance premium even further by granting 3% for employers who are party to an approved collective bargaining agreement; up to 3% for employers who request consultative loss control services from their insurer; and up to 2% for employers to comply with statutory return-to-work requirements.

Criteria Determined by the Insurance Company

As reflected by the content of this chapter, most of the state workplace safety premium credit laws require insurance carriers to provide a premium discount to employers who adhere to very specific criteria in implementing safety programs, safety committees or drug-free workplace programs. However, at the writing of this book, at least one state (Alaska) has taken a somewhat different approach. They placed the responsibility for establishing the criteria for workplace premium credit in the hands of the individual insurance carriers in that state. This means that it is very likely that each insurance carrier's criteria for offering workplace safety premium credits will differ. If you are a small business in Alaska, hopefully you view this as an opportunity for your company to take a bite out of your workers' comp premium. Before you solicit premium quotes for your upcoming policy year, you (with the help of an independent insurance agent) should learn the criteria and the potential amount of the workplace safety premium credit offered by each workers' compensation insurance carrier in your state.

Workplace Safety Premium Debits

This entire chapter is directed at informing small businesses owners and managers of workplace safety premium credits that may be available. On a less positive, but equally important note, it is imperative that small business employers also be aware that some states grant insurance carriers the right to debit (increase) the premium of businesses that fail to address loss control recommendations issued as a result of an on-site loss control consultation.

Initiative Required

Although the laws of a handful of states were referenced within this chapter, their reference was merely to demonstrate the unique nature of workplace safety premium credits among the various states. Workers' compensation legislation is much too dynamic to include a comprehensive listing in a book such as this. Therefore, to learn what (if any) legislation exists in your state that provides for workplace safety premium credits a degree of initiative is required. Contact your insurance agent and employ his help in learning the credits for which you might be eligible. Reference the resources in the appendices of this book and search the legislation in your state for pertinent statutes and administrative rules. Contact the loss control staff of your insurance carrier. Remember, if you don't take the time and effort to learn of these credits, it is unlikely that your company will benefit from them.

CHAPTER 6

Who's Wearing the Safety Hat?

Certainly safety is everyone's responsibility. But when no one is designated to coordinate company safety efforts, that's exactly who does it. This chapter will help you identify the individual best-suite for that roll.

Designating a Safety Coordinator

Often owners and managers in small businesses wear many hats. Frequently in small businesses there is no particular person designated to coordinate safety efforts for the company. Instead, the "safety coordinator hat" collects dust on the hat rack... at least until an injury, inspection or other event necessitates that someone (often the company owner) puts it on.

The role of a safety coordinator differs in each company. In small businesses it is normal for that role to be a collateral duty. Depending upon the size of the workforce and the type of industry, the safety coordinator role may only consume a small percentage of the designated employee's time.

Holding the title of "safety coordinator" does not imply that the designated employee will be held responsible for ensuring that the workplace is free of hazards or for ensuring that employees engage in safe behavior. The responsibility for implementing the company's various safety initiatives should to be borne by all of the supervisors and managers. Instead of bearing the burden alone, the safety coordinator, ideally, will serve in a leadership capacity and will be a resource regarding safety issues.

In businesses in which no one particular person has been designated to wear the safety coordinator hat, the default attitude might be that "safety is everyone's responsibility." However, when a specific person is not designated to wear the safety coordinator hat, that's exactly who coordinates the company's safety efforts – no one guides the company in identifying and correcting hazards before they translate into injuries. No one is held accountable for failures that place employees at risk. No one ensures that safety-related training is conducted and is effective. And, no one challenges the company as a whole to improve their injury prevention efforts.

Certainly this does not suggest that employee safety is ignored when nobody has been officially dubbed the company's "safety coordinator." It does mean that the safety efforts of the company will likely suffer because of the lack of purposeful planning and leadership.

If your company has not yet identified someone to coordinate safety efforts, you are urged to select a person to fill that role based upon the characteristics of the individual, as opposed to simply designating the most convenient employee. This chapter will provide a picture of the ideal candidate for that role.

A Healthy Perspective

Perhaps the most important consideration when assigning the role of safety coordinator should be the individual attitudes and underlying beliefs relating to both occupational safety and leadership.

There are certainly a great number of people that have a defeatist attitude toward workplace accidents (particularly relating to incidents that do not result in significant injuries). Likely, everyone has heard someone say, "Accidents just happen. That's why they're called them accidents." A person with that attitude, regardless of his other qualities, is not the right person for the job. Instead, the right person to fill your company's role as safety coordinator should be one who views safety as an immutable value, placing the prevention of injuries and human suffering at the top of his priorities list. Along the same lines, he should a have a healthy level of optimism concerning the ability to improve your company's injury prevention efforts, viewing no hazard as an insurmountable hurdle.

The role of safety coordinator is no place for someone who wants to use that position to leverage power over others in the company. Instead, the person selected as your company's safety coordinator should view the role as that of a mentor and resource. As such, he should have high standards for himself and view part of his responsibility as being a role model within the company. He should desire to teach, train and mentor. Furthermore, he should possess the ability to coach, encourage and motivate others to get involved.

A Key Figure

In addition to having a healthy perspective concerning workplace safety and leadership, the ideal candidate to be fitted for the safety coordinator's hat should be a key figure within the company. He should have knowledge of the operation, access to the decision-maker(s) and should be accessible to all employees.

The individual selected for the role of safety coordinator should have an understanding of the entire operation (or at least be capable of learning it). It may be someone who has been employed with the company for a long time and has performed many of the jobs during his tenure. By selecting an individual with broad knowledge of the various tasks performed by employees, it is likely that the safety coordinator will more readily see the different needs of various departments (or functions); and will be more apt to understand how the actions or activities in one part of the operation impact employee safety in another part. Choosing an employee with knowledge of only a few aspects of the business will likely be a stumbling block to effect positive change throughout the company.

In addition to having a broad-base of knowledge concerning the operation, the individual should have direct access to the company owner or top decision-maker(s). If the safety coordinator must channel each request, criticism, and plan for change through one or more supervisors, the message (and its urgency) may likely be diluted before making it to the decision-maker.

The person selected for the role of safety coordinator should be accessible to supervisors and others responsible for enacting company safety measures. He should also be accessible to the entire workforce, as he will be the company's resource for safety-related matters. For this reason, an outside salesperson or a company owner who is only sporadically at the company facility would likely not be the ideal choice to wear the safety coordinator hat.

An Effective Communicator

Another characteristic that should be present in a person to be considered for the safety coordinator role is good communication skills. He must be able to speak convincingly to individuals in all levels of the company, from the newest employee to the company owner.

He should be a competent educator, trainer and promoter. For this reason employers are urged not to quickly overlook their sales force for a potential candidate. Salespeople must be effective communicators to promote the product that they are selling and if they have been in that field for any length of time, you could likely conclude that they have developed some marketing skills that may translate well into marketing safety internally, a topic discussed in greater depth in the chapter titled "Marketing 101."

Being an effective communicator does not merely imply that the ideal candidate is clear and convincing. Communication is a two-way street. For that reason, in seeking an individual with effective communication skills, consider that person's willingness to listen and learn from others, irrespective of their position in the company.

The Ideal Candidate

If your company has not yet designated someone wear the "safety coordinator" hat, you are urged to put more thought into the identification of that individual than merely looking for the person whose plate is not already too full with other responsibilities. You are encouraged to consider the personal qualities described in this chapter and select the person who would do the best job. After all, you are considering the person who will coordinate your company's safety efforts, which will greatly impact the degree to which your company's greatest asset (your employees) will be protected. Collaterally, if those efforts are effective, you can expect to be rewarded through lower workers' compensation premiums.

Certainly each of the above-described qualities is desirable. But the chance of finding each of those characteristics in one individual is unlikely. It is quite possible that the employee whom you select for this position will have strengths and weaknesses. For that reason, after designating a safety coordinator, you are encouraged to routinely affirm his strengths and intentionally develop the qualities in which there is visible room for improvement. Invest in that person by purposefully sending him to training and education seminars or classes as a part of your company's overall plan to enhance employee safety.

If your company already has an individual filling the role of safety coordinator, and you are that person, evaluate yourself against the traits and qualities mentioned above. Then strive to improve upon those in which you have the least strength. Seek out professionals in other companies that wear the safety coordinator hat and build a network of colleagues who will encourage and support one another in this role. You have the most important role in your company.

CHAPTER 7

Accident Prone

Even within small businesses, a small percentage of employees submit a disproportionate number of workers' compensation claims. These employees can be an incredible source of frustration for business owners trying their best to prevent injuries and to keep workers' compensation premiums within reach. This chapter addresses the topic head-on and provides a means countering the problem, regardless of how small the workforce.

Unlucky at Life

All too often a small percentage of employees submit a disproportionate number of workers' compensation claims. Some even contend that 20% of employees are responsible for 80% of the workers' compensation claims. Whereas that contention may not necessarily be accurate, it does provide cause to consider the indisputable anecdotal evidence that there is often a small group of employees who seem to be injured at work at a greater frequency than the rest of the workforce.

Employee's who repeatedly submit workers' compensation claims can be an incredible source of frustration; a thorn in the side of a business owner who is trying his best to prevent injuries and to keep his workers' compensation premiums within reach. Such employees are frequently accused of being careless or inattentive. However, out of earshot, the labels are frequently harsher. An employee who submits multiple workers' compensation claims is often called clumsy or accident prone, or is described as an accident waiting to happen.

Is that true? Are some people simply more prone to injuries than others, with no other logical explanation? If so, are you powerless to turn things around and break the cycle? After all, what can a small business owner who is already overtaxed with other responsibilities change about a person who simply has two left feet?

Before that question is answered, it is first important to take a look at what employers have historically done when confronted with this dilemma.

The Errors of Our Ways

The most common response to addressing "injury repeaters" is to simply do nothing. Understandably, many employers feel helpless to transform a clumsy, accident prone employee with two left feet into a graceful, coordinated, safety-minded, model employee. So they throw their hands in the air, bang their head on their desk or mutter under their breath that they wish the employee would simply quit.

Obviously doing nothing begets nothing. Injury repeaters will continue to be injury repeaters unless something is done to throw a stick in the spokes (figuratively speaking). You can wait for the individual employee to change something on his own, or you can take control and guide the process. If you are in a position of authority within a small business, you presumably got there because you make things happen. You are a leader. So when it comes to addressing the problem of injury repeaters, follow your natural tendency and lead.

Simply taking the initiative and being committed to the task of leading employees out of a cycle of injury repetition is not enough. If you are leading based upon your best guess of what needs to be done, you could very well be leading the injury repeaters in circles. Some employers who have been moved to action by the frustration of feeling helpless try techniques that are almost guaranteed to fail. Among these techniques are the guilt trip, the shame game and the screen play.

The guilt trip, as you may have guessed, involves confronting the injury repeater with his poor performance and the impact that it is having upon the company as a whole. The objective is that the onset of guilt brought about by being tagged as 'the problem employee' will cause a sudden change in behavior that will eliminate future injuries. In extreme cases of poor judgment, some employers even use peer pressure to intensify the guilt. In these situations the employer, either directly or covertly, informs the workforce of the subject employee's personal responsibility for higher workers' compensation costs and the impact that those costs will have on pay raises, benefits and the like. More often than not, the result that this brings about is not a dramatic change in behavior for the better, but a pent-up hostility and resentment toward the employer. For a host of reasons, hostility and resentment are the very things that should be avoided in the midst of a workers' compensation claim.

The shame game is somewhat similar. However, instead of attempting to capitalize on the emotion of guilt, the employer exploits the sentiment of pride. Nobody wants to be viewed in a negative light. Fully aware of this, some employers label injury repeaters with a variety of unflattering titles, believing that the shame of the label will magically transform them. However, like the guilt trip, this frequently brings about the exact opposite of the intended result. Instead of being magically transformed, the employees who have been belittled by what amounts to little more than an adult version of name-calling, live down to the expectations of being the accident prone, problem employee.

The screen play is a somewhat different, but an equally ineffective method of addressing injury prevention. It does not address the current injury repeaters at all, but instead, attempts to prevent any more from getting through the front door and becoming a problem for the company. Simply put, the screen play involves screening-out prospective employees whom the employer believes have the propensity to be injury repeaters. Although there are commercially-marketed tools for achieving some success in screening-out employees with a higher statistical propensity for injuries, the most common method used by small business owners and managers who employ this method is a "gut feeling." Not only is this unreliable, it may result in passing over a good prospective employee.

Identify the Repeaters

Certainly there are significant problems with some of the traditional responses to injury repeaters. Now it is time to concentrate on what works. Even for very small businesses, a systematic, well conceived approach will yield the greatest result. The first step is to identify the injury repeaters.

This may seem unnecessary for small businesses, particularly small businesses with few injuries. But following this systematic process may identify employees whom you may not have considered being injury repeaters, or may omit employees whom you would have sworn fit the injury repeater mold.

First, contact your insurance agent and request loss runs for the past five years (or more). These loss runs may need to be retrieved from several different insurance carriers, depending upon how much your company bounced from one insurance company to another during the previous 5 years. A note of caution, since some business owners ask for loss runs only when soliciting new quotes on insurance, you may need to reassure your insurance agent that you are not shopping insurance companies through another agency.

Once you have five years of loss runs at your fingertips, tally the number of claims for each employee represented on the loss runs. Then develop criteria identifying what constitutes an "injury repeater." There is no standard formula. It could be anyone with two or more claims in five years, anyone with three or more claims in five years, anyone with five or more claims in five years. It is entirely up to you. It is that simple. The employees identified through that 15 minute process are the ones who will be the subject of your efforts.

In this process you may be tempted to exclude individuals from consideration who are no longer employees of your company. After all why should you be concerned about someone who may be an 'injury repeater' if he is no longer employed by your company? The answer lies in the reality that former employees of small businesses often return, seeking employment at some point in the future. This process will help you assess their need for specialized attention in the event that they return and are rehired.

Focus on the Problem

The next step is to take a close look at each incident to determine why it happened. Perhaps the biggest hurdle with which you will be faced in this process is that small business owners and managers typically fail to take small claims serious enough to seek-out the real causes underlying the injury-producing incidents. When an employee bumps his head, trips over his own feet, or cuts his finger with a utility knife the injury is typically minor – some may even say the injury is insignificant. Because the injury is perceived to be insignificant, no time is "wasted" attempting to really understand why it happened. The result is that prevention of future similar injuries is disregarded until there is a severe injury or until a trend of injuries is identified.

With that in mind, intentionally give equal consideration to addressing the "why" questions for each reported incident, regardless of the severity of the injury. It may not seem logical to place equal importance on understanding why someone cut their finger with a utility knife and received two stitches versus understanding why someone else fell ten feet from a platform and now is permanently impaired. But for the purpose of addressing employees who have submitted more than their share of workers' compensation claims, what happened is far less important than why it happened.

In attempting to address why an incident occurred, consider the myriad of factors that may have contributed to make the incident happen. Do not be satisfied with identifying one cause for an incident. Instead, attempt to identify as many as possible. You may even be well-served to solicit the input from the injury repeater himself. Under most circumstances, nobody is in a better position to identify the things that contributed to an injury than the injured party himself.

Search for Common Ground

By following the steps outlined above, you will have identified one or more employees that fit the mold of an injury repeater and the claims that they have submitted in the past five years. For each of those claims you will have identified several contributing factors. The next step is to search for commonalities. For example, if one of the employees identified through this process had five injuries in the past five years, consider what those injuries have in common. More importantly, consider what the factors that contributed to those injuries had in common.

Armed with this information, you can exercise your ability to reason. Why would the commonalities that you have identified result in one employee being injured more often (or at least reporting claims more often) than his coworkers? What makes this employee, his work environment or the level of guidance he has received from management different from the majority of the other employees?

Although this is often the most difficult step in the process, your ability to accurately pinpoint why an employee is overrepresented on the workers' compensation claims history is critical to solving the problem. To help guide your thoughts in this process, a partial list of possible explanations for employees reporting injuries at a disproportionate frequency is provided below.

Reporting Differences

Simple as it may seem, one explanation for some employees being overrepresented in injury statistics is that they report injuries at a lower threshold than the average employee. A sore back might be shrugged-off as an inevitable part of life by some employees, while other employees may quickly associate their discomfort with a task that they performed at work and report it as a work-related injury.

Risk Taker Tendency

Each person has behavior tendencies shaped by his personality and social influences. Some people seemingly live for things like skydiving and motorbike riding, while others consider it too risky to even travel the posted speed limit on an interstate highway. Employees who fit the risk-taker mold may frequently be caught performing tasks without personal protective equipment or may engage in other risky activities.

Medical Problems

Occasionally medial problems increase the propensity for an employee to have more than his fair share of injuries at work. Beyond physical handicaps that may be obvious to you and others, employees may have medical problems that are not readily detectable. Sleep disorders, hearing problems, hypertension and a host of other medical problems could be impacting claim frequency.

Emotional Stress

Everyone experiences stress in their lives. Occasionally that stress is fairly well hidden while at work, but has an impact nonetheless. Consider an employee whose teenage daughter is in a prolonged state of rebellion. It is not likely that her dad will openly discuss this at work, but it can be a tremendous distraction, keeping his focus away from the job he is performing.

Fatigue

Nobody is at the top of their game when they are physically fatigued. They are understandably more prone to the types of injuries that are commonly blamed on carelessness or inattention. Couple this with the reality that many Americans are so deep in financial debt that they need a second job just to make ends meet and it explains why employees drag themselves to work, seeming worn-out before the workday begins.

Physical Condition

According to numerous studies, your employees (collectively) are in the worst physical shape ever. It stands to reason the employees who are less physically fit are more prone to physical injury. As such, consider the physical condition of employees who have been identified as injury repeaters.

Ineffective Training

Training is a key component of a company's efforts to prevent employee injuries. Unless employees know how to perform their jobs safely, injuries can be expected. However, even if training is conducted for all employees, that does not mean it will have an equal impact on all employees. Some people simply learn differently than others and require training that is conducted in a different manner to be effective.

Unsavory Motives

It is a disheartening and unfortunate reality that some people have a moral fiber that is no stronger than an overcooked linguini noodle. When such people are employed and have multiple workers' compensation claims, it is only logical to consider the possibility that their motives for submitting a claim are suspect. Much more will be discussed about this the chapter titled, "To Catch a Thief."

Drug-Induced Impairment

Much is written about the use of illegal drugs and alcohol and their impact upon workplace safety, and it should certainly not be discounted. But don't gloss-over the impact of legal drugs. Some over the counter (OTC) drugs taken for colds and allergies can significantly affect performance, even when taken properly.

Workstation Characteristics

Thus far, the list of possible explanations for employees reporting injuries at a disproportionate frequency has concentrated on the individual employee. However, the characteristics of that employee's workstation may be a factor contributing his frequency of injuries. Consider if the tasks require awkward positions, or if repetitive tasks that increase the potential for cumulative trauma injuries. Also consider the general condition of the work areas in which the injuries have occurred. A work area that is not orderly generally increases the hazards to which employees are exposed.

A Plan of Attack

Although the above is only a partial list of explanations for why employees report injuries at a disproportionate frequency, the diversity of these explanations attests to the fact that there can be no one-size-fits-all approach to addressing the problem of injury repetition. Although improved training may halt the problem of repetition in some circumstances, it will do nothing to stop an injury repetition problem caused by a medical impairment. Similarly, redesigning the workstation of an employee who has submitted several workers' compensation claims may be the perfect cure in some situations, but it will do little to impact an employee who reports to work impaired by allergy medications.

As such, you must come together with the injury repeater and openly discuss the possible causes for injury repetition. Then, jointly identify a plan of attack. Knowing that doing nothing, begets nothing, you and the injury repeater are obligated to identify a plan of attack that addresses how the problem of repetition will be brought to an end.

Because the employee will likely feel intimidated or threatened with this type of discussion, you should make a concerted effort to communicate that the problem being addressed is injury repetition, not the individual.

Finally, to promote accountability for the actions agreed to in this plan of attack, a quasi-contract should be written between you and the employee, identifying the commitments of both. This will not only serve to make a more significant impact upon the employee and remind him of his commitments to you, but will hold you accountable for your commitments to the employee. Furthermore, the simple written contract will provide a clearly visible demonstration of your concern for the employee, which may be just the cure that was needed in the first place.

CHAPTER 8

Erecting Roadblocks

Many small business owners feel at least partially immune from the threat of workers' compensation fraud. Whereas workers' compensation fraud may very well be less prevalent within those small businesses in which strong bonds of trust exist between the employer and the employees, the only employer immune to claimant fraud is one with no employees. Nonetheless, small business employers can erect roadblocks to make the road to workers' compensation fraud more difficult to maneuver.

You're Not Immune

Because of the close-knit, family atmosphere that is fostered and exists in many small businesses, a number of small business owners feel at least partially immune from the threat of workers' compensation fraud. Such employers reason that they know their employees well and are confident that none of their employees would ever engage in workers' compensation fraud. Whereas workers' compensation fraud may very well be less prevalent within small businesses in which strong bonds of trust exist between the employer and the employees, the only employer immune to claimant fraud is one with no employees. In reality, some of the people who you would never suspect of doing anything illegal or even underhanded, are swayed into a lapse in ethical behavior by financial pressures, fear of an uncertain future, or a well-worded enticement.

If you have ever had the misfortune of deciding to turn on your television during the daytime on a weekday, you have no doubt been inundated with commercials advertising attorneys who specialize in workers' compensation cases. In large measure, these commercials attempt to convince the viewers that they deserve a disability settlement and are sitting on a cash cow if they have a workers' compensation claim. In addition to promoting a get-rich-quick mentality, these advertisements paint insurance companies as being conniving and deceitful (the enemy). Laying aside judgment of the ethical character of these attorneys, the truth is that they are not stupid. They are buying up air-time on television stations during the very time that their target audience is sitting in front of the television. Couple that with billboards, clever taglines and full-page yellow-pages advertisements and you will realize that there is an active and very aggressive campaign to drum-up business from workers' compensation claimants. Even if this form of advertising is not successful in influencing an injured employee to initiate a law suit, the repetitious message undoubtedly helps promote a victim mentality and the perception that the employer and the insurance company could not possibly be ethical and honest. It is not a very big leap to believe that the tactics do their part to promote workers' compensation fraud.

Now, consider how the personal financial pressures facing an employee might entice an individual to engage in workers' compensation fraud. Based upon conservative estimates, the average personal credit card debt carried is over $8,000. Most Americans have at least one car payment, and many of those owe more than the car is worth. Many depend upon two steady incomes just to make ends meet. The sad reality is that the number of Americans living paycheck to paycheck is alarming. Faced with the opportunity to relive some of their financial strain, some roll the dice in hopes that they can bend the truth enough to earn a settlement, or earn a little money under the table with another company while drawing indemnity benefits from their workers' compensation insurance company.

How do small businesses counter these and other factors that steer your employees down the road of workers' compensation fraud? The unfortunate answer to that question is that most small businesses do little or nothing intentionally and consistently to prevent workers' compensation fraud.

Although a majority of people have a strong enough moral fiber not to be swayed into committing workers' compensation fraud, the odds are good that (under the right circumstances) one or more of your current employees could be swayed. For this reason, every business (large and small alike) should have an aggressive campaign of its own to counter the external influences that push employees toward workers' compensation fraud.

While there is no sure-fire way to make your business fraud-proof, you can erect roadblocks to workers' compensation fraud. These include employing sound injury prevention measures, exercising due diligence in hiring, educating employees, maintaining open lines of communication, and promoting early return-to-work following injuries.

Injury Prevention

The first and most important roadblock to workers' compensation fraud that should be erected is to employ sound injury prevention measures. Throughout this book you are encouraged to implement measures to prevent employee injuries. Largely this is because injuries (workers' compensation claims) have a direct impact on your insurance premium. However, it is important to know that employing sound injury prevention measures produces less obvious benefits. One of these benefits is that preventing injuries also lessens your company's exposure to workers' compensation fraud.

To illustrate how preventing injuries also lessens your company's exposure to workers' compensation fraud, consider the many ways in which workers' compensation fraud is perpetrated by an employee. Workers' compensation fraud can involve an employee fabricating an injury or reporting an off-duty injury as being work-related. However, workers' compensation fraud also includes an employee who is legitimately injured on-the-job, but exaggerates the extent of his injury to receive additional compensation. It includes an employee who works another job where he is paid under-the-table to receive income from both the insurance carrier and an employer. It also includes an employee who draws unemployment benefits concurrently with workers' compensation indemnity benefits. In fact, there are likely more ways of turning a legitimate workers' compensation claim into fraud than there are ways to commit fraud in the absence of a legitimate work-related injury.

Another element of this "injury prevention" roadblock is thoroughly and consistently conducting accident investigations. As a part of your company's injury prevention efforts, accident investigations serve the primary function of identifying why an injury occurred, so that it can be prevented from happening again. Additionally, within the context of preventing workers' compensation fraud, thoroughly and consistently conducting accident investigations discourages employees from fabricating a claim. To illustrate, imagine that you are an employee and were injured playing softball with your friends over the weekend. Because money is tight, you are concerned about the co-pay amounts on your health insurance -- particularly if there are to be repeat doctor visits. For that reason, you are contemplating about reporting the injury as a workers' compensation claim. You may feel fairly confident that you could get away with it if your employer does not conduct accident investigations. You would be less likely to fabricate a story about how the injury occurred at work if you knew that your employer would gather facts through conducting an accident investigation

Due Diligence

Another roadblock that should be erected to deter workers' compensation fraud is the exercise of due diligence in the selection and hiring of employees. In short, it should be your goal to screen-out applicants who pose a threat to your company because of their propensity to engage in workers' compensation fraud.

The first step in this process is one that is often overlooked by businesses with twenty employees or fewer – the use of a formal application for employment.

Another step in the process of exercising due diligence in hiring is to ensure that references and background information are verified. This includes verifying that the previous employer exists (or existed) and that the applicant was actually employed there. The legitimacy of previous employers listed on an application can be determined by reconciling the telephone number of the business, as provided on the employment application, with the telephone number in the local phone book or through a web-site, such as www.switchboard.com. The latter enables you to enter the telephone number that the applicant provided and searches for the residence or business to which that telephone number is assigned. Once contact is made, prospective employers generally have little trouble verifying that the applicant was employed there.

Although the applicant's former employer may only volunteer the individual's dates of employment, do not stop there. At least try to get more information. For example ask directly if the individual would be rehired if he returned. If you have no luck soliciting the information you want from former employers, try to get it from the applicant himself. A cleverly worded question may get the applicant to reveal more than he wanted to. For example, in the interview process, try asking the applicant, "I plan on contacting your former supervisor at ABC Manufacturing. What do you think that he will say about you?"

Drug-screening of applicants is another means of exercising due diligence in hiring. Although the chapter titled, "A High Priority" discusses drug-screening in much more depth, it is important to mention here because illicit drug use is, by definition, a violation of criminal law. An individual who violates laws relating to illicit drug use may lack the moral character to refrain from workers' compensation fraud.

For the same reason as listed above, criminal records checks should be conducted of applicants. Despite the popularly-held worldview that character does not matter, a person who has a criminal record may lack the moral character to refrain from workers' compensation fraud.

You may be tempted to evaluate a job applicant's propensity to engage in workers' compensation fraud through directly questioning him about past work-related injuries or past workers' compensation claims. You are, however, cautioned against employing that tactic. As a result of the Americans with Disabilities Act (ADA) it is no longer acceptable, under most circumstances, for employers to ask pre-employment questions regarding past injuries. Instead, it is best to arrange a post-job-offer physical examination and let the healthcare professional conducting the physical ask questions of the prospective employee regarding health history, prior injuries and the ability to perform essential job functions.

Education

Yet another roadblock to workers' compensation fraud involves educating your employees. Many employers train employees how to perform their jobs safely and efficiently; and even how to report a work-related injury if necessary, but far too few include information about workers' compensation fraud in employee training. The more employees know, and the more they are aware that you (their employer) know about workers' compensation fraud, the less likely they are to engage in it.

First, employees should be made aware of the costs associated with workers' compensation fraud. Let them know how fraud influences your workers' compensation premiums, and in-turn how an increase in insurance costs influences profitability of the company. Avoid presenting them with the published figures associated with workers' compensation fraud. Although the nationwide statistics are big and impressive, talking about billions of dollars is simply incomprehensible to individuals who are accustomed to household budget figures.

In addition to educating employees about the financial impact that workers' compensation fraud has on your company, employees should also be educated about the consequences of engaging in workers' compensation fraud. Since each state is different, it is best to check your state's workers' compensation web-site for the specifics. This is an opportune time to additionally educate your employees that the company has a "zero tolerance" policy relative to workers' compensation fraud and is committed to punish violators to the full extent of the law.

Although some of this information may be construed negatively by employees, it need not be that way. By interspersing the information concerning penalties and zero tolerance with general instructions (such as injury reporting and modified duty) you can send the overall message to your employees that they will receive prompt, professional medical treatment, and compensation for lost wages without resorting to fraud.

Communication

A fourth roadblock to workers' compensation fraud is erected when you effectively communicate with your employees. Effectively communicating with employees is a thread that runs throughout this book and is said by some to be the single most important factor for controlling the costs of workers' compensation claims. Failing to effectively communicate with employees can quickly turn a once satisfied employee into one who feels abandoned, under-valued and unimportant. Such feelings can be the spark that ignites an adversarial relationship, which is a key ingredient in many situations of workers' fraud.

Luckily, because of the limited size of their workforce, most small businesses do a good job at developing and maintaining a bond of mutual respect and trust with their employees. Communication is the key. Although you hired your employees to perform specific work tasks, you will be well served to take an interest in knowing what is important to your employees apart from their job. While at work make sure that your employees know that you will not ignore their complaints and concerns about working conditions. Let them know that you will take their recommendations seriously, and that you value their contribution to the company.

Following an injury, communication with the injured employee is equally important as it is before the injury. It is more important. After an injury, your employee is waiting to see if that bond of trust and respect was real or not. With that in mind, do not be quick to place blame, or to let your zeal for preventing workers' compensation fraud shatter the relationship between you and your employee by unjustly jumping to the conclusion that claim is fraudulent. Your actions and attitude expressed in front of the employee could very well cause the very thing that your fear. Instead, understand that communication is a two-way street that begins with listening. Gain as much information as you can about the incident. However, ensure that the message that is communicated to the employee is your concern for his wellbeing and the desire to prevent this incident from happening to him or another employee in the future.

Maintaining effective communication is perhaps even more critical when an employee is off work as a result of a work-related injury. Remember that they are likely sitting in front of a television that is feeding them the message that insurance companies are evil and that they are entitled to a windfall. At a minimum, you should be in contact with the injured employee several times per week, expressing your concern for his recovery. Although your words are important, your actions communicate more than your words ever can. If you are serious about preventing fraud, communicate that you value the injured employee by offering to do some of the things that the employee's injury might make difficult. This might include picking-up a few items for the employee at the grocery store and delivering them to his house, or driving the injured employee to a doctor's appointment or church. You will not likely see that type of care and concern in a large corporation. But, yours is not a large corporation.

By communicating in both word and deed that you value your employees, you establish a bond of trust and respect and an allegiance to your company that serves as a roadblock to workers' compensation fraud.

Early Return to Work

The fifth and final roadblock to workers' compensation fraud is a whole-hearted commitment to an early return-to-work (modified duty) program. Your employees should know up-front that your company will find work for injured workers as soon as it is conceivably possible for them to return-to-work.

An early return-to-work program serves as a roadblock for employees who want to abuse the workers' compensation system for personal gain. How it accomplishes this feat is quite simple. Individuals who intend to commit workers' compensation fraud generally seek to be off work as a result of their injury, as there is typically little potential for personal gain associated with no-loss-time injuries. When employees know up-front that their employer provides modified duty assignments consistently, they realize that they are less likely to be off work for any significant amount of time following an injury. Faced with that realization, an employee may not even try to engage in fraud, or may quit and become a thorn in the side of an employer who chooses not to erect this roadblock.

Difficult to Maneuver

Short of firing all of your employees, there is nothing that can be done to completely eliminate your exposure to workers' compensation fraud. However, erecting the five roadblocks in this chapter will make it difficult for any employee to maneuver his way down that road.

CHAPTER 9

To Catch a Thief

Although there are specific steps that small business employers can take to deter workers' compensation fraud, the unfortunate reality is that fraud may still rear its ugly head. When that happens, the goal is to identify and expose the fraud as quickly as possible. This chapter presents the most common and strongest indicators of workers' compensation fraud and instructs employers how to use that information effectively.

A Thief by Any Other Name

Fraud, in no uncertain terms, is theft. A perpetrator of theft is called a thief. Using any other term to describe the individual diminishes the gravity of the crime. Although the thief who commits workers' compensation fraud does not stick a gun in your ribs and overtly demand your wallet, the result is the same. He steals benefits from your workers' compensation carrier that are not rightly his. And as far too many small business owners have learned the hard way, the enormous drain on insurance companies created by workers' compensation fraud is not merely absorbed by the insurance companies. It is passed onto the policyholders through increased insurance premiums. Particularly for small businesses with very limited operating capital, the impact of increased premiums due to fraud can not only inhibit competitiveness and growth, but can threaten the very existence of a small business.

For many small businesses, workers' compensation insurance is the second or third most costly recurring expense, outside of payroll. Although spiraling healthcare costs are indeed a big factor, the high cost of workers' compensation premiums can be partially attributed to the lack of success that many businesses have had in combating workers' compensation fraud. The reality is that it takes more than a desire not to become a victim. It takes a plan. The first part of that plan, as described in the previous chapter, is to erect roadblocks to discourage would-be thieves from attempting to commit fraud. The second part is to identify when there is a thief in your midst before he cracks the proverbial safe and places a black mark on your workers' compensation loss history that will remain for years. In other words, the second part of the plan is to catch the thief before he takes the money and runs.

No Small Business Immunity

Many small business owners underestimate the pervasiveness of workers' compensation fraud and are under the false assumption that they are immune to the problem. If you are one of those small business owners, or hold similar views, you likely justify your belief by pointing to the family-like atmosphere in your businesses or the fact that you have known many of your employees and their families for years. However, the ethical character of others is not always something that is visible to the naked eye.

Since 98% of all private-sector businesses in the U.S. are small businesses, it is clear that the problem of workers' compensation fraud cannot rest solely within big corporations. Frankly, if your company has employees it is not immune to workers' compensation fraud. The intent of this chapter is to help you identify employees who may be flirting with the idea of committing workers' compensation fraud, or who are actively and aggressively involved in an attempt to steal workers' compensation benefits.

Are Red Flags being Raised?

Although workers' compensation fraud may be perpetrated by medical providers and employers, the focus of this chapter is "claimant fraud." Claimant fraud happens when an employee intentionally provides false information to collect benefits. Such an employee may claim an injury was work-related when it was not. He may exaggerate an injury in order to remain off work or to obtain a disability award. Furthermore, he may secretly continue working on the side while collecting benefits. An employee engaged in workers' compensation fraud may allege an injury that does not exist and then fabricate a story to corroborate work-relatedness.

The pervasiveness of the fraud problem causes some employers to become overly pessimistic, viewing almost all workers' compensation claims as being suspect. This leads to an unhealthy relationship with employees, even those who have never submitted a workers' compensation claim. Conversely, other employers would fail to recognize workers' compensation fraud even if the employee overtly bragged about how he is milking the system.

Injury Reporting

One of the most common red flag indicators of workers' compensation fraud is an injury that reportedly occurred early on a Monday, or the first day after returning to work after one or more days off work. An employee who reports and injury on a Monday morning may actually be reporting an injury that he incurred while he was off work over the weekend.

Another red flag relates to the amount of time that has lapsed before the injury is reported to the employer. Occasionally an employee who is legitimately injured at work does not report the injury to his supervisor or employer immediately. Instead, when the injury occurs he shrugs-off the pain believing it will subside, or has a delayed onset of pain from the injury. However, injuries are occasionally reported days or even weeks after the alleged incident. When the length of time between the injury and the time that it is reported is unreasonable the claim should likely be considered suspect.

What Other Employees Say

A fairly reliable red-flag indicator of workers' compensation fraud is rumors or outright allegations circulating among employees that a coworker's injury is not legitimate. These rumors are frequently based in fact, rather than mere suspicion. For example, an employee may have previously informed coworkers of an injury sustained outside of work, which is later submitted as a workers' compensation claim.

Employees are also your eyes in the community. It is often your employees who will inform you when a coworker has been seen working for another employer or engaged in work which he is allegedly unable to perform.

Description of the Injury

The injured employee's description of the injury itself can raise a red flag. One example is an employee who describes how he was injured, but does so without being specific, even when prodded for more detail. This may point to the possibility that the injury was fabricated. An employee who offers only a vague description of what happened may indicate that the employee did not anticipate you to question the him about the incident and has not completely thought-out a believable story to corroborate his injury claim.

Another red flag is raised when the employee's description of how he was injured just does not seem to be plausible. Unlike huge corporations, small business owners and managers are typically well acquainted with each and every task performed by their employees. Therefore it is quite reasonable for you to use your own knowledge of those tasks to question the legitimacy of a claim.

Similarly, a red flag is raised when an incident allegedly results in a significantly more serious injury than would be reasonably be expected. In such cases the employee may be exaggerating the extent of the injury for the purpose of getting additional time off work or in hopes of receiving a permanent disability settlement.

Inconsistencies in the employee's description of the incident also call the legitimacy of the claim into question. Just as prosecutors of criminal cases uncover inconsistencies in subsequent statements made by defendants, employees who attempt workers' compensation fraud can be revealed by inconsistent statements about the how the injury occurred.

Employment Status

Although new employees are statistically more likely to be injured at work, a red flag should be raised when a new employee reports an injury. It is an unfortunate reality that some individuals view the workers' compensation system as an opportunity to get rich quick. There is little benefit for these employees to remain employed by your company for years before attempting to abuse the system. For that reason, many take the very first opportunity to roll the dice with hopes of cashing-in.

On the other side of the spectrum are employees for whom employment termination is eminent. Particularly in small businesses, employees know in advance when they are going to be laid-off or terminated. A red flag is raised when an employee for whom termination or layoff is looming, submits a workers' compensation claim. Although an employee who is terminated or laid-off may be eligible for unemployment benefits, a workers' compensation claim offers the potential for indemnity benefits which can far exceed the maximum received from state-mandated unemployment benefits. This is a particular concern with older workers who may perceive that they will be unable to find another job.

Financial Pressures

As evidenced by the pervasiveness of insurance fraud, an alarming number of Americans do not view insurance fraud as immoral behavior. That combined with the financial indebtedness of the average working family is a recipe for fraud. A number of people may view the potential to score a financial settlement in order to pull them out of a debt hole to be a strong motivator for committing workers' compensation fraud. For that reason, knowledge that an employee who submitted a workers' compensation claim is having significant personal financial problems raises a red flag. However, just as any single red flag indicator is likely insufficient reason to leap to any conclusions about the legitimacy of a claim, an employee's poor personal financial status alone is not a strong indicator of fraud.

Closely related to the personal financial pressures of employees is the absence of healthcare insurance. Employees who do not have health insurance may try to have an injury or illness which is not work-related treated as a workers' compensation claim because they cannot afford, or do not want to pay, the out-of-pocket expense for medical treatment. For this reason, a red flag is raised by employees who submit a workers' compensation claims when they don't have healthcare insurance coverage.

Evasiveness

Some red flags are raised as a result of the injured employee's apparent evasiveness. As mentioned in the previous chapter, maintaining contact with an employee who is off work as a result of a work-related injury is very strongly encouraged. However, a red flag is raised if you are frequently unable to make such contact with the injured employee. Not being able to contact an employee who is too injured to come to work, or only being able to contact him through a friend or relative, may indicate that he is working elsewhere while receiving workers' compensation benefits.

Another red flag relating to the evasiveness of employees exists when the only home address that the employee provides is a post office box. Employees who commit fraud realize that concealing the physical address of their residence makes it much more difficult for you to visit them at their home, or to have surveillance conducted.

Personal Ties

Red flags can also be raised when certain ties and relationships exist outside of work. For example, a red flag may be raised when an employee who submits a workers' compensation claim has close friends or relatives who have submitted workers' compensation claims in the past which have resulted in indemnity benefits or settlements. More frequently than many people outside of the workers' compensation insurance industry may believe, workers' compensation fraud is contagious among friends and relatives. Individuals who see their friends or relatives committing fraud without detection are more prone to try it themselves. They may even get advice from those who have been successful in the past. Similarly, individuals who have submitted legitimate claims in the past may unknowingly instill the motivation for a friend or relative to seek similar benefits through illegitimate means. Such personal relationships are often brought to light when your employee has an unusual familiarity with the workers' compensation system and workers' compensation legislation.

Attitude

Red flags can also be raised by an employee's attitude. A disgruntle or uncooperative attitude may appear either before or after an employee reports an injury. Regardless of when this attitude becomes evident, it should be considered to be a possible indicator of fraud.

One manifestation of an undesirable attitude that constitutes a red flag is the employee's resistance management. More specifically, a red flag is raised when an employee is resistant to the very measures that have been implemented to control the costs of workers' compensation claims. For example, considering the family-like atmosphere that exists in many small businesses, an employee who objects to you visiting him at home may indicate that he is frequently not at home due to another job, or that he engages in activity at home which he is allegedly unable to perform. Similarly, an employee who opposes modified duty assignments may be a possible indicator of fraud.

Seeking a Settlement

Another strong red flag indicator of fraud exists when the employee is actively seeking a rapid financial settlement. This is sometimes done with the hope that the insurance carrier will take the bait and not look into the claim with as much scrutiny as it may warrant.

Because the goal of most workers' compensation litigation initiated by the employee is a financial settlement, another red flag indicator of workers' compensation fraud is raised when the employee obtains legal representation soon after submitting a workers' compensation claim. This is particularly true when the attorney has a reputation of litigating questionable claims, or who gain notoriety from television commercials touting workers' compensation as a specialty. The workers' compensation process is designed to be effective without the need to involve attorneys. As such, the involvement of an attorney at the onset of a claim is likely a strong indicator that the motives of the employee are questionable.

Medical Treatment

The medical treatment received by an employee can also raise red flags. One such red flag is raised when there are contradictions in the medical diagnosis of the employee's injury. Whereas it is not uncommon for an employee to be treated by more than one doctor for a single injury, when those doctors' diagnoses are inconsistent, there may be cause to question the legitimacy of the employees' claim. This may indicate that one of the doctors is collaborating with the employee to exaggerate the severity of a claim, or that the employee was able to influence one doctor's diagnosis with subjective claims of pain or restricted mobility.

A red flag may also be raised when the employee does not keep his medical appointments. An employee who misses doctors' appointments or rehabilitation treatments may indicate that he knows that the treatments are unnecessary.

Yet another red flag raised by medical treatment is dubbed "doctor shopping." If the employee changes medical providers in the middle of the treatment process, he could be doing so in hope that he will find one who will prescribe time off work or a permanent disability. This red flag is a particularly strong indicator of fraud if the employee waits to switch doctors until initial doctor releases him to return to work.

Unmasking the Thief

Red flags alert you to the possibility that an employee may be attempting to commit workers' compensation fraud. Generally, the more red flags, the more questionable is the claim. So when a claim is characterized by several red flags that seem to point to the possibility that a claim is fraudulent, you must take some type of action. This generally involves reporting your concerns to your workers' compensation insurance carrier. However, understand that not all questionable claims warrant the insurance company dispatching a private investigator to try to catch the employee on videotape. Much of the investigative work done by insurance companies is done through closely reviewing the employee's prior medical history and other less spectacular means.

Many states now have fraud investigative units as a part of the body that governs workers' compensation in the state. In addition to being good sources of information and advice concerning suspected workers' compensation fraud, many of these state investigative units will additionally conduct investigations of their own, either in concert or apart from the efforts of your insurance company. Contact information for these workers' compensation fraud units is provided in Appendix A.

Lastly, if you suspect fraud, it is not the time to wash your hands of the situation and turn it over to the insurance company. Instead, it is time to ensure that you are doing everything in your power to discourage the employee from going any further down the road of workers' compensation fraud. As suggested in the previous chapter, this is done through maintaining close contact with the employee and doing your best to prevent the relationship from becoming strained.

Although nothing short of terminating all employees will completely eliminate the risk of workers' compensation fraud, small business owners have the power to make a difference within their company. By erecting roadblocks that discourage fraud and by having a plan to unmask the thieves that perpetrate it, you will decrease your attractiveness as a target for those individuals who threaten your business.

CHAPTER 10

Don't Shoulder the Burden Yourself

When accidents happen in a small business, there is a tendency for the business owner or manager to shoulder the burden of investigating and analyzing the accident on his own, and then to announce what will be done differently to prevent a future similar incident. This chapter identifies the flaw in that tactic and presents a team approach that is compatible with small businesses.

No one Man is an Island

When an injury occurs at your company, what happens after the dust settles? After the employee has gone to the doctor – after the workers' compensation form has been completed, and even after your own internal incident form has been filled-out – what happens next? The injury has already happened. The time to be proactive has past. It is now time to react. You can't stop the tape and rewind. You can't turn back the hands of time. The only thing you can do is figure out why the injury happened and come up with a solution to prevent it from happening again. How do you do it?

If yours is like many small businesses, "what happens next" is that the owner or a manager reviews the known facts surrounding the incident to determine what caused it and what (if anything) can be done to prevent it from happening again. If that describes you, then your goal of "stopping repeat injuries" is both noble and necessary. It is certainly wise to look at the details of every single injury to determine how similar incidents might be prevented in the future. But, it is <u>not</u> wise to rely upon one person to arrive at a conclusion on his own... even if that person is you.

It makes no difference if you are the sharpest crayon in the box – if you know more about the business than any 3 other people combined – or if you have an uncanny ability to apply deductive logic. The fact is (brace yourself... this may come as a shock) you don't have all the answers. Furthermore, you don't even know all the relevant questions to ask. I hope that this revelation has not caused irreparable harm to your psyche. The truth is, your limitations are normal. The fact that you don't have all the answers is something that you have in common with every person who lives and breathes

The way you see things is shaped by your present position and past experiences. As an owner or manager, you don't see safety rules and procedures in quite the same light as a new employee sees them. As someone who is involved in the day-to-day operation of your company, you don't see the inherent hazards of the work quite the same as a person whose background is in a different industry. Your unique perspective shapes the way you view employee injuries and their causes. Based upon your perspective, you will be inclined to ask certain questions. Also, you will likely be predisposed to a limited set of solutions for addressing injury prevention.

This chapter provides a way for you to break free from the "one man show" routine. It provides a new way to examine the facts surrounding injuries – a way that draws benefits from the collective knowledge and insight of others. Lastly, it provides a way to arrive at injury prevention solutions that work consistently.

Like all of the topics addressed in this book, there is nothing complicated, difficult or even sophisticated about this process. The difference between this process and the "one man show" method used by most small businesses is that this process considers the fact that you don't have all the answers. You need the input, insight, intuition, intellect and ingenuity of several others to get the full picture. Unless you have a full, accurate picture of why an employee was injured, you are not going to be very successful in preventing future similar injuries.

A Firm Foundation

Any builder will agree that a solid foundation is essential for constructing a building. The same is true for just about anything; including the process used to stop repeat injuries. Because you are limited by your unique perspective, relying solely upon yourself for this process does not constitute a firm and reliable foundation. Although you may have success for a time, sooner or later you will fail to see what might have been clearly evident to someone else. This part of your company's safety efforts will crumble and fall like a building constructed on a weak foundation. In the rubble may be an employee who was seriously injured because you failed in your efforts to stop repeat injuries. For this process to be effective, you and the other people involved in the process must buy into the following belief system.

First, you must acknowledge that a group of individuals working as a team can brainstorm much more effectively than any individual alone. There is simply no need to elaborate further. If you are hesitant to buy into this fundamental view, stop reading now and start again at the beginning of this chapter.

Second, you must realize that sometimes the people furthest removed from the situation have the best insight. This is a relatively important concept to grasp, since you, as the owner of a small business or a manager within that business, will be fairly close to most situations that occur there. It is only after you acknowledge this reality that you will be receptive to a clerical employee's insight concerning the hazards to which your company mechanic is exposed.

Third, you must understand the following psychological phenomenon. When your employees are involved in identifying problems and solutions, they have a vested interest in implementing the solution. You have probably issued edicts within your business (like Moses descending from the mountain-top) only to find that not everyone embraced your wisdom and even fewer adhered to the rules consistently. Grandma's wisdom seems fitting here; "Those convinced against their will are of the same opinion still." When employees feel like the new rules or new procedures are theirs,' the reluctance to accept them can magically turn into eagerness to implement them.

Lastly, you must maintain the perspective that each and every employee injury could have been prevented. This perspective is difficult for some employers to embrace. You may be quick to throw out an example of how an employee just tripped over his own feet, or how an employee was hit by another car while she was stopped at a traffic light. However, both of those injuries and every other one that you can dream-up could have been prevented if something in the sequence of events that led up to the incident was different. This is not to say that the solution is always in the hands of the employer. However, if you fail to be steadfast in your conviction that every injury is preventable, soon you will stop trying to find a way to prevent the reoccurrence of all injuries, except those for which there are quick and easy solutions.

Assembling the Team

To use the process that is being discussed in this chapter, you will need to assemble a team of 3 to 5 employees. These employees must accept the four tenets listed above, just as you must.

Additionally, you must remember that there is strength in diversity. That sounds like a catchy politically-correct phrase. But with respect to the process being discussed in this chapter, it rings loud and true. You should seek people with different job titles, people with different employment longevity and people with varied backgrounds. If you choose two people for this team who are very similar with respect to these characteristics, one of them is unnecessary.

How it Works

You should already have a process for gathering information, completing the workers' compensation reporting form and completing your company's own internal incident form following an employee injury. Those processes are done merely to collect and document information. Although that is an important step, simply collecting and documenting information has never prevented any injury. What is done with that information is of paramount importance.

If injuries at your company have historically been less frequent than one per month, you should assemble the team of 3 to 5 employees that you have selected following each and every employee injury. However, if the frequency of employee injuries is greater than one per month, it is advisable to have a standing meeting time for the team every month.

At the beginning of each of these meetings, the ground-rules should be voiced to serve as a reminder to employees and to keep individuals from leading the discussion away from its intended focus – preventing the incident that caused the injury from happening again. First, the employees should be reminded that the meeting is not intended to find fault. For that reason, there should be no attempt to place blame for the incident. Secondly, employees should be reminded that the meeting is not a forum to discuss disciplinary action. In fact, at least one or two of the employees in the meeting should be non-management employees who have no voice in the discipline of their peers. Thirdly, the participants should be reminded that the discussion will be limited to facts, as opposed to opinions. Lastly, the employees in this meeting should be reminded that their first responsibility is to identify the underlying cause of the incident through continually asking questions until there are no more logical questions to ask concerning the incident.

Once the ground-rules have been voiced, the injured employee (if available) should be present and should be asked to describe his account of the incident. However, before the employee begins to speak, the person directing the meeting should put him at-ease by assuring him the process is not for the purpose of placing blame. Once the injured employee begins to speak, he should not be interrupted, unless he gets off on an unrelated tangent. When he is finished, the employees that you selected to be on the team can begin asking questions concerning the incident. This may even include questions concerning the employee's knowledge, training, etc. However, the questions should never be worded in a manner as to sound accusatory. Lastly, the questioning of the injured employee should be concluded by asking for his suggestions for preventing the incident from happening to someone else in the future. It is important that this final question be worded in that manner (as opposed to asking the employee what he could have done to prevent the injury). These two forms of the same question will invariably elicit quite different responses.

Although not the purpose of this process, the mere fact that the injured employee must make a verbal statement concerning the injury and be questioned can be a deterrent to workers' compensation fraud. The employee had to explain the incident previously (for reporting purposes) but now he is faced with telling the same story again. If the incident actually happened, it will be no problem for the employee to keep the two stories the same. However, if the first description of the incident was a lie, the employee will be challenged to remember the details surrounding the lie when he provides an account of the incident for the second time.

The next step in the meeting is to determine the causes of incident. This is the most challenging part, because there are frequently one or more contributing factors that are readily apparent and are hastily labeled as "the cause." Regardless of whether the conditions that are identified are simply "contributing factors" or if they can be considered to be the "underlying cause" of the incident, these conditions fall into one of three categories:

- Unsafe acts
- Unsafe conditions
- Managerial/administrative deficiencies.

"Unsafe acts" are the behaviors that directly contribute to the cause of the incident. These may involve the injured employee's action or omission of action, or may result from the action or failure of another person. Unsafe acts include such things as failure to look in the direction of travel when operating a forklift, removing a guard from a machine, using improper lifting techniques, failing to obtain assistance from another employee when warranted, and failing to use available material handling aids.

"Unsafe conditions" are the attributes of the workplace that directly contribute to the cause of the incident. Unsafe conditions are also called "hazardous" conditions, as the existence of an unsafe condition creates a hazard. Unsafe conditions may be either physical characteristics or environmental conditions. Physical characteristics that may constitute unsafe conditions may include such things as a spill on the walking surface that creates a slip hazard, or a poorly designed workstation that requires the employee to move in an awkward manner. Environmental characteristics that may constitute unsafe conditions include such things as excessive temperatures, excessive noise, poor lighting and inadequate ventilation. Although environmental characteristics are not tangible features of a workplace, they nevertheless may constitute unsafe conditions.

"Managerial/Administrative Deficiencies" are conditions within the structure of the company that directly contribute to the cause of an accident. These are often determined to be the underlying cause. Examples of managerial/administrative deficiencies include ineffective training, inadequate supervision, the absence of effective safety inspections, and the tacit approval of policy violations.

The participants are encouraged share their thoughts out-loud and to continually ask "why" for each contributing factor listed. By doing this they are digging to uncover the underlying cause(s) of the incident. For example, consider an employee who slipped and fell in a puddle of oil on the floor. Without digging to find the underlying cause, you might come to the conclusion that the cause of the incident was a puddle of oil on the floor. However, if you continued to ask "why" until you had exhausted all logical questions, you might have come to the conclusion that the underlying cause of this incident was no routine preventative maintenance performed on the particular piece of machinery which leaked oil onto the floor.

Once the underlying cause(s) have been identified, it is then time for the group to discuss potential corrective measures. In keeping with the group process, this is not the time to issue edicts. It is at this time more so than any other in the process that you (the company owner or manager) should sit-back and listen to the insight of the others on team.

Lastly, it is important to recognize that when "nobody" is assigned responsibility for ensuring that a corrective measure is implemented, that is exactly who will ensure that it gets done. Therefore, for every corrective measure recommended through this process, a specific individual within the company must be identified (by name) as being responsible for ensuring that the measure is implemented. Furthermore, that individual must be held accountable. When possible the worker assigned with responsibility for implementing a specific corrective action should also be provided with a target date or deadline.

Summary

If yours is like many small businesses, you or someone else in your company takes it upon himself to review the circumstances surrounding each employee injury and then, with command decision, determines what caused the incident and what can be done (if anything) to prevent something similar from happening in the future. However, that solo act negates the input, insight, intuition, intellect and ingenuity of your company's most valuable resource – its employees.

A wise business owner or manager recognizes the benefit of addressing something as serious as employee injuries and workers' compensation claims by using a small diverse group of employees who are willing to invest themselves in a process that may prevent a peer (or even themselves) from being injured in the future. The entire process will likely take the group a little longer at the beginning, but will become easier and will require less time as the employees get accustomed to the process. Through encouraging, active participation from selected employees and consistently applying corrective measures, the number of injuries will steadily reduce, as will the rate of worker' compensation claims.

CHAPTER 11

A "High" Priority

The relationship between substance abuse and workers' compensation claims is so profound that it demands to be made a "high" priority, and should likely take precedence over many of the recommended practices in this book.

A Pervasive Problem

Substance abuse is certainly a huge problem. Unlike the commonly misconceived image of drug-abusers as a subculture of people with whom most of us do not interact, the majority of adult substance abusers are employed. In fact, it is estimated that 75 percent of adults who admit to current illicit drug use (at least once per month) are actively employed either full-time or part-time. This number represents more than 12.4 million individuals[1]. Although those statistics are eye-opening, the problem of substance abuse is particularly distressing

---

[1] Substance Abuse and Mental Health Services Administration, Results from the 2002 National Survey on Drug Use and Health: National Findings, September 2003.

within the context of workers' compensation. You may have suspected that substance abusers, including those who abuse alcohol, are more prone to injuries, but you may be surprised to learn the extent to which that is true. One study reports that 38 to 50 percent of all workers' compensation claims are related to the use of alcohol or drugs in the workplace.[3] Another study suggests that 47 percent of serious workplace accidents and 40 percent of the workplace fatalities can be linked to alcohol consumption and alcoholism.[2] Clearly, substance abusers are overrepresented among workers' compensation claimants. In fact, at least one study suggests that substance abusers file three to five times as many workers' compensation claims as employees who are not substance abusers.[3] As if that is not enough cause for alarm, the National Institute on Drug Abuse (NIDA) reports that employed drug abusers cost their employers about twice as much in medical and workers' compensation claims as their drug-free coworkers.

Certainly those statistics provide the evidence that substance abuse is an enormous and pervasive workers' compensation issue. But that's not the whole picture. There are plenty of statistics that point to substance abuse as a cause for increased employee turnover, absenteeism, violence, decreased productivity and a host of other ills. Each of these can contribute to stress on the employees that do not abuse drugs and can make them more likely to incur injuries at work.

The problem of substance abuse is so significant that any serious attempt to take a bite out of your workers' compensation premiums must (without exception) confront the issue of substance abuse. In fact, the relationship between substance abuse and the frequency and cost of workers' compensation claims is so profound that it demands to be made a priority – a "high" priority as the chapter title suggests. For this reason, addressing substance abuse should likely take precedence over many of the other recommended practices in this book.

---

[2] "Bernstein M & Mahoney JJ, "Management Perspectives on Alcoholism: The Employer's Stake in Alcoholism Treatment," *Occupational Medicine*, Vol. 4, No. 2, 1989, pp. 223-232.

[3] "Working Partners", National Conference Proceedings Report: sponsored by U.S. Dept. of Labor, the SBA, and the Office of National Drug Control Policy.

Through the Eyes of Small Business Owners

Unfortunately many small businesses owners and managers are blind to the near inevitability that the problem of substance abuse will surface within their company. They are equally blind to the reality that substance abuse can have a direct, negative and long-lived impact on their workers' compensation premiums.

An unfortunately common perspective of small business owners and managers is often reflected in comments such as this… "I know each and every one of my employees, and I know none of them are drug abusers." Certainly some businesses exist and have no substance abusing employees. However, the prevalence of substance abuse in the United States makes that anything but common.

If you are among those small business employers who feel somewhat immune to the problem of substance abuse, consider how many younger workers you currently employ. Nearly one in four employed Americans between the ages of 18 and 35 has illegally used drugs.[4]

Many small business employers who hold the view that their workplace is immune to substance abuse, have fallen into the trap of placing too much faith in their employees. Such employers simply trust each member of their workforce not to become snared into the use of illicit drugs or the abuse of alcohol.

Others place undue faith in their own ability to discern. The latter may likely be heard saying, "We're small enough that I get to interact with my employees every day, and I could tell if any of my employees are under the influence." Many parents, spouses, close friends and others who have more frequent and more intimate interaction than an employer, have been shocked to learn that someone close to them has a substance abuse problem. Many are also shocked to learn how long the problem went undetected.

Although there are certainly signs and symptoms that point to substance abuse, the presence of some of these behaviors could be the product of stress. Others may be symptoms of depression or a host of other problems. Relying upon mere observation as a means of detection

---

[4] *"Drug Free Workplace Information Kit"* Tennessee Department of Labor and Workforce Development, Drug Free Workplace Program

is misguided and fails to deter substance abusers from seeking employment within your company.

Small Businesses are Targeted

Ironically, while many small business owners and managers feel that their company is somewhat immune to the problems of substance abuse, the reality is that small businesses are targeted by substance abusers. Recent data suggests that overall, 7.7 percent of all full-time workers abuse illicit drugs. However in very small businesses (those with 25 employees or fewer) 8.6 percent of workers reported current illicit drug use. The same study found that almost 90 percent of employed active illicit drug users and over 80 percent employed heavy drinkers work for small and medium sized firms.[5]

The overwhelming majority of large businesses have active substance abuse programs that make all employment offers contingent upon the applicant's ability to pass pre-placement drug screening. When substance abusers are aware that they will be required to submit to drug-screening, many do not follow through with the rest of the application process. Instead, they walk out of the door and look for a company that does not conduct drug-screening. As a result, many of these substance-abusing job applicants turn to small businesses. They are well aware that only 5 to 10 percent of small and medium sized businesses have implemented active drug-testing programs. [6]

The Solution

The solution for small businesses is the same as it is for large companies, a drug-free workplace program. Many people automatically associate a drug-free workplace program with drug-screening. But there's more.

---

[5] Substance Abuse and Mental Health Services Administration, Office of Applied Studies. Worker Drug Use and Workplace Policies and Programs: Results from the 1994 & 1997 NHSDA. OAS Analytic Series #11, DHHS Publication No. (SMA) 99-3352, Rockville, MD, 1999.

[6] *"Drug Free Workplace Information Kit"* Tennessee Department of Labor and Workforce Development, Drug Free Workplace Program

While drug-screening is important, a drug-free workplace program generally includes five components:
- written policy
- supervisor training
- employee education
- drug screening
- employee assistance

A written drug-free workplace policy typically defines what behavior is prohibited, when drug-testing will be conducted, how the policy will be enforced, and what will occur if the policy is violated. It may also address issues such as confidentiality, searches of persons or property, and reporting of drug-related convictions. Many times, a written drug-free workplace program also identifies how and when the policy is to be communicated to employees.

Supervisor training is essential. At a minimum, this training should familiarize supervisors with their specific responsibilities in implementing the drug-free workplace policy. Additionally, it should train supervisors to recognize and deal with employees who have job performance problems that could be related to alcohol and other drugs.

Just as supervisor training is essential to an effective drug-free workplace program, so is employee education. The purpose of employee education is to familiarize employees with your company's drug-free workplace program, to provide general awareness education about the dangers of alcohol and drug abuse, and to make employees aware of the types and sources of assistance that may be available.

Drug-screening is yet another essential element of an effective drug-free workplace program. There are 6 primary triggers for drug-screening. Although you may not elect to use all of them, each trigger serves a valid purpose.

Pre-placement drug screening is generally conducted after a contingent offer of employment has been made and is intended to deter drug-abusers from applying for a job with your company.

Random drug screening is conducted intermittently with no advance warning or justification and is and is intended to serve as a deterrent to existing employees.

Reasonable suspicion drug screening is conducted when employee behavior suggests a possible substance abuse problem, and is intended to identify employees violating the company's drug-free workplace policy before they are injured or injure someone else.

Post-accident drug screening is generally conducted following a work-related incident and in many cases can provide the justification for denial of a workers' compensation claim or a reduction in the amount of benefits paid.

Return to duty drug screening is generally conducted of previously suspended employees before they are permitted to return to work. This type of testing enables employers to keep valuable employees without diluting the company's drug-free standard.

Follow-up drug testing is conducted of previously suspended employees after their re-hire. This helps deter employees who are known to have had a substance abuse problem from engaging in future drug use.

Lastly, employee assistance programs are common elements in many drug-free workplace programs. However due to cost, some companies (particularly small businesses) do not include this element. Instead, they direct employees to substance abuse counselors where the employees can get the help they need at their own expense.

Overcoming Obstacles

Surely many small business owners acknowledge implementing a drug-free workplace program is beneficial. However, many of those same employers are discouraged to the point of inaction because they fear that implementing a drug-free workplace is too costly, too difficult or too risky. The reality is that is none of these things should stand in the way of implementing a drug-free workplace program.

For employers who are discouraged by the anticipated cost of implementing a drug-free workplace program, a case can be made for the exact opposite. Failing to implement a drug-free workplace program is where the cost really lies. Employers who fail to implement a drug-free workplace program eliminate the chance of getting a drug-free workplace credit from their workers' compensation carrier (see chapter titled "Jumping Through Hoops"). In many cases that premium credit alone will more than cover the cost of the entire drug-free workplace program. But beyond that, employers who do not actively confront the threat of drug abuse in the workplace increase the risk of employee injuries, theft, workplace violence, absenteeism, employee turnover, and a myriad of other problems that can erode the company's bottom-line.

For employers who are discouraged from implementing a drug-free workplace program because they are apprehensive about its complexity, they have quite a number of options at their disposal. Many of these resources were not available to small business employers in previous generations. A few of these are listed at the end of this chapter. They include a toll-free phone number (1-800-WORKPLACE) staffed by employees whose sole job is to help you develop a drug-free workplace program. Also mentioned at the end of this chapter is an interactive Internet-based drug-free workplace program tool that will help you develop a drug-free workplace program, customized to your company. Also don't forget your workers' compensation carrier's loss control staff. They have a vested interest in your success and may be able to provide you step-by-step instructions, sample policies and other assistance. Finally, there are firms and consultants who specialize in assisting employers who want to implement and administer a drug-free workplace program, but do not have the expertise or the inclination to do it themselves.

For employers who are concerned about the risk of having employee drug- screening challenged in a court of law, they should rest in the knowledge that the courts consistently rule in favor employee drug-screening that is based on procedures that are clear, fair, consistent, and communicated in a written policy statement.

Drug-Free Workplace Resources

If your company does not yet have a drug-free workplace program, it is time to take action. Reviewing the following sources of assistance is a great starting point. However, prior to implementing any drug-free workplace program that involves drug-testing, it is advisable to first consult with competent legal council, as a handful of states prohibit or restrict drug-testing in the workplace under some circumstances.

The Workplace Helpline

The Workplace Helpline is toll-free telephone consulting service that provides technical assistance and guidance in developing and evaluating programs and policies designed to address alcohol and drug problems at work. It is staffed by trained specialists who can help design a program that meets your specific needs. Consultation is provided on policy development, supervisor training, employee education, employee assistance programs, and drug-screening. This service is provided free by the Center for Substance Abuse Prevention. It can be accessed through the telephone number 1-800-WORKPLACE, or HELPLINE@SAMHSA.GOV. More information about this service is available at www.workplace.samhsa.gov/HelpLine/Helpline.htm

Making Your Workplace Drug Free: A Kit for Employers

"Making Your Workplace Drug-Free" is a kit which offers guidance, specific strategies, and easy-to-follow steps for creating a drug-free workplace program or for enhancing an existing one. It was designed for owners and managers in businesses of all sizes, but especially smaller businesses. The kit suggests low-cost approaches and should be especially helpful for employers who do not have much time to develop a written drug-free workplace program. Get the kit on-line online at the website www.workplace.samhsa.gov/WPWorkit/workitindex.html

The Drug-Free Workplace Advisor

The Drug-Free Workplace Advisor provides information to businesses on how to establish and maintain a drug-free workplace. This is one of several e-tools on the Department of Labor web-sites. These interactive web-tools are intended to simulate the interaction you might have with an employment law expert. It will ask questions and provide answers based upon your responses. Included in this e-tool is the Drug-Free Workplace Program Builder, which is designed to assist you develop and customize a program that reflects your company's needs and culture. As you move through the Program Builder, you will be provided with information that will help you choose among various options to create a program suitable to your company. Try the Drug-Free Workplace Advisor at www.dol.gov/elaws/drugfree.htm

State and Territory Resources

Many states offer publications, help-lines, training aids and other resources to assist employers in the development of a drug-free workplace. See what your state offers at the website listed below: www.dol.gov/asp/programs/drugs/said/StateResources.asp

CHAPTER 12

Less than Full Strength

Because they have bought-in to some of the myths surrounding modified duty, far too many small business owners and managers disregard it, claiming that modified duty is not feasible for their company. Such attitudes cost these small businesses dearly. This chapter addresses these myths, explains the many benefits of using modified duty, and discusses the unique challenges faced by small business owners and managers when attempting to use modified duty to control workers' compensation costs.

The Choice is Yours

Imagine that one of your employees has just returned from the doctor after injuring his back in a fall at work. He hands you a slip of paper from his doctor that indicates that he is able to return to work, but cannot lift over 25 pounds until he is seen again in three weeks. He is a fairly good employee. However, he only knows how to do one job. You are aware that the only job he knows involves some lifting that exceeds the 25 pound restriction, as well as some other relatively strenuous tasks. At that point you are faced with making a decision. Will you tell the injured employee and the insurance company that you just cannot accommodate the doctor's restrictions, or will you make some temporary adjustments and allow your injured employee to return to work within the doctor's restrictions?

The latter is a workers' compensation claims management technique that is known by several names. The two most popular names are "light duty" and "modified duty." Because it is more accurate in its description, the term "modified duty" is quickly gaining more popularity.

There is nothing new about the concept of modified duty. It has been a successful management tool since the very earliest days of workers' compensation insurance. In fact, most companies that have grown into medium or large business have wholeheartedly embraced the concept of modified duty.

However, a significant number of small business owners and managers do not know as much as they should about this topic. Because they do not have a full understanding of the benefits (or because they have bought-in to some of the myths surrounding modified duty), far too many small business owners and managers disregard it, claiming that modified duty is not feasible for their company. Such attitudes cost these employers dearly.

For that reason, this chapter will address some of the myths surrounding the topic of modified duty and will explain the many benefits of choosing to use this technique. It will also discuss the unique challenges faced by small business owners and managers when attempting to use modified duty to control workers' compensation costs.

What's in it For Me?

Using modified duty is not easy. It will require time and effort. It sometimes involves shuffling the job duties of others or trying to create productive work for the injured employee out of thin air. It may even require that training be conducted for one or more employees to perform tasks that they have never performed before. Since your time is valuable, and probably in high demand, it is legitimate for an already over-burdened small business owner or manager to ask the question, "What's in it for me?" Before you invest your time and effort, you should know the benefits that you can expect from your effort.

If you are already familiar with the concept modified duty, you may be aware of some of the benefits. However, there are quite a few of them that you may not have considered.

Not only does a commitment to use modified duty lower your workers' compensation premiums, it also deters workers' compensation fraud, helps injured employees heal more quickly, and improves the general morale of employees.

Lowers Premiums

To understand how a commitment to using modified duty can result in lower workers' compensation premiums, you need at least a cursory knowledge of how premiums are calculated. In Chapter 3, the experience-rating process was introduced and was said to influence your company's workers' compensation premium based upon the company's claim history. Plain and simple, given two identical companies, the company with more costly workers' compensation claims in the recent past will pay a higher workers' compensation premium.

Consider again the example at the beginning of this chapter. An employee presented you with a slip from his doctor stating that he could return to work if you could accommodate lifting restrictions. If you would have chosen to work with the employee and find something he could do without lifting over 25 pounds, the employee would not have missed work because of his injury and therefore would not have been paid wage replacement benefits from the workers' compensation carrier. However, if you had chosen not to use modified duty, the employee would have been off work for at least 3 weeks (hypothetical), while drawing indemnity benefits. Obviously, the latter would appear on the workers' compensation claims history to be a more severe (costly) claim and would have a more negative impact on future workers' compensation premiums.

Discourages Fraud

There is a certain percentage of the population that may otherwise be "ethical," but who have no moral problem taking advantage of insurance companies. But, fraud not only hurts the insurance companies. The unethical individuals who perpetrate workers' compensation fraud have a very real and direct impact upon their employer as well. In fact, small business owners feel the impact of workers' compensation fraud much more than multi-million dollar insurance companies.

Employees who are bent on abusing the workers' compensation system often do it by attempting to remain off work for as long as possible – far past the time that is medically necessary. A company that is committed to using modified duty places a road block directly in their path, as the effect of modified duty is that injured employees are returned to work as quickly as possible.

As mentioned in the chapter titled "Erecting Roadblocks," modified duty can even identify and weed-out employees who are trying to milk the system. How it accomplishes this feat is quite simple. Consider again the scenario presented at the beginning of this chapter. You are faced with a decision. You can either provide modified duty to the injured employee or tell him that he must remain off work until fully released by his doctor. The employee seeking to milk the system is counting on the latter. If you offer modified duty to such an employee, he will likely decline it and offer a lame excuse for his refusal. This is a fairly good indication that the person with whom you are dealing was counting on the time off work, and would likely develop into a malingerer, if permitted to do so. In such situations, know that the insurance company (once informed of your offer of modified duty and the employee's refusal) will likely stop the wage-replacement payments immediately, foiling the scheme.

The benefit of using modified duty to counter fraud does not end there. In fact, modified duty can discourage fraud even if it is never used. Simply by being committed to using modified duty and being vocal about it, you will be sending a message to employees that time off work is not an automatic benefit afforded to everyone who has a workers' compensation claim. On the contrary, employees know ahead of time that you will make every effort to keep them at work, insofar as their doctor permits it. The unfortunate reality is that some employees view time off work as an entitlement due to them as a result of being injured while at work. Individuals with this mentality can easily convince themselves that malingering to prolong a workers' compensation claim is acceptable as well.

Helps Healing

The very fact that an employee is in a position to be given a modified duty assignment means that there is some physical task that his doctor does not want him to perform, at least for a short time. The physical restrictions imposed by the doctor are imposed for a reason. It is not because the doctor is concerned about your company's productivity. The reason that doctors impose temporary physical restrictions is to help the employee heal better and quicker.

By using modified duty, you increase control over the recovery process. Although you cannot watch the injured employee 24 hours per day, by allowing him to return to work, you can make sure that the doctor's orders are being followed at least for the 8 hours per day that he is under your control. Conversely, when the employee is off work (presumably laying on a sofa recovering) you have no idea what activities he is engaged in. Furthermore, you have no control over whether he is adhering to doctor's orders.

In addition, numerous studies have revealed that employees who return to work following a work related injury recover at a more rapid pace than those who do not. Why this happens is debatable. Maybe it is because of the therapeutic benefits of work. Maybe it is routine contact with peers at work that is the key. Why it happens is not important. What matters is that you can count "healing" among the benefits of modified duty.

Improves Morale

Not only can the practice of using modified duty lower your premiums, combat workers' compensation fraud and aid in the recovery process of injured employees, it can also improve morale within your company. This includes both the morale of the injured employee as well as the workforce as a whole.

Ask ten people to describe themselves to you and nine of them will mention their job within their first three sentences. Good or bad, your job is a large part of your identity. The same is true of your employees. With that in-mind, it is easy to understand that an employee's sense of self worth decreases when he is off work and increases when he returns to work. Permitting an employee to return to work within the scope of modified duty can boost his sense of self worth.

Additionally, an employee's morale and sense of self-worth is bolstered by the very message that is being sent by an employer who is willing to use modified duty. Simply by taking the extra effort to keep the employee working, you are communicating to an injured employee that you value him. Your commitment to modified duty tells each employee that he is worth the extra effort that it takes to find something productive for him to do until he is able to return to his regular job. In short, by using modified duty, you are communicating to employees that they are valued not only when they are at 100 percent, but also when they are not physically up to par.

Now consider the impact that modified duty has on the employees who are not injured; the ones who keep on working at their regular jobs while the injured employee gets your attention. Their morale is heightened through the use of modified duty as well, as they are not asked to take-up the slack for a coworker who is off-work (on the sofa at home).

Confronting the Myths

There are some myths surrounding the topic of modified duty that prevent some small business owners and managers from using it. Unfortunately many simply accept these false notions without challenging them and without asking the opinion and advice of someone in the insurance industry. As a result, these employers shy away from modified duty and forego all of its benefits.

Some employers fear that they will be sued if the employee re-injuries himself while on modified duty. In today's society no one is immune from being sued for virtually anything. However, the fear of being sued if an employee is re-injured at work is not warranted. Workers' compensation is not only a protection for employees – it is a protection for employers as well. In the absence of negligence, workers' compensation is the sole remedy for an injury arising out of, or in the course of employment. Therefore, it is a generally true statement that the only employees who can successfully bring a civil suit against an employer for a work-related injury are those who can point to employer-negligence as the cause of their injury.

Another myth is that using modified duty will create morale problems with other employees. Ironically, this fear is so dramatically unfounded, that the exact opposite is true in almost every circumstance. Employers who hold this fear believe that employees will see a peer performing "light duty" work and view him as getting off easy and not pulling his fair share of the load. Although this mindset is far less prevalent than some people believe, it does exist to some extent. However, it is quickly and easily reversed when disgruntled employees are assisted in visualizing the alternative, in which the injured employee is off work, makes roughly the same amount of income, and does nothing to help the work get done.

Yet another myth is that using modified is just too much trouble. This myth is rarely voiced. But it nevertheless keeps far too many small business owners and managers from using modified duty. The reality is that it is a very simple process. No lengthy policy is needed. No forms are required. It simply takes knowledge of the tasks performed by employees, a general idea of the physical requirements to perform those tasks and a commitment to cash-in on the benefits that modified duty provides.

Modified Duty within Small Businesses

Whereas large businesses almost universally embrace the concept of modified duty, the same is not necessarily true for small businesses. When faced with the opportunity to provide an injured employee with a modified duty assignment, some small business employers quickly resist, claiming that their company does not have any "light duty" jobs. They assert that everyone who works for them does a wide variety of tasks and that each employee is likely to perform some type of strenuous work at some point during an average work day. However, with only extremely rare exceptions, small businesses (even very small businesses) are able to able to use modified duty.

The stumbling block that many small business owners and managers have is not that modified duty can't work for them. Nor is it that they are too stubborn try something different. The most significant obstacle is that many small business owners and managers have a preconceived and limited view of modified duty. Some employers falsely believe that modified duty can only be implemented if the company has an existing full-time clerical job that is not currently staffed by someone else. Others with a similar, limited view of modified duty think it is feasible only if the injured employee is capable of performing the job assignment without training or without affecting the job duties of other employees.

The easiest way to break free from a limited view of modified duty is to begin viewing each employee's job as being comprised of many different tasks. The injured employee may be temporarily unable to perform every task that comprises his own job. But that does not necessarily mean that he cannot perform the other tasks, even while he has a physician-imposed physical restriction. Similarly, there may not be a vacant job within your company for which the injured employee can perform all of the required tasks. But that does not mean that he cannot perform some of the tasks associated with one or more jobs until he is released to return to work at full-strength. In other works, using modified duty may require assembling a job (in piece-meal fashion) for the injured employee to perform using the existing tasks that are normally being performed by several employees. Furthermore, as an overburdened small business owner or manager, you may be well-served to have an employee who is unable to perform all the tasks of his own job, help lighten your workload for a period.

But don't paint yourself into a corner by limiting your view of modified duty to tasks that are currently being performed in the normal course of business. Also consider the tasks that are performed only periodically (such as counting inventory) and the tasks that there never seems to be enough time to do (such as filing, reorganizing a particular area of the facility, spring cleaning or painting).

In fact, how modified duty can be used to keep an injured employee productive is limited only by your imagination. Depending upon the physical limitations of the injured employee and the physical requirements of the task, an employee with temporary physical limitations can be used to train other employees, to greet customers, to distribute promotional flyers, or to keep the facility clean. He may be used to serve as a night watchman, conduct safety inspections, provide support to an overburdened supervisor, or may be just the right person for your pet project that you have never found the time to start.

The underlying message however, is that modified duty is both feasible and beneficial. Although it requires more effort than simply telling an injured employee to come back to work when he is 100 percent, the effort that it requires pays back tremendous dividends.

CHAPTER 13

Let the Games Begin

When insurance companies are pitted against one another to win your business, the clash almost always manifests itself in competitive pricing. This chapter provides guidance on obtaining competitive quotes, as well as instructions for basing the selection not only on the amount of the premium, but also on the ability, liability, stability and dependability of the insurance carrier.

Competition Breeds Lower Premiums

At the writing of this book, a popular tagline used by the mortgage broker, Lending Tree, is "When banks compete, you win." The same is true about insurance companies. When several insurance companies are pitted against one another to win your business, the clash almost always manifests itself in competitive pricing. In short, competition breeds lower insurance premiums. And when it does, you win.

However, there is one caveat. For insurance companies to compete for your business to any measurable degree, your business must be attractive to insurance companies. In insurance terms, your company must be perceived to be a good risk.

For your company to be viewed by insurance companies as being a good risk, it is likely necessary for your company to have a favorable loss history. In practical terms, this means that the number of workers' compensation claims and the cost of the claims incurred by your company over the past several years should be less than the industry average. Another factor that influences the insurance companies' perception of risk is the level of comfort that they (the insurance companies) have with your particular industry and with your operation specifically. Additionally, the level of cooperation that the insurance companies can expect in managing claims costs and responding to loss control recommendations may also be factored into their perception of your company as a workers' compensation risk.

Employing the strategies throughout this book will help to make your company a good risk in the eyes of insurance companies. However, for the purpose of addressing how competition can help you take a bite out of your workers' compensation premiums, this chapter will assume that your company is already a good risk in the eyes of most reasonable insurance underwriters.

Monopolistic States

Sorry folks. If your business is located in a monopolistic state (a state that does not allow competition within the workers' compensation insurance arena, but instead requires all workers' compensation insurance to be placed with or through a state fund) and you have no exposure outside of that state, you cannot use competition as a strategy to take a bite out of your workers' compensation premium. The very nature of a monopolistic system implies that there is but one authorized provider, and since workers' compensation is mandated for most employers, you are simply stuck with paying whatever the state fund charges.

Competition Among Agents and Brokers

Although the object of using competition is to influence the premiums charged by the insurance companies, as a small business employer you generally do not have direct access to the insurance companies. Instead, you will typically work through an insurance agent or broker. These are the intermediaries between you and the insurance company underwriters.

In simple terms, an insurance "agent" is an individual who is licensed by a state to sell insurance for one or more insurance companies. If an insurance agent is working exclusively for a single insurance company he is called a "captive agent." If an insurance agent represents multiple insurance companies, as opposed to just one, he is referred to as an "independent agent." Even though independent agents work with multiple insurance companies, that does not mean that they have a working relationship with all of the insurance companies that offer workers' compensation in your state. First, they generally do not have access to direct writers of insurance (the insurance companies that use captive agents). Second, independent agents are generally limited to working with insurance companies with which they (or the agency for which they work) have signed a contract defining the commission structure and the minimum requirements for the volume of business that the insurance company expects.

Insurance "brokers," on the other hand, generally do not have contracts with any particular insurance companies. Instead, they work on a commission or negotiated fee basis trying to find the buyer the best policy by comparison shopping. In reality, the line separating agent and broker can be blurry. For example, in many cases independent agents can work in the capacity of an insurance broker and comparison shop coverage from insurance companies other than the ones with which they maintain a contract.

Particularly for small businesses, insurance agents and brokers are often selected based upon personal relationships, rather than allowing multiple insurance agents to compete for your business. That is not necessarily a bad thing. After all, it is important to trust your insurance agent or broker to work in your best interest, which is likely more feasible when some level of personal relationship exists. However, the occasional introduction of competition among insurance agents may help to keep your agent or broker working aggressively to find you the best coverage for your dollar.

Furthermore, even if your agent is aggressively working in your best interest, not every independent agent (as mentioned above) has access to quotes from every insurance provider. For that reason, it may be advisable to occasionally employ the tactic of competition with respect to your agent or broker; simply to see if other insurance companies (ones to which your agent does not have access) can offer a more competitive quote.

If you do decide to allow a competing agent or broker to solicit insurance quotes on your behalf, it is important to consider the fact that insurance companies cannot provide a quote to multiple insurance agents for the same company for a given policy period. For that reason, you should select a competing agent that has access to insurance carriers different from the ones your current agent uses. If there are some insurance companies used both by your current agent and the competing agent, protect your current insurance agent's access to those insurance companies by writing a letter that identifies your current agent as the "agent of record." This will limit the competing agent to insurance companies not used by your current agent. You may even choose to simplify the process by selecting a captive agent to provide the competition, as a captive agent works only for one insurance company, and will therefore not be attempting to solicit a quote from the same insurance companies as your existing agent.

Lastly, with respect to using competition among agents and brokers, be transparent and open with your current agent. Let your agent know that you are seeking additional quotes from another agent and why. You have nothing to gain by acting covertly. In fact, the mere knowledge that you are soliciting competitive quotes from another agent may be enough to cause your current agent to exercise whatever influence he has with insurance companies to yield a lower quote and retain your business.

Competition among Insurance Carriers

The first and most important principle to remember when using competition among insurance carriers to take a bite out of your workers' compensation premium is simply to "make the choice yourself." Don't delegate to your insurance agent the responsibility to choose who will be your insurance carrier. Instead, request to see the quotes that were obtained from each insurance carrier, compare them and ask questions.

Certainly you should seek the council of your agent or broker. Recognize and respect the fact that he is a licensed professional who has sworn to a code of ethics. His knowledge not only of the insurance industry, but of how specific insurance companies treat their clients will be of benefit to you. But ultimately, the choice should be made by you (the employer). By committing to make the choice yourself (with the council of your agent or broker), you will help counter the potential for an agent to select the insurance carrier that simply has the best commission structure for him.

Comparing Apples to Apples

If you are willing to take the advice set forth in this book and make the ultimate decision yourself, you must be able to objectively compare the insurance quotes provided by your agent or broker and ensure that you are comparing apples to apples. As explained in a previous chapter, three very fundamental building blocks in calculating workers' compensation premiums are the classification code, the estimated payroll, and the experience modifier. For that reason, it is essential when comparing insurance quotes that the same information be used to develop each quote. This information should be clearly indicated on each quote.

In addition to ensuring that competing quotes use the same classifications, payroll and experience modifier, as an "apples to apples" comparison of workers' compensation quotes requires that you consider the impact (if any) that workers' compensation coverage might have on other lines of insurance. Occasionally, multi-line insurance carriers will provide a quote for workers' compensation coverage that is dependent upon securing other lines of insurance from that same insurance company. In such situations, the quote from the multi-line insurance carrier may be the least expensive workers' compensation premium presented by your insurance agent or broker, but the overall cost of insurance (all lines combined) may not be competitive. Conversely, mono-line insurance carriers (those that provide workers' compensation coverage only) may be able to provide you with the lowest workers' compensation quote, but may cause you to lose a discount offered by a multi-line insurance carrier for placing all of your insurance business with them.

More than Premium

Since workers' compensation benefits are defined by state statutes, many small business owners fall prey to the misconception that there is no significant difference from one insurance carrier to another. For that reason, the tendency of many small business owners is to focus solely upon the price. In short, the insurance company with the lowest quote gets the business. This thought process is short-sighted and can have unfavorable consequences for the employer. Although price is indeed an important factor (perhaps the most important factor) it should not be treated as the sole consideration.

Employers should protect themselves from potential negative consequences of making a hasty decision when selecting their next workers' compensation carrier. To do this, they must look beyond price to consider the ability, liability, stability and dependability of each insurance carrier from which a quote has been obtained.

Ability

If your business involves employees performing work in states other than the state in which your company is domiciled, one consideration you may want to address up-front is the ability of the insurance provider to meet your needs. Many self-insurance funds are limited to providing coverage in one state and thus may force you to secure workers' compensation coverage through a different provider for work performed outside of your primary state. In addition to being an administrative hassle, this could very well cause your total workers' compensation premium to be higher than coverage obtained through an insurance carrier that is able to provide workers' compensation coverage in all states.

In addition to the ability of your insurance carrier to provide coverage in each state in which your employees perform work, you should also consider foreseeable changes in your business that may impact the ability of particular insurance carriers to provide coverage. Yes, even a slight change in your operation may render an insurance carrier unable to continue coverage. To illustrate this, imagine that you own a convenience store that closes at 11:00 pm nightly. If you decide to stay open 24 hours per day (and your insurance company gets wind of it), you might receive a cancellation letter from your insurance carrier, because their underwriting guidelines exclude 24 hour convenience stores from coverage. For this reason, you will be well served to discuss foreseeable changes in your operation with your insurance agent or broker before selecting a workers' compensation insurance carrier.

Liability

Another very important consideration in selecting a workers' compensation insurance carrier is the degree of liability the insurance carrier assumes. In this regard, one of the most fundamental distinctions to be made is the contrast between fully-insured insurance products and self-insurance funds. Whereas insurance companies assume all the financial risk for compensable work-related injuries, employers who maintain workers' compensation coverage through self-insurance funds retain some of that financial risk themselves. In essence, each of the employers with coverage through a given self-insurance fund sign an agreement that makes them not only liable for their own losses, but also for all other employers in the fund. Although the premium charged for coverage through a self-insurance fund is typically lower than that charged by an insurance company, there is a potential to be financially assessed for losses incurred by the fund as a whole. And in many cases, that potential for a financial assessment lags several years after you cease maintaining coverage through the self-insured fund.

Another means by which some employers assume some of the liability for workers' compensation losses is through loss-sensitive plans, such as retrospective rating plans and deductible plans. Retrospective rating plans are generally offered only to larger employers and are workers' compensation policies in which the premium is modified retrospectively (after the end of the policy year) based upon losses incurred during that period. With such plans, employers are not provided with a guaranteed cost for insurance dependent only upon payroll fluctuations. Instead, they assume some of the risk themselves. Similarly, workers' compensation plans with built-in deductibles to be paid by the employer do not result in the full liability of workers' compensation losses being transferred to the workers' compensation carrier.

Stability

The stability of an insurance carrier is another characteristic that should be taken into consideration when selecting a workers' compensation carrier. There are several rating organizations that measure and report on insurance carriers' financial strength and viability to meet claims obligations.

	Rating	Descriptor
	A.M. Best Company Financial Strength Ratings	
	Rating	Descriptor
Secure	A++, A+	Superior
	A, A-	Excellent
	B++, B+	Very Good
Vulnerable	B, B-	Fair
	C++, C+	Marginal
	C, C-	Weak
	D	Poor
	E	Under Regulatory Supervision
	F	In Liquidation
	S	Suspended

Figure 13.1

The most widely used rating organization is A.M. Best Company. This rating system is analogous to school report-card grades. Figure 13.1 depicts each of the potential ratings within that system.

It is important to select a workers' compensation carrier with a relatively strong financial strength rating ("A" and above)... Just ask any employer who had the misfortune of being insured by a workers' compensation carrier during the insurer's decline into liquidation. Such insurance carriers have little motivation to effectively manage claims, which can have a long-lasting unfavorable impact upon your company's experience modifier.

Dependability

In addition to ability, liability and stability, selecting a workers' compensation provider should include consideration of the insurance carrier's dependability. As a small business, your success depends, in-part, on the alliances that your company forms with other companies. Relative to workers' compensation the most obvious alliance that exists (or should exist) is the one between your company and your workers' compensation carrier.

For such an alliance to be beneficial, you must be able to depend upon your workers' compensation carrier to provide advice and services when needed. You should be able to depend on your workers' compensation carrier to act in your best interest. Furthermore, you should be able to depend on your workers' compensation carrier to exercise some degree of loyalty.

Too often when big-ticket purchases are made, the buyer must take the promises of the salesperson with a grain of salt. That should not be the case with your workers' compensation insurance purchase. You should be able to depend upon your workers' compensation carrier to deliver the loss control services that were promised. However, no assumption should be made regarding the availability of loss control services (except in states in which loss control services are required to be provided upon request). For this reason, the type of loss control services and the limitations on the availability of those services should be discussed up-front, as a part of the decision-making process. This may be particularly important for companies that are so small that they have not received loss control services from workers' compensation providers in the past, or for companies that have unique hazards and would benefit from the professional guidance of an occupational safety or industrial hygiene professional.

In addition to being able to depend upon your workers' compensation carrier to provide loss control and other services touted by their marketing literature (and perhaps by your insurance agent) you should be able to depend upon your workers' compensation carrier to act in the best interest of your company in circumstances in which they have some degree of latitude. In practical terms, this means that your insurance carrier takes into consideration the effect that subrogation for a workers' compensation claim might have on your business if sought from your best customer. It also means that your insurance carrier considers the impact to your company's loss history when determining how ardently to fight suspected cases of workers' compensation fraud.

Dependability in a workers' compensation carrier can also be measured by the carrier's willingness to retain long-term clients when the occasional bad loss year rears its ugly head. Obviously an insurance carrier would not be acting in the best interest of its shareholders if it retained bad risks for the mere sake of being loyal. However, an insurance company that is poised to send a non-renewal letter every time an insured company's loss ratio crosses the 70% threshold means that you may be only one claim away from being tossed into the assigned risk pool.

Price

Although ability, liability, stability and dependability are important considerations, the fact remains that price (justifiably) carries the most weight in the insurance carrier selection process. After all, if you were not driven to lower your workers' compensation premium, you very likely would not be reading this book. Nonetheless, allowing price to play too significant of a part in your decision can have negative consequences.

As presented earlier in this chapter, loss-sensitive plans (such as retrospective plans and deductible plans) shift some of the financial risk to you. Self-insured funds that have joint and several liabilities do the same. Choosing an insurance carrier that is headed for bankruptcy or one that does not provide dependable and professional loss control services may result in higher claims costs and ultimately land you a higher than necessary experience modifier.

With those caveats having been expressed, quite often letting competition within a free market economy work to your advantage can yield your company a significantly lower premium with a very stable and dependable workers' compensation carrier. Lastly, if you have worked hard to make your company desirable in the eyes of insurance underwriters, you may even be able to work through your insurance agent to secure a lower quote from the insurance carrier of your choice.

Chapter 14

Marketing 101

If you are the individual within your company who is responsible for overseeing employee safety efforts, there is one more hat that you should be wearing... the hat of the "marketing director."

Time for Another Hat

If you already have salespeople employed by your company, don't merely skip-over this chapter and move onto the next. This chapter is not about marketing the product or service that your company provides to external customers. In fact, the marketing espoused in this chapter is not intended to be directed toward external customers at all. Instead, the product that this chapter advocates that you market is "safety" and the intended audience is your employees.

The authors of this book are well aware that most small business owners and managers who oversee issues such as employee safety and workers' compensation also wear a variety of other hats. Many perform traditional human resources functions, such as hiring and firing. Many also wear the hats of trainer and compliance-specialist – not to mention the hats of accountant, supervisor, counselor, and others. However, if you are the individual within your company who is responsible for overseeing employee safety efforts, there is one more hat that you should be wearing – the hat of the "marketing director."

Over the past several decades, the US economy has continued to transition away from traditional manufacturing jobs. Now with more service-oriented businesses than ever before, employees are working without the direct and constant supervision that was so central to many company's injury prevention efforts. In fact, in many small businesses the employees frequently work alone or with very small groups of coworkers.

Without constant and direct supervision, employers must rely more and more upon individual employees to perform their work-related tasks safely on their own accord. To do this, employees must keep "safe behavior" foremost in their minds.

For example, when a truck-driver is opening a trailer door, he should instinctively think about the possibility that the load has shifted and is leaning against the trailer door; or that that a load-lock came loose in transit and may fall out when the trailer door is opened; or that a gust of wind may rip the trailer door from his hands.

Although it would be great if "safe behavior" was the foremost thought in the mind of each employee all of the time, the reality is that safety is competing with an immeasurable number of thoughts every minute of every day within every employee. An employee may be dealing with anger after someone has cut him off in traffic earlier in the day. He may be frustrated by unrealistic expectations at work. He may be worried about financial problems; concerned about some family issue; or may merely have drifted off into thought about his plans for the remainder of the week.

Regardless of what thoughts an employee may have, if those thoughts are not furthering the objective of preventing injuries, then they are competing for something that marketing professionals call "top of mind awareness."

Creating Top of Mind Awareness

"Top of mind" refers to that which comes to mind first. In marketing circles, the product, brand or company name that a person thinks of first has achieved "top of mind" status. Think of a psychological test in which you are given a word and are asked to say the first thought that enters your mind. The resulting word is "top of mind"

The concept is not too different when the product being marketed is injury prevention and the intended audience is your employees. The twist is that the triggering event is no longer the potential customer's need for a product or service. Instead the triggering event is the employees' awareness that he must perform a specific task. For example, if you were to need computer repair, the need for that service might trigger the thought of a particular person or company who could provide that service for you. When the product you are marketing is safety and the audience is your employees, it might look a little something like this. An employee is aware that he must perform a task involving the use of a handheld grinder. That awareness might trigger his recall of specific safe work practices, such as checking to ensure the guard is secure; checking the area for flammable materials, and donning the appropriate personal protective equipment.

Repetition

The impact of marketing efforts is gradual. Consider your own company when you first hung your "Open for Business" sign. There likely was not a line of customers beating down your door. One cannot expect to announce the availability of the product or service and then sit back and wait to be overwhelmed with sales. In fact, seasoned marketing professionals are well aware that it often takes 12 to 15 (or more) impressions to close a deal. That's 12 to 15 incidents of calling, mailing, visiting, or having their product seen in advertisements before an individual makes the decision to purchase the product.

The message here is that effective marketing efforts demand persistence. One of the challenges that you are bound to face in your quest for creating top of mind awareness (as an injury prevention tool) is that the human brain more closely resembles a sieve than steel trap. In short, what goes in doesn't always stay there.

In 1885, researcher Thomas Ebbinghaus did a study on people's ability to retain information. He called the results of the study "The

Curve of Forgetfulness." Ebbinghaus found that a person forgets 75% of what he has learned in the previous week. After three weeks, he forgets 90%. After four weeks, he forgets 95%.

The results of that study do not bode well for small businesses that have taken the traditional route for promoting injury prevention. A large number of small businesses rely upon safety meetings as their sole means by which specific safe work behaviors are intentionally and routinely reinforced. These safety meetings often address a different topic each meeting and generally cycle once every calendar year. Employers who follow that traditional path are very likely not having as big of an impact as they might have thought. Instead, it is likely that much of what is being disseminated in the safety meetings is seeping out of the employees' active memory long before the topic cycles through the list to be addressed again.

If employers expect to make safe work behaviors "top of mind" among their employees, they must make an intentional effort to place a consistent message in front of their employees frequently enough to make an indelible mark.

Variety of Mediums

Certainly successful marketing campaigns repeatedly expose their target audience to their message. However, few successful marketing campaigns attempt to achieve that repeated exposure through a single medium. Instead, they use a variety of marketing mediums to ensure that their message reaches the target audience. Consider virtually any successful company or product and attempt to identify the different mediums that are used for promotional purposes.

Although any successful company would suffice for an example, consider one of America's most successful entrepreneurial ventures – McDonald's. The McDonald's company and products they sell are marketed through radio and television commercials, billboards, movie and television product placement, contests, event sponsorships, coupons, and a host of other mediums. Even within the restaurants they leverage every conceivable marketing opportunity. From the paper bags, to the wrappers on every sandwich, the floor mats, highchairs, employee clothing, and plastic trays – virtually everything bears the logo of McDonald's. Even the roofs of McDonald's restaurants bear the image of their world famous french-fries.

Certainly a degree of McDonald's success is attributable to their marketing efforts. There is much to be learned form their example and the example of virtually every other successful company. In attempting to instill safe work behaviors in your employees, follow the lead of these successful companies and endeavor to use a variety of mediums to convey your message and to create top of mind awareness.

Commit that every newsletter, paycheck stub, e-mail message, or other written correspondence given to an employee intentionally attempts to advance the goal of achieving "top of mind awareness" of specific safe work behaviors. As all effective marketing professionals do, think outside of the box. Create contests within your company that advance the goal of creating top of mind awareness. Make it fun. In 1975 McDonald's got the whole world to memorize the ingredients of a Big Mac and 30+ years later most people who were at least 10 years old at that time can still recite with ease "Two all beef patties special sauce lettuce cheese pickles onions on a sesame seed bun." What do you want your employees to know and to stick in their minds forever? In what creative and innovative ways can you remind your employees of the key safe work behaviors that (if implemented consistently by all employees) will have a noticeable impact upon your company's loss history?

Perceived Importance

The same study that gave us the Curve of Forgetfulness also found that the brain retains information it considers important and "forgets" information deemed less relevant. Therefore, if you are charged with the management of employee safety efforts and intend to overcome the human limitations of memory, your message must not only be frequent, it must be perceived by your employees to be important and relevant.

Many small businesses see commercially-produced safety videos as the best means to disseminate and reinforce their safety message. After all, most safety videos are brief, packed with information and address the particular safety-related topic in more depth than many small business owners or managers feel that they can. Many times safety videos are made available for free through insurance carriers and trade associations. Although, commercially-produced safety videos and other generic efforts can be beneficial when used as one of many mediums through which to reinforce a specific safe work practice, they are not a panacea. Furthermore, they can send an unintended message to employees when used alone. When used as the primary means of promoting safety, generic efforts such as standardized safety videos can communicate to employees that the message is not important enough to be customized to their situation. Generally, a more positive impact will result from two minutes of the company owner or supervisor discussing safe work practices relating specifically to the work that employees perform, versus a twenty-minute safety video that is not reinforced through company-specific training.

That is not meant to imply that a company owner or supervisor who leads a safety meeting or safety training session will cause the topic to be perceived by employees as important and relevant. To achieve that goal, the content must be directly related to what employees do and the hazards they face. For that reason, each effort to reinforce a specific safe work practice should attempt to relate specifically to tasks that employees perform, or should review the past incidents that have (or could have) resulted employee injuries.

Creating Buzz

Repeated exposure to a message that is perceived as important and relevant through a variety of mediums will go a long way towards creating top of mind awareness. But if you want to cement the success of your efforts – if you want to install a turbo-booster to your internal safety marketing plan, there's one more thing to do. Create buzz.

The term "buzz" is used to describe marketing efforts that capture the attention of the target audience to the point where the potential customers are not only talking positively about a particular company or brand, but that particular company or brand becomes entertaining, fascinating, and even newsworthy. This is not to say that the measure of success of your internal marketing efforts hinges on whether or not your safety meetings make the 11 o'clock news. However, on a much smaller scale, if you can generate positive buzz and cause safety be become the "news" among employees within your company, you will have achieved a measure of success that many small businesses think is unattainable.

If your well of creative ideas is dry, feel free to follow the lead of a trucking company with which the authors of CHOMP COMP are familiar. To generate buzz about preventing falls when entering/exiting trucks, that company management encouraged several of their drivers participate in a dramatization. Photographs of those employees were taken depicting both safe and at-risk behaviors relative to entering/exiting trucks. These photographs were assembled in a display and placed in an area of the facility frequented by their truck drivers. After a short time, employees began to write notes on the display. Rather than remove the display or discourage employees from defacing it, the management of that company recognized that what they had done was create buzz about a specific safe work practice that has plagued the trucking industry for years.

Developing a Marketing Strategy

Obviously creating top of mind awareness is easier said than done. Nonetheless, it is possible with a sound plan and persistence.

Many larger companies have latched onto this concept of marketing safety and use catchy phrases such as "Think Safety," "Safety First" or other such slogans. However, these slogans do little to influence employee behavior. Many small businesses make a similar mistake by repeatedly and consistently telling their employees to "be careful" or "be safe." Instead, of catchy phrases that promote safety as a general concept, or safety well-wishes that do little more than to show your concern for employees, efforts to gain top mind awareness among employees should focus on specific safe work practices.

As with any effort to prevent injuries at work, begin with a goal in mind. Hence, the first step in creating top of mind awareness is to identify your objective. What specific behaviors do you want to influence through your internal safety marketing efforts? That may sound simplistic, but it requires that you (at least mentally) assess the likelihood of injury and well as the potential severity of injury associated with virtually every task that employees perform to help determine where emphasis should be placed. It also requires that you narrow your list to a manageable number of behaviors – likely no more than 3 to 5 behaviors at any given time.

The next step, more than any other, may make you feel like a marketing executive. Once the objective has been determined, a marketing plan (of sorts) must be developed. This should be more than a list of creative ideas for instilling 3 to 5 safe work behaviors in the subconscious of employees. It should define the methods, mediums and strategies for achieving your goals. It should identify who will be responsible for performing each task involved in your marketing campaign. Furthermore, it should identify a timeline or triggers for the implementation of each marketing effort. Lastly, it should establish targets (or standards) so that progress can be monitored.

The creation of a marketing plan is an ideal time to solicit the input of your employees. You will not only benefit from their creativity and varied perspectives, but involving them in the process will yield a host of additional benefits. Your employees will see the value that you place on their safety, as well as the time and energy that you are investing. They will also become intimately familiar with the specific safe work behaviors upon which your internal safety marketing efforts will focus. But perhaps the greatest benefit of soliciting their input and involvement is that it will foster a sense of ownership of the safety marketing process. In short, their solicited involvement in the planning will almost assure their voluntary involvement in the implementation.

The final step is to implement your marketing plan. Far too many times, wonderful ideas for promoting safe work behaviors are never implemented because of other responsibilities that compete for the finite time and energy of the company's management. Assuming that your marketing plan was thoughtfully conceived let it serve as your guide.

CHAPTER 15

You Didn't Hire Guinea Pigs

While most small business owners would rather themselves be injured than one of their employees, they sometimes unintentionally and unknowingly allow employees to become occupational guinea pigs. This chapter explores the true essence of being proactive by stressing hazard identification prior to an accident or near miss, and by exploring management characteristics of truly proactive companies.

Truly Proactive

As a preface statement to this chapter, the authors want you to be absolutely clear that they do not ascribe to the philosophy that eliminating 100% of risk is a feasible or even desirable business objective. Accomplishing such a degree of risk elimination is achieved only by locking the doors and going out of business. Let's face it, eliminating all risk means you have no need for safety and loss control professionals, nor do you have a need to read this book. Small business owners should be aware though, that the reality that some risk will always be present can be embraced to the point that it breeds complacency and thus lead to a subconscious (and sometimes conscious) tendency to manage safety from a reactive stance rather than a proactive stance. There are numerous, very sincere business owners and managers that state, "We're proactive when it comes to safety" when in reality they're reactive. While the concept sounds cruel and may even appear to be something ripped from liberal media headlines, small businesses can have employee guinea pigs and not even give it a second thought. For example, many companies start-up new process equipment with only a limited, formal safety review, if any review at all. As long as everything works and no one is hurt, there's no safety intervention. However, when an injury does occur, there's a knee jerk reaction and the company is quick to keep "another employee" from being injured in the same manner.

In reality, only a small, very dysfunctional segment of business owners would concede that employees are dispensable and that it's ok to address safety and loss control after employees get hurt. Most business owners are compassionate and care deeply about their employees. It is extremely tough balancing the many balls of business management and ensuring that all risks are properly managed. Unfortunately though, many small business owners have simply accepted that accidents are going to occur as part of doing business and that's why they purchased insurance. When talking with these business owners, they often reveal that near misses and accidents are what prompt them to address hazards. When these same individuals report that they manage safety proactively, loss control professionals simply want to pull their hair out! One can only wonder if they would even be in business if their entrepreneur spirit said something similar, such as, "when we see people buying this service or product, then we'll go into business." As obvious as knowing that in order for a business to gain any significant market share, they must be poised before customer demand comes to fruition, so should be the perception that to successfully manage loss, a company must be poised to address hazards before accidents occur.

The Term Proactive and its Misuse

The term "proactive" was popularized in business during the late 80's and early 90's when management focus was turned to such influences as Steven Covey. Covey, a rightfully, well-respected personal and organizational leadership guru urged individuals to address matters before they surfaced as problems. The occupational safety profession hopped on this bandwagon very quickly as it clearly expressed the message that they had been preaching to upper management for so long. It's no secret that the very successful, upper echelon safety programs are built on the fundamental principles of managing safety by preventing accidents before they occur, forecasting safety regulation, and designing safety into processes and equipment before they become operational. The term "proactive" has been popularized to the point that is has almost become a meaningless cliché. This popularization and overuse has led to one problem with respect to occupational safety – many folks now use the term without really knowing what it means! This has led to many companies and business owners learning the hard way that they really weren't proactive.

A perfect illustration of this problem was provided during a consultative loss control visits to a fairly "good" small business. The owner of a small, concrete oriented, construction business was being interviewed and the issue of foot protection for his employees entered into the conversation – specifically the prospect of employees wearing steel toed shoes was discussed. The business owner did not feel that steel toes were necessary. A quick review of the tasks that his employees were involved with revealed a real hazard for foot injuries from falling chunks of concrete. He also admitted that field employees frequently handled heavy pieces of portable equipment such jackhammers and were exposed to falling pieces of concrete, etc., Despite this clear need for protective footwear, he held his position that steel toes were not necessary. Toward the end of the discussion, he commented that his company would be "proactive" and address the matter if a trend of foot injuries or near misses occurred. While many of you may have read this scenario and quickly detected that this business owner doesn't understand the concept of being proactive, don't assume you are the norm or that you have a firm grip on being proactive (even though it's the authors' hope you do). You are challenged to examine your management philosophies and see if you have ever told anyone in your organization, "We want to be proactive when it comes to safety." Then, honestly evaluate what percentage of actions you take to improve safety are based upon near miss and injury incidents (which are, by the way, not just incidents where someone escaped bodily injury) as compared to the percentage of actions taken when a hazard is first realized or detected. If you are truly proactive, the big majority will be taken simply as a result of knowing hazards exist rather than seeing the hazards come to fruition through either a near miss or accident.

How Do You Select the Guinea Pig?

In continuing this mission to impress upon you the need to examine your organization's culture and evaluate your proactiveness, an interesting and sobering perspective to consider is the "prompts" for safety action. Reactive safety cultures that are driven by trailing indicator measures (i.e., workers' comp loss data, injury rates, etc.) pay an expensive price just to obtain the data necessary to direct their efforts. Sadly enough, the price to the individual employees and their families cannot be measured in dollars and cents. This not to say that all employers who have had employees get injured from unaddressed hazards are careless, ruthless slave drivers without regard for human life, but simply a challenge to consider the ethical and monetary implications of detecting and hazards after incidents occur. Experimenting with safety using real people is dangerous business – and a practice that could very well take your business under should circumstances align just right.

During the consultative meeting with the concrete-oriented business owner in the above illustration, the temptation arose to pose the question, "Which employee(s) would you prefer get hurt first?" The hazard was there, the lack of hazard control was recognized and the only thing left to do was to "test" and see if the two combined would produce a foot injury. While refrain and professional courtesy was exercised to avoid posing this question in such a poignant manner during the visit, you should consider the last time a hazard with feasible controls was detected in your company. Did you think about which employees could be injured by this and imagine how it would affect them if it occurred? The analogy to experimental animal test subjects is more accurate than most would think, and maybe even more cruel. In laboratories, scientists are performing deliberate tests where there is a level of uncertainty in exactly what kind of outcome will be produced. With the workplace, it is fairly certain what the outcome of experiments involving uncontrolled hazards will be – injury and loss. Really, the only questions left to answer is how long it will take and what subject will be affected. Do you really want to perform such an experiment?

How to be Proactive with Safety

It's not enough to simply be encouraged to be proactive and to limit the description of a "proactive approach" to safety management as addressing hazards before near misses and injuries occur; even though that is (in a nut shell) what it is. Similarly, it is difficult to provide a definitive list of activities and characteristics applicable to all organizations that exercise true proactiveness when it comes to workplace injury prevention. Therefore, some fundamental characteristics and activities that are fairly germane to all businesses that have a proactive approach to safety management are given below.

**Essential Activities of
Proactive Safety Management Approach**

- Conducting routine physical work environment inspections.

- Performing regular audits of established safety systems / programs / procedures to verify their applicability, efficacy and adherence.

- Conducting routine observations to determine and measure percent employee safe and at-risk behaviors.

- Communicating with employees through an established means about actions taken to evaluate and address detected hazards.

- Fostering safety engagement by all employees – training and charging each individual with responsibility to identify, report and in some cases the ability and responsibility to correct hazards.

Just because your organization does not currently posses all the above characteristics or perform any of the above activities, it does not mean that your organization cannot adopt a truly proactive approach to safety management. As with many parts of your small business, you started small and grew, and most likely have plans to grow even more. Treat safety management just like any other part of your business plan. Ensure that safety plans grow with the business. Effective loss control does not happen overnight, and if you try to force it to, you'll take two steps forward and later on three steps back.

The existence of some of the characteristics mentioned may not be best judged by you. It is recommended that those stable organizations with employees that are in a position to be objective (i.e., not currently in labor disputes, downsizing, excessive overtime etc) administer a well designed, independent safety perception survey to determine how well your communication and management systems are working. There are several sources and methods to conduct such. However business owners must realize that such surveys, in order to be reliable, must be designed according to proper research protocol and have a degree of reliability. Safety consulting firms and even some loss control departments of workers' compensation insurance carriers offer such surveys. While the surveys are many times not free, they can quickly reveal roadblocks in the company's attempts to be proactive. Safety perception surveys are not imperative to be proactive, but they certainly are an invaluable edge.

Being Reactive is Important Too

While this chapter has really hammered the message that a proactive approach is key to effectively controlling loss, it is not meant to overshadow the need for an equally aggressive reactive approach. A problem less rampant with general managers and business owners than with safety professionals is the tendency to overlook reactive measures out of frustration. Those head strong for a proactive approach are often overcome by the perceived failure when an injury occurs, and in defeat they loose focus on finding opportunities to improve safety and prevent a future recurrence of the same incident. Always remember that the approach to managing loss should be proactive, but proper reaction to incidents is just as, if not more, important. To fail to be proactive is not good business sense, but to fail to be reactive is simply negligence.

The Bottom Line

We've all heard the expression that you must learn from your mistakes; and that is sound advice. However, when dealing with an organization's livelihood, not to mention the lives and personal wellbeing of its employees, business owners are encouraged to learn from others' mistakes – not their own! Waiting for injuries or even near misses is a reactive approach to safety; regardless of how you slice it. Small businesses must adopt the same philosophies on proactiveness that some of their larger counterparts. Hazards must be identified through purposeful efforts; not by accident. Hazards must be controlled when identified – prior to an injury event – in order for an organization to be truly proactive.

CHAPTER 16

Think You're Too Small for a Written Program?

Many small business owners summarily dismiss the notion of needing formalization and written documentation when it comes to safety. In some cases, they assume that a formal safety program is just for the "big companies". This chapter exposes the fallacy in that thought-process and provides a foundation for formalizing your safety efforts into a documented safety management system.

Think Again!

Many small businesses across America have workforces that are so small the business owners get to know each employee personally. In many instances, this familiarity is due largely because the small business owner works alongside employees and a quasi-peer relationship develops. Besides being fully versed on all the extra curricular activities that each employees' children are involved with, the business owner in this type of workforce gains an in-depth understanding of each person's work habits. Just as common are small businesses where operations and employment levels have crossed thresholds that force business owners to be concentrated in management and administration functions. Still yet, many of the business owners in this situation are tightly tied to the workforce and have some degree of daily interaction with a considerable contingent of the workforce. No matter which of these organizational structures the small business owner may be in, this close interaction with employees is a wonderful experience that provides a unique insight that executives in larger corporations could only dream of. By all means, small businesses should capitalize on this closeness to improve safety and prevent loss. Nonetheless, there is an ominous pitfall that small business owners must avoid with such close knit work environments; failing to adopt formal, safety programs. Assuming those "familiar" employees do not need formal guidance in identifying and correcting hazards – and subsequently dismissing the need for formality in safety – is a misstep that small business owners should do their best to avoid.

This chapter deals with the importance of all businesses formalizing their safety efforts into what many refer to as a "safety program." Before progressing any further, the term "safety program" should be clearly explained. Safety program in this chapter refers to a formalized, written plan that defines roles and responsibilities for safety and loss control; clearly states safety and loss control policies; dictates activities (i.e., inspections, audits, training, safety committee meetings, toolbox talks, safety meetings, etc.) that will take place to prevent loss events; and dictates reaction to incidents when they occur. Simply put, a "safety program" would be better served to be called a "formal safety management system." However, since so much of the business world, OSHA, trade associations and others refer to this as a "safety program," this chapter will refer to it that way as well.

Why is a formal, written program so important?

If you're a small business owner or manager who firmly believes in putting everything in writing, this portion of the chapter may simply be preaching to the choir. (Please know also that you are in the minority of small business owners with this sound business practice.) Unfortunately though, it's quiet typical for many small business owners to wonder why such formalization is necessary when they can simply communicate their expectations through informal, daily conversations with the employees they know so well. After all, that's how they've done it for years and they've not experienced any problems – right? Discussion in the legal liabilities chapter certainly provides sufficient justification for documenting one's safety and loss control efforts. However, if that doesn't convince you, maybe the forthcoming benefits can.

Demonstration of commitment is one of the most fundamental reasons for formalizing safety efforts. By developing a written safety program and communicating it to all the employees, the company minimally shows the employees that injury prevention was at least important enough to the owner(s) of the company that time and care was taken in order for it to put in writing. Obviously such a program should serve to be more than paper on a shelf, but the simple act of establishing the safety program with paper and ink creates somewhat of burden to follow through with its requirements. While there are "safety culture" risks associated with a putting a program in writing that may not be the current practice of the company, it is better to err on the side of having the program. Employees can distinguish commitment by management and they'll certainly detect more commitment from having a written program than from not having one.

The written program is also important in that provides a clear road-map for safety performance in the company. So many employees fail to act in a safe manner simply because they are unclear of their role in preventing injuries. With an accessible, well-developed and communicated safety program, employees don't have to guess what they should be doing to prevent injuries, or what actions they should be take when certain work circumstances arise. Obviously, language and literacy barriers must be considered when dealing with the matter of written safety programs; however these are barriers that, with a small amount creativity and effort, can be accommodated and overcome by the employer.

Another important reason for having a written program has some overlap with legal justification for such, but has a distinctly different purpose. A written program is an objective way to hold employees accountable for safe behavior and to judge their overall job performance. Aside from the legal protections, a written program provides a concrete "measuring stick" for employers to look to when identifying strengths and weaknesses of individual employee performance. In the absence of a written program, if a supervisor conducts a job performance review with an employee and admonishes that employee for their safety performance on the job, the supervisor is doing little more than simply telling the employee that she or he is not being "careful enough." Have you ever wondered how you measure careful? How do you tell the employee how much "carefulness" is satisfactory, excellent, outstanding or, in some cases too obsessive compulsive? With a written program that has been properly communicated, it is much easier to give objective criticism for employee safety performance.

Finally, another reason for developing a formal safety program revolves around the fact it can (and should) serve as the minimum standard for safety in all operations. The safety program should establish minimum expectations that supervisors can utilize to ensure that they set a good example to subordinates and drive accountability. The written safety program establishes a boundary, which if followed, will help ensure a higher degree of safety culture and serve as a baseline for continuous safety improvement.

While there are many more reasons for developing a formal safety program than those listed in this chapter, these represent some of the most fundamental business reasons. In order for injury prevention to be more than a "peripheral function" of the business, it must receive equal attention as other business initiatives that get the chance to be "formalized." If you say that you don't afford many other business initiatives the opportunity for formalization, you may find that some of the same justifications for formalizing safety will hold true for other areas such as quality, operations, etc. Know though that there's no better justification for formalization than the children who look forward to seeing their mother or father returning home from work in the same physical and mental condition that they left in.

Important Characteristics of a Good Safety Program

There are numerous keys to developing a sound and effective safety program. In fact, if you were to talk to just 10 safety professionals across the nation you could probably compile a rather exhaustive list that could be expanded into a very lucrative safety textbook. You may also find that many safety professionals may disagree on intricate details on how programs are worded, arranged, communicated, etc. However, I think you would find that almost all of the safety and loss control professionals worth their salt would agree on the following three characteristics.

Characteristic One: Customized

Before progressing too far into this point, it should be clear that the authors of this book are not advocates of "reinventing the wheel." However, a cookie-cutter approach is not a very fruitful endeavor when it comes to impacting safety within a company. Trade associations, workers' compensation insurance carriers, OSHA, the competition and colleagues can all provide sample safety programs. These programs should be evaluated and looked to as guides, not as fill-in the blank, change the company name "forms." An intended purpose of the formal safety program is for it to serve as a living document that is utilized by employees in their work. If indeed the employees do access it, they can quickly identify wording or elements (sections) that either don't apply to their work or simply stand out as "canned." When employees detect the generic way in which such programs were constructed, the credibility of the safety program and its implementers are quickly viewed in a negative fashion. Furthermore, this type of approach provides the impression that the company simply "threw something together" to satisfy OSHA or the insurance company; not because it was serious about preventing injuries.

When a distinguished regulatory scrutinizer, such as a savvy OSHA compliance officer, reviews programs developed with cookie-cutter approach, they often perk up and start searching for other safety efforts the company may have taken with the same, minimal effort approach. Granted, a cookie-cutter safety program can appease an OSHA inspector or even the OSHA standards in many cases, however business owners need to be aware that this "low bar" standard may come back to haunt them in several ways; namely ineffectiveness when it comes to preventing workplace injuries.

To be effective, a company's safety program must be developed for the company's specific operations. While this doesn't mean that good ideas from sample programs and the programs of other companies can't be implemented, it does mean that each of those templates and sample elements should apply to your company's operations. Your employees don't work for your neighbor's company or the fictitious company the template was developed for. It is commonly said in the safety profession the companies should adapt templates – not adopt them.

Characteristic Two: Understandable

As mentioned earlier, successful safety programs must be living documents that are used routinely by employees to guide their actions. As such, the program must be written to a literacy-level that accommodates the reading abilities of the vast majority of the workforce (95%). For those employers who have a considerable percentage of illiterate employees, the program should be designed for easy verbal explanation by a supervisor or manager and be frequently reinforced verbally.

Unfortunately and too frequently, safety programs read like OSHA standards; a language that even degreed safety professionals argue about and don't always understand. In cases where OSHA mandates certain language in a program, it must be written in that manner, however, seldom is the exact language of a company's written program dictated by OSHA. Therefore, the safety program's language should be straightforward, and its content should be concise and applicable to the work environment employees will encounter. If employees and supervisors find the program too cumbersome to understand and navigate, they'll simply choose to ignore it, thus defeating the fundamental reason for having the program to begin with.

Characteristic Three: Flexible

As we begin to see more and more small businesses compete on a global level, their processes must be flexible and have the ability to change with a minute's notice. As other elements of a company's infrastructure must be able to change with the business demands, so should its safety program. Too often companies back themselves in a corner by only thinking of the present operations when developing their safety program. If the program has no flexibility and adaptability, when the wheels of business change course suddenly, key safety activities are frequently left unattended – thus uncontrolled. In fact, one of the most common times to see spikes in workers' compensation claims is when a company experiences growth, downsizing or venturing into uncharted territory. The safety program should be flexible and should be developed with checks and balances to account for these times. Activities such as regularly scheduled program reviews, management safety meetings, etc., are just a few examples of things that are written into safety programs and consistently performed to ensure the program remains flexible.

In Summary

No business is so small that it doesn't need formality with its safety program; some less so than others but none completely void of need. A formal written safety program should be a living document that is used by employees and supervisors alike to guide their actions and serve as their established standard for safety accountability. As part of being a usable document, the programs should be written in plain, easy to understand language that is appropriate to the majority literacy level of the workforce. There are basic characteristics such as flexibility and understandability that all programs should possess, however one of the most important characteristics is customization. Business owners are strongly encouraged to avoid the temptation to implement completely "canned" programs that at best only provide compliance with governmental regulations.

CHAPTER 17

Looking for Trouble

Before any hazard can be controlled, it must first be identified and evaluated. This chapter explores risk perception and acts as a catalyst for small business owners to proactively evidence hazards and do something about them before a negative outcome occurs.

Identifying and Controlling Hazards

This book provides numerous strategies, tips and insight for small businesses to take a bite out of their workers' compensation premiums. A significant portion of the information presented deals with how companies can best react to injuries in order to minimize costs and control the impending rise in premium. As reducing 100% of risk in not practical, small businesses must know how to react when the injuries occur. However, as pointed out in the "Truly Proactive" chapter, just mitigating the losses of an accident that has occurred is not sufficient. Continuous improvement efforts must focus on preventing injuries. Prevention of injuries is the true essence of safety! In order to be effective at preventing injuries, it is imperative for companies to take a systematic, purposeful and proactive approach to identifying and controlling hazards.

As pointed out before, this book does not intend to make the small business owner an occupational safety professional. In maintaining that theme, this chapter will present the most fundamental and foundational elements of identifying and controlling hazards. However, though the chapter will take a non-safety professional approach, it is necessary to venture into the world of safety academia and clearly define what the authors mean by the term "hazard." This defining of hazard is necessary because even the insurance and safety fields' definitions of hazard are somewhat different. For the purposes of this chapter, we'll present a definition of hazard that is taken from the occupational safety world's view of the term. After all, it's the occupational safety world that is focused on PREVENTING injuries.

> **Chomp Comp Definition of Hazard**
>
> A HAZARD is any condition, action, event, equipment, process or procedure that is the source of injury or increases the likelihood that an injury will occur.

While hazards can be effectively tackled by any one of the three main methods that will be presented, the small business owner may find the best method to be impractical and the lesser effective methods undesirable. When such is the case, the discussion at the end of the chapter should loom in the back of the small business owner's mind. Some hazards simply pose too much risk.

Identification of Hazards

Successfully identifying hazards can occur through a variety of methods, at various times and as a result of a different of events. In fact, some hazard identification is simply fortuitous. Unfortunately, in such cases an accident is driving the hazard identification process; tragically it's too late to be proactive. What's more disturbing is the fact that many small business owners feel this is an acceptable method. Sure, they would never state such nor would they ever verbally endorse such a policy. However, when examining the ratio of reactive safety initiatives (those taken after an accident and involving more than informal encouragement) to proactive safety initiatives (enacted before an accident occurred) in most small businesses, the ratios are either 1:1, 2:1, or always : never. For the most part, the failure to make the ratio of proactive initiatives higher is not rooted in willful disregard for employee well-being or safety. In many instances, the small business owner simply failed to recognize a hazard that caused the accident and resultant injury until after such occurred. This "day late and a dollar short" identification is often a source of heart burn and worry for the business owner more so than anyone else.

Now that it has been established (or at least eluded to) that the optimal time for hazard identification to occur is before an accident, a company must define its process of hazard identification. While there are several different methods and tools for identifying hazards, there's one common theme; hazard identification must be a systematic and purposeful process. Just like any other aspect of the business, a plan must be in place. The company must determine and document:

1. the systematic process for identifying hazards;
2. how frequently the activities of hazard identification will take place; and
3. who is responsible for identifying hazards?

This chapter really focuses on #1 as there is no "one size fits all" approach to address #2 and #3. Purposeful efforts to identify hazards before accidents occur should take place as frequently as the company can support. As for who identifies hazards, all levels of the organization should be involved, at least to some extent, in the identification process. Even though there will be several involved in the process, it is certainly the person "wearing the safety coordinator hat" that should champion the cause by monitoring identification activities; both for completion and quality.

Even though identifying hazards prior to an accident is the optimal time, identifying and analyzing hazards after an accident is an absolute necessity. Proactive is desirable – reactive is a given. Companies must strive to be proactive, but if they fail to be reactive, they're negligent. This may seem like a series of redundant statements. They are – and it is for a purpose.

Hazard Identification Process

Inspections / Audits

Distinguishing between an inspection and an audit is simply an exercise in semantics to some – even to some in the safety profession. However, upon closer look the terms are not mere synonyms even though there are some shared attributes. Regardless of whether it's an inspection or an audit, the business owner must perceive the process as a hazard identification opportunity. Furthermore, an audit or inspection must not be thought of as just "an event." Both are tools that can be used to drive injury prevention efforts. They must be regarded as a process that is a spring board for corrective action and a precedent for how the workplace will be viewed in future inspections and audits.

An inspection is a process where a company checks to see if employees are adhering to a particular company policy (i.e., wearing required personal protective equipment); evaluates the level of safety in a given work environment; or verifies the presence and operability of established safety equipment. In essence, an inspection is simply a snapshot at particular given time as to whether or not an area and its employees meet a particular established standard of care. Inspections are much more suited to pass-fail type checklists where simply the status of safety at the time is recorded. For the most part, inspections are simply quantitative.

An audit, as opposed to an inspection, is more qualitative and not only looks at compliance but also the "why" of non-compliance. Maybe more importantly, an audit provides much more in-depth evaluation of safety performance. Audits look at how well a company is performing relative to established systems, but may also evaluate the need for additional systems or the reengineering of existing systems. An inspection examines status at a particular given moment, whereas the period of time that an audit focuses on is normally much more expansive. Audits naturally require open ended responses to findings and promote systematic change as opposed to correction of a given condition.

Whether or not the business owner is conducting an audit or an inspection, there are guiding principals that apply to both. This book has condensed the principals into four:

1. First, the process should be systematic; both in the scope and method. Companies should utilize checklists and other documents that provide a game plan for evaluation.

2. Secondly, the findings of inspections or audits must be properly documented and communicated to the necessary parties. This communication involves both the positive reinforcement of safe performance and the admonition of improvement for substandard performance.

3. Thirdly, communicated findings should have corrective action assigned by those involved with the finding. As part of the communication, all involved parties should know beforehand that they have a part in providing a solution for deficiencies.

4. Finally, a plan of action to remedy any substandard performance should be documented with assigned responsibilities and established timelines.

Actually, this principal is one that applies to any identified hazard. Businesses must know that such a process of identifying and developing corrective action warrants diligence in follow-through. Once problems and their solutions are documented, action is expected. This proverbial "hitching of one's wagon" causes some small business owners to ostracize themselves from correcting problems. However, everyone reading this is encouraged to take the high road as the long term payoffs for addressing findings of inspections and audits is superb to ignoring a problem.

Reporting Systems

Probably the most effective hazard identification method is the most obvious and straight forward; nevertheless it's the least used in small business. This method is the most effective because it's also the most efficient when done correctly. It simply involves engaging the employees that interact with particular work environments and processes on daily basis. This method is a well developed hazard reporting system. Hazard reporting systems allow employees at all levels in a business to properly document hazards at any point during their workshift and slate them for further evaluation and correction.

Employees, through their experiences, are the most well equipped individuals in your workplace to identify hazards. Being well equipped though, and even noting hazards, is to no avail unless there's an established system for reporting those identified hazards. Employers must establish a formal line of communication, maybe even a formal document system, which allows employees a means of conveniently bringing their observations to the attention of the right people at the moment they're detected. Time and again, it has been shown in accident investigations that workers were aware of the dangers that caused the incident and would have reported the hazard if they would have simply known how or to whom is should be reported. Too often it's erroneously assumed that employees of a small business know they can simply voice a concern whenever it comes to mind. Many times employees in small businesses are so close they don't want to appear to be a whiner or a complainer, so they'll simply keep hazards to themselves. While these employees may have good intentions, companies must make sure these employees know there is a genuine desire for hazards to be made know to management, and to provide a well advertised means by which they can do it.

Job Safety Analysis

A job safety analysis is formalized approach utilized within the safety profession to break down a particular worker's job into the particular tasks that comprise the job. Each identified task of the job is evaluated to determine if it possess one or more types of hazards normally contained in a long list; for example lifting hazards, laceration hazards, repetitive motion, etc.

There are numerous examples of job safety analysis forms present on the worldwide web and in most general occupational safety management textbooks. Regardless of the format utilized, the benefit of breaking a job down into its individual components and evaluating it is a tremendous tool for identifying hazards.

Hazards to Consider when Analyzing the Tasks of a Job

- Laceration (knives, sharp edges of materials, etc.)
- Crushing / Impact (falling or moving objects that may potentially strike head, toes or other body parts)
- Slip, Trip Fall
- Ladders
- Walking surfaces
- Construction heights
- Burns (thermal and chemical)
- Ergonomics (as one category increases, it greatly affects the tolerance of another)
    - Repetitive motion (repetition
    - Force (lifting heavy items, forceful gripping, forceful pulling, forceful squeezing, etc.)
    - Posture (bent wrists, overhead reaching, bending at the waist, any non-neutral position)
- Inhalation of vapors, fumes, dusts or mists
- Radiation (infrared / UV as in welding; x-rays in the medical profession, etc.)
- Flying particles (dust, chips, etc.)
- Splashing liquids
- Electrical (hazards from improperly maintained equipment and hazards from servicing and troubleshooting electrical appliances)

Safety Committee Involvement

Another method of identifying hazards is to employ the service of a well organized safety committee. An effective safety committee is one that has assigned responsibilities and activities beyond meeting once per month over pizza or doughnuts to create a laundry list that only seems to grow. Properly trained members of a safety committee can be utilized to perform inspections, audits, job safety analysis and even serve as accident review board members.[7] Involving safety committee members not only serves to identify hazards, it gives the members a strong sense of responsibility and value when they are charged with a specific role. Successful safety committees inevitably have members involved in the hazard identification process in one or more ways.

Controlling Hazards

Small businesses must develop systems for identifying hazards. Moreover, they must know how to control hazards that are identified; regardless if they're identified through a well established, proactive system or as the result of a tragic accident. While researchers are constantly searching for the most effective controls for specific types of hazards and mechanisms of injury, their recommendations will always fall into one of three major categories of controlling hazards. Sometimes a combination of three is used to minimize risk to the lowest degree possible, but each element will still be one of the three. These three categories include: engineering controls, administrative controls and personal protective equipment. If a business owner understands these three categories and their hierarchy, they're well on their way to effectively controlling hazards.

The hierarchy of hazard controls dictates that attempts to eliminate the hazard should always be made first. As eliminating a hazard altogether is not always feasible, the hierarchy next dictates that exposure to the hazard should be minimized. Since minimization of exposure does not always create a tolerable level of risk, temporary

---

[7] While serving on accident review boards, safety committee members need not know the extent of injuries or the outcomes of loss. They only need to know the causation of accidents as there are overriding legal privacy issues relating to knowing the extent of injuries.

barriers must be erected between the employee and the hazard to minimize or preclude its effect. In essence, the three methods of controls are preferred accordingly:

- personal protective equipment = ok/good;
- administrative controls = better;
- engineering controls = best.

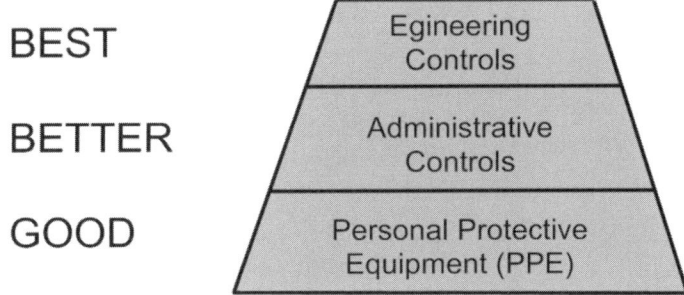

Order of Attack For Controlling Hazards

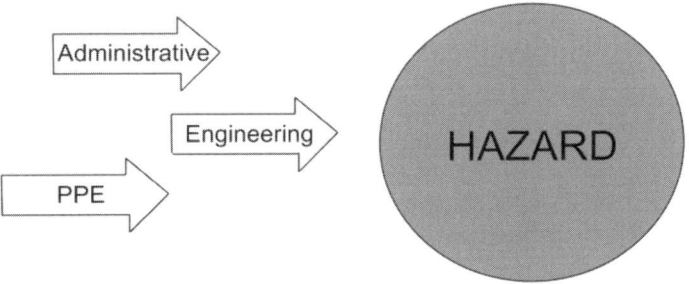

To the non-safety professional, the terms engineering, administrative and personal protective equipment may not be perfectly clear. Therefore, a discussion of each with examples is provided.

Engineering Controls

Engineering controls are those controls which eliminate the hazard from a particular operation either by isolation, substitution or providing an alternative to a work process. An example of isolating a hazard would include completely and permanently enclosing a machine process to prevent workers from being able to access hazardous areas, or better yet automating a process. Examples of substitution are best exemplified by finding an alternative chemical that performs the necessary work without posing a particular hazard. Purchasing smaller sized materials to reduce the amount of force required for lifting or maneuvering is also an example of substitution. Finally, an alternative work method may include the provision of a lift assist to replace the need for manually handling materials or product.

Administrative Controls

Administrative controls involve minimizing exposure to hazards or increasing employee knowledge and skill so that they know to work safely with the hazard exposure. A common example of an administrative control involves rotating workers so as to minimize their exposure to a particular hazard such as repetitive motion, noise, etc. Another example of minimizing the extent of exposure is sometimes argued to be an engineering control; this example is that of machine guards. Many contend that since the hazard itself is still present, and since machine guards may, in some cases, be removed by employees, they are actually administrative controls. Finally, the most common administrative control happens to be one of the most common "perceived" solutions to many problems in the workplace: training. Training is consider the most obvious of administrative controls for it only provides knowledge and hopefully skill for employees to work with hazards that will inevitably be part of their job. As you can tell, administrative controls are susceptible to employees electing to not use them or bypass them. For this reason, administrative controls are considered inferior to engineering controls.

Personal Protective Equipment (PPE)

Personal protective equipment is self explanatory. It involves the donning of eye protection, protective clothing, hard hats, etc. Personal protective equipment is considered a "last resort" effort to control hazards and is almost always accompanied by the administrative control of training; if for nothing else training on how to use the PPE properly. PPE is considered the most inferior method of controlling hazards because the control does nothing with the hazard itself; only the person subjected to the hazard. In many cases the only barrier between the person and the hazard is a piece of plastic or piece of rubber. The temptation for employees to not wear PPE is great (due to comfort, convenience, forgetfulness, etc.), and this further makes it a less desirable control.

Too often companies look to PPE controls first; either because of habit, convenience or ignorance. This is a shortsighted approach and all companies should first seek to eliminate hazards before looking to options that only mitigate them or minimize their effects.

Other Strategies for Dealing with Risk

After hazards are identified and possible options for controls have been evaluated, some business owners may still have a great deal of apprehension about exposing their workers to the amount of risk that remains from the hazards. In other cases, the expense and regulatory burden of providing certain administrative controls (i.e. a confined space entry and rescue program) or PPE (respiratory protection program) are daunting. Whether the reservations are from expense, regulatory burden or sense of uneasiness, business owners often and legitimately question whether or not a particular venture is worth undertaking. This represents a very sensible concern that must not be ignored. Business owners should carefully consider if after putting the necessary hazard controls in place, a venture is still profitable or justifies the remaining risk. If the answer is "no," or "probably not," then the option of "risk avoidance" should be considered. Particularly in situations where risk comes from ancillary work (i.e. certain maintenance tasks, peripheral businesses) that does not contribute to the overall mission and market of the business, risk avoidance may be even more attractive. While the authors do not advocate businesses running in a constant state of fear, nor do they believe that eliminating all risk is practical, there is a point where businesses would be better off staying away from risky work that isn't essential to their business.

Risk avoidance can be accomplished in a variety of ways. The easiest way to understand simply involves a company abandoning a certain type of business or deciding not to venture into a particular operation. Another way involves one of the most common and fastest growing trends in American workforces – the use of contractors. While using contractors can remove the employer/employee relationship, the contracting company must be diligent in demanding, obtaining and maintaining proper proofs of workers' compensation insurance from the contractor to avoid being charged premium for the contractor payroll anyway. Finally, employers are looking to outsourcing certain aspects of their business to other firms or purchasing materials that require little or no prep from their employees.

Summary

Identifying and controlling hazards is essential to significantly lowering workers' comp premiums. Companies cannot simply rely upon accidents and informal processes to point out hazards. Purposeful, systematic methods for identifying hazards must be in place for optimal safety. There are numerous strategies for systematically identifying hazards and companies must utilize as many of them as their resources will allow. After hazards are identified, companies must be diligent, and once again systematic in controlling them. While many companies traditionally look to buying personal protective equipment first, they must transition to immediately evaluating engineering controls which eliminate hazards and not merely mitigate them or their effects. Finally, some risks don't make good business sense and options for avoid risk should be analyzed.

CHAPTER 18

Measuring Up

Understandably business owners question company safety efforts when there is a spike in the number of employee injuries. However, the frequency of injuries does not measure the effectiveness of safety efforts. Instead, safety performance is the proper measure of safety efforts. This chapter will explain the importance of gauging safety efforts with proactive measures and will provide you with the knowledge to properly measure safety efforts in your business.

An Honest Perspective of Safety Performance

Most all business owners and managers could surmise that the central purpose of any organization's safety program should be to reduce, if not totally eliminate those events and circumstances that produce accidents. Certainly one does not need to consult a safety professional in order to arrive at that conclusion. Furthermore, everyone can understand that the whole purpose behind all hazard controls is proactive in nature and involves the prevention of injury. Therefore, it only goes to reason that the mark of a good safety program is the lack of injuries, and conversely, the mark of a poor safety program would be presence of injuries, or at least a high rate of injuries – right? The vast majority of businesses, both large and small, quickly give an affirmative response to this argument and conclusion. Even though the vast majority agrees, this is truly an example where the vast majority is wrong.

While the presence of injuries, and certainly the presence of high injury rates signal safety failures, the lack of injuries does not necessarily indicate good safety performance. The previously stated evidence and conclusion make for an easy connection with the traditional way of thinking that has created the system by which we measure safety performance. However when the concept of safety performance is examined in further detail, we see that the very nature of accidents (unlikely events) make such a carte' blanche assumption inaccurate. Measuring safety performance is actually concerned with measuring those things we "do" to prevent injuries; not the outcomes (which are injury statistics).

The issue of measuring safety performance is one not only of concern to large corporations interested in benchmarking and comparing various entities and divisions, but also to small businesses as they strive to protect profitability by keeping workers' compensation costs to a minimum. As we explore the pitfall of relying solely on the absence or presence of accidents to judge how well a company is performing regarding safety, small business owners will see how imperative it is measure safety performance, not just outcomes.

Trailing Indicators vs. Leading Indicators

At the writing of this book, safety performance measurement has become one of the hottest subjects discussed by safety professionals in America, and is arguably already the topic that stirs some of the most passionate cries for a paradigm shift by those that insist experience modification ratings and OSHA recordable incident rates are "the" measuring sticks for safety performance. While this is an issue that will for some time consume articles in professional safety trade journals and be the focus of safety management system revamps in large corporations, it is just as imperative for small businesses that do not have full-time safety professionals or elaborate safety management systems to understand and apply. In order to do so, a fundamental knowledge-base must be established pertaining to the two broad categories of safety performance measures – "trailing measures" and "leading measures." As most of the current literature regarding this matter refers to these measures as "indicators", this chapter, for the sake of consistency, will also refer to them in that manner.

Trailing indicators are measures based upon outcomes without respect to how outcomes are achieved. Examples of trailing indicators include OSHA recordable incident rates, lost-time accident rates, experience modification ratings, workers' compensation loss data, etc. As you can see these all represent negative outcomes and in order for us to obtain such data, undesirable events (accidents) must occur. You may quickly take exception to this and state that the absence of data (i.e. the absence of injuries) represents accomplishments. However, you are cautioned to carefully consider your position by asking yourself if there is a way to achieve a favorable accident rate and still be unsafe. We'll explore this more very shortly.

Leading indicators represent those measures of actual activities and accomplishments that promote safety in the workplace. As leading indicators are ideally organization-specific, it is hard to develop a definitive list of examples, however a few are given below. As you can see, leading indicators measure things that are actually being done to further employee safety. They represent activities that, if done or monitored, will prevent or reduce the likelihood of accidents and thus affect trailing indicator measures in a positive way.

EXAMPLES OF LEADING SAFETY INDICATORS

- % Accident Investigations Completed On-Time
- % Job Safety Analysis Completed
- Application of Skills Taught in Safety Training
- Retention of Information from Safety Training
- Safety Audit Scores
- % Safe DOT Roadside Inspections
- # of Safety Behavior Observations Made
- % of Personal Protective Equipment Worn Correctly
- % Safe Seat Belt Usage

The Problem with Trailing Indicators

As you have probably discerned by now, this author is not supportive of measuring safety performance by solely looking at trailing indicators. It is not held that trailing indicators are worthless and have no purpose – just that they don't accurately indicate safety performance. Obviously trailing indicators should be, and must be tracked for a variety of reasons. First and foremost, trailing indicators assist in identifying areas where more immediate attention to safety is needed, thus providing a basis for prioritizing safety efforts. Trailing indicators must also be tracked and documented to satisfy regulatory requirements set forth by OSHA's recordkeeping standards and the Bureau of Labor Statistics data collection efforts. Also, trailing indicators (specifically workers' compensation loss data) provide valuable information useful in determining how premium increases and decreases will affect a company's finances and profitability. Thus, one can see that the problem with trailing indicators is not necessarily with the data, but with how the data is used.

One of the biggest problems associated with trailing indicators involve their lack of reliability. As accidents are events that are unlikely to happen in the first place, the absence of them may not be the result of safe behavior or sound safety systems, but rather from luck or the natural odds associated with a given hazard. In order to better understand this matter, one simply needs to consider driving habits. Many individuals exceed the speed limit on a daily basis – probably even you or someone you know. If one were to examine the number of speeding tickets issued as compared to the number of individuals that actually speed, you would see a great disparity and find out that only a small population actually gets caught. If you speed, think of what percentage of occasions where you exceeded the speed limit and got caught versus those you didn't get caught. The lack of a ticket doesn't mean that someone didn't speed, it simply means that a negative outcome (for the driver anyway) didn't occur. Similarly, and maybe more powerfully, since speeding is generally accepted as unsafe behavior, think of the times that speeding takes place with no accidents occurring. In this scenario, the lack of an accident doesn't equate to a presence of safe behavior. It only attests that no negative outcome occurred. The lack of an accident does not even indicate the occurrence of an event that "could" have produced a negative outcome.

Along the same lines as the speeding examples, think of the times that an employee lifts an object unsafely but never gets a back injury. Are there ever any times that employees ignore safety policy or procedures and never get injured? On numerous occasions, the authors of this book have visited small businesses and witnessed extremely unsafe behavior, (such as an employee riding the forks of a forklift) at companies that boast long periods (months or years) with no employee injuries. Just like with the speeding illustrations, the lack of back injuries or other work place injuries does not necessarily indicate employees were working in a safe manner. It could simply mean that the employees have been riding a nice, favorable wave of luck. Unfortunately, the wave of luck will eventually run ashore and an undesired event will take place.

The problem of unreliability for trailing indicators is even worse for small businesses. Fundamental research statistics teaches us that the smaller the sample group, the more unreliable the data. By definition, small businesses employ relatively few workers. Because of the limited size of the workforce, the fact that injuries have not occurred for some time does not carry the same weight as with large companies with respect to the effectiveness of hazard controls or hazard validation. Thus, small businesses are more susceptible to developing a false sense of security in their safety efforts when they have low injury rates. This is not to say that all small businesses with low injury rates are necessarily unsafe, simply that the opportunity is greater to become somewhat complacent when injuries do not occur for extended periods.

Another problem associated with trailing indicators involves the very nature of the measures; they are exclusively outcome-oriented. Imagine if someone told you to be the most profitable company you could be, but the only measure you could take was year-to-date profit. Obviously you would immediately label this as an absurd proposition – and rightfully so! This would be similar to a basketball coach trying win a game by only watching the scoreboard – not by reviewing real-time statistics and watching the court. By now it's probably not surprising to you that the central theme of measuring safety performance is no different than measuring any other aspect of your business. Just like you measure efficiency, market share, revenue-flow and the many other things that affect profitability, the activities that impact injury statistics and other trailing indicators must be measured to truly know how well a company is performing from a safety standpoint.

Some small businesses, particularly those in the construction arena are well aware of their experience modification rating (EMR). They realize having a low EMR is desirable and can often be the difference in being awarded a contract over their competitor. For years the EMR has been touted as a much better "measure" of safety performance than other trailing indicators since it considers loss costs, not simply a rate of occurrence for accidents. Furthermore, since the actuaries who helped come up with EMR built in a mechanism that was intended to account for injury severity and frequency, many think it to be a reliable measure of safety performance. The authors of this book contend that while the EMR might make sense as a means of determining equitable premiums based upon past losses (which is what it was designed to do), and can be a good indicator of claims management, it is not a good measure of safety performance. Various allowances and ways that loss expenses are manipulated in the EMR calculation provide breaks for companies who do a good job managing claims. However, claims management and safety management are two different issues. Some may counter the argument by saying really low EMRs only occur with the absence of injuries, and while this is true, keep in mind that the absence of injuries do not necessarily equate to good safety performance.

To further illustrate the shortcomings of EMRs in indicating "safety performance," two examples will follow. Before examining these examples, some terminology review is necessary. The National Council on Compensation Insurance (NCCI) is the rating bureau that calculates the EMR for most employers; except in states where a state rating bureau does. In all NCCI states, workers' compensation insurance companies provide the NCCI with data at the end of each policy year concerning the claims and associated loss costs for each insured company.

In the information reported from insurance companies, claims are classified as medical-only (where employee claimants missed no time from work and the only expenses are medical) or lost-time (claimants missed time from work). Only 30% of the loss costs for "medical-only" claims are used in calculating the EMR. However, 100% of the loss costs for "lost-time" claims are used in the calculation of the EMR.

While those states that have exclusive state rating agencies may have their own specific allowances for medical-only costs versus lost-time claim costs, there is usually some type of differentiation between the two to promote reporting of minor claims. While not explicit in publications, the discounting of medical-only claims is also thought to equate "lower severity injuries" to "lower risk."

Two more terms include "ratable loss" and "non-ratable loss." In most states, the ratable loss of a particular claim is the amount of loss up to $100,000. In other words, most states set a limit for the amount of an individual loss that will be used to calculate the company's EMR; in most states it is $100,000. Non-ratable loss is that loss of a particular claim over $100,000 or the particular state's established limit. Generally speaking in most states, only the first $100,000 of loss of each claim is used in calculating a company's EMR.

Finally, the terms "primary loss" and "excess loss" must also be considered. In the NCCI rating system, the first $5000 of any claim is considered primary loss. Loss over $5000 is considered to be excess loss. Excess loss is discounted when calculating an EMR.

Example 1

Company A
Carpal Tunnel Claim
Loss = $99,999

Company B
Catastrophic Claim
Loss = $247,345

Loss Counting Toward Company A's EMR = $99,999
Loss Counting Toward Company B's EMR = $100,000

NOTE: Only $1 difference in EMR calculation

In example one (above), the concept of ratable loss versus non-ratable loss is presented. One can see that the claim incurred by Company B could very likely be attributed to a serious safety performance failure (such as the failure to use fall protection that resulted in an employee's death), while the loss incurred by Company A may or may not even be attributable to the claimant's employment. Nonetheless, there's only $1 difference in the amount used to calculate the company's EMR. No reasonable person would say that such a small difference of $1 accurately reflects the "safety performance" of these two companies.

Example 2

Company A	Company B
John M. Doe	Justin X. Sample
Lumbar Strain Lifting	Lumbar Strain Lifting
Treated by Dr. Doogood	Treated by Dr. Shyster
Conservative Treatment	Less Conservative Treatment
No Lost Time	16 Days Lost Time
Claim Costs = $5000.00	Claims Cost = $5,000

Loss Counting Toward EMR of Company A = $1,500
Loss Counting Toward EMR of Company B = $5,000

NOTE: 70% Less of the loss is considered for medical only

In example two (above), the terms "medical only" and "lost-time" are at work in EMR calculation. Since the care received from Dr. Doogood for John M. Doe is conservative, only $1500 of loss will be used in calculating the EMR of Company A. As for Company B, Dr. Shyster's decision to put Justin X. Sample "off work" will cause 100% of the $5000 claim cost to be used by the NCCI to calculate their experience modification factor. With both Mr. Doe and Mr. Sample, the injuries are the same, the circumstances are the same and "safety" is the same. The only difference in the two claims was the physicians' choices of treatment. These choices drastically changed how the claims were handled and what category of loss they fell. Truly this shows claims management and not safety management (the aspects of preventing these two back injuries).

When one considers the discounts given for various aspects of loss, it is clear that the EMR is an intricate calculation that is largely influenced by how well a claim is managed and the type of treatment plan an individual physician (or other licensed health care provider) "chooses" to give. That's right – the subjectivity of a physician's opinion can greatly impact a company's EMR. It is just as easy to see that EMR is not a very good measure of safety performance.

As the subject of safety performance measurement is broad enough to consume a separate book, there are many other limitations and problems associated with trailing indicators that cannot be addressed in constraints of this chapter. However, it is important for small businesses to understand one additional matter dealing specifically with trailing indicators such as the OSHA recordable and lost time incident rates. Aside from the susceptibility to inconsistency of reporting, such injury rates and their calculation methods were never developed with the intent of individual businesses using them as a measure of internal safety performance. The rates were largely developed so that federal and state OSHA agencies would know which industry classifications to develop emphasis programs and focus compliance efforts. These rates have been utilized by businesses because simple calculation methods are available to present what is thought to be "hard figures" – sadly the only language that some managers and business owners know. Only a small percentage of degreed safety professionals realize that these calculation methods are derived from BLS formulas developed shortly after the turn of the 20th Century and that they have been revised numerous times to improve their validity.

Now that some of the more substantial limitations of trailing indicators have been revealed, it easier for the small business owner or manager to see the need to adopt leading indicator measures, or at least be cognizant of the fact that the absence of injuries does not necessarily equate to good safety performance. The usefulness of trailing indicators lies in prioritizing and directing safety efforts, evaluating financial impacts and regulatory diligence.

Leading Indicators: Yes it is Feasible to Use Them!

Earlier when we defined leading indicators some examples were given and you may have become instantly skeptical concerning the feasibility of using them. Many people consider leading indicators to be those "soft things" that you can't put numbers to. Others may agree that leading indicators are truly the way to measure safety performance but dismiss using them because they feel they do not have the resources. These concerns are certainly understood. However, one cannot ostracize leading indicators without first examining if indeed numbers can be used for these "softer things" and if resources are as demanding as was initially thought. Leading indicators can be used and used effectively – even in a small business.

Some consider leading indicators to be the "softer side of safety" that present room for gray issues and subjectivity in comparison to OSHA recordable incident rates and EMRs. However, leading indicators can actually be more concrete and definitive. For example, through a simple observation process, one could measure the percentage of time that employees are compliant in their use of personal protective equipment. Prior to observation, determine what items of personal protective equipment each employee is required to be wearing while performing a particular observed task. Award one point for every item of personal protective equipment worn correctly. After a sample population of employees has been observed, divide the total points earned collectively from all employee observations by the total number of points possible – thus yielding a percent-compliant measure. This describes a very simple percentage calculation and a very straight-forward data collection method. In comparison to determining whether or not an injury was actually "recordable" (according to OSHA's definition) and then utilizing the formula to determine recordable incident rate, arguably this leading indicator (percent-compliant) proves to be an easier measure to establish and is actually less subjective.

The degree of difficulty involving the use of leading indicator measures is actually less than that of trailing indicators. However, the effort and time investment for obtaining leading indicators may be more. This helps explain why trailing indicators are more widely used -- you can do them from the desk and they're convenient. Being a small business owner, you know that the easy way is seldom the best way. Indeed leading indicators do take more creativity and do require more effort than looking at the OSHA log or workers' compensation loss run; however the rewards are much greater and are long-term.

Finally, it should be pointed-out that employees can relate to leading indicators much better than trailing indicators. Few if any of your employees understand what the OSHA recordable incident rate or the workers' compensation EMR is – let alone what they (as an individual) can do to improve them. However, understanding that a department or crew didn't meet their goal on personal protective equipment inspections is easily understood by every member of the workforce, and each employee clearly knows what he or she did to contribute to the result – whether it is a positive or negative contribution.

In summary, safety performance is all about the efforts expended to prevent injuries. Traditional measures of safety such as accident statistics and workers' compensation loss rates are not accurate measures of safety performance and are actually "rear view mirror data." If a company wants to impact their workers' compensation premiums in a positive and lasting way, they must focus their measurement efforts on "windshield data" that measures efforts to prevent injuries. While leading indicators may take more time and effort to calculate, they produce better results and give employees feedback on what they can do to continuously improve safety performance. Small business owners must embrace measures that may not be as commonly accepted and traditional, but certainly point them in right direction for improvement.

CHAPTER 19

Safety and Loss Control Training

Too often, it's said that employees need more training as method of preventing recurrence of an incident that resulted in an injury. In many cases, it's actually the training that's the problem. This chapter explains barriers to conducting effective training and sound, fundamental principles for providing effective training to the adult learner.

Maximizing Value

Training is often perceived to be a "silver bullet" that eliminates all at-risk behaviors and poor job performance issues. Business owners, supervisors and even some "safety professionals" commonly record on accident reports "employee needs more training" as the solution to preventing recurrence of an accident event – many times without serious consideration. Unfortunately, conducting more training is not the solution for a vast majority of workplace accidents. Many times the root of accident causation can be traced to a safety program (or lack of), management oversight and company culture issues. These are obstacles that even the best training initiatives can't overcome! However, despite these concerns, quality training can be an effective loss control strategy. Please note that it is not merely training, but "quality" training that is advocated as a loss control strategy. In order to get the maximum benefit from training, companies must decide that changing skill and behavior is a primary goal of training and then make a conscious effort to ensure that this goal is accomplished. Training can provide a powerful and positive impact on loss control; however it doesn't happen by "accident."

Businesses, both small and large, are normally not strangers to conducting training in some form or another. In fact, many small businesses invest thousands of dollars each year just for safety training. There are a myriad of motivators for conducting safety training that include regulatory compliance, effect on insurance premiums, customer requirements, etc. While these are all inarguably sound reasons for performing training, they are not the best reasons. Training is a business investment and, like any other business investment, its objective should be to obtain the greatest return. If positively affecting employee behavior is not the "main reason" your company performs training, your investment return is certainly diminished. Furthermore, proper motivation alone is not enough to ensure maximum return on your training investment. This fact is certainly at the heart of many companies' frustrations with failed safety training efforts.

Safety and loss control training is a vast topic that could consume an entire book – in fact there are several excellent books published on that topic already. Therefore, this chapter alone cannot serve as an exhaustive guide to great training. Furthermore, this chapter's purpose is not to make the reader an expert trainer, training designer or training manager. It does however serve to provide the reader with a sound foundation to make better safety training choices. It is essential for small business owners to have a basic understanding of the key training principles, the role training plays in improving safety performance and how to evaluate training effectiveness.

Training vs. Education

Before we begin discussing training in a little more detail it is important that you can make a distinction between the terms "training" and "education." Believe it or not, there is a notable difference between training and education – aside from being two different words.

Education deals strictly with imparting knowledge, primarily through a traditional instructional method (i.e., lecture, reading, etc.), and challenging participants to internalize that information and draw conclusions that are more theoretical in nature (i.e., explaining the science the behind a particular health problem). Those participating in education are not ordinarily expected to draw upon their preexisting knowledge and experiences. In education, the teacher is almost exclusively in control of the learning environment, and educational objectives can be met with or without participant buy-in. In other words, education describes the traditional learning vehicle that children, teenagers, and (to a lesser extent) college students experience. While education may establish a foundation for performing a skill, it does not, in itself, produce the ability to perform a skill or exhibit a desired behavior.

Training has many characteristics that distinguish it from education. Summarily, training is a process that provides less theoretical framework and attempts to produce in its participants the ability to perform a task or exhibit a particular behavior (i.e., erect scaffolding, perform an equipment safety inspection, apply lockout/tagout etc.). Training may be delivered through a variety of vehicles (i.e., formal instruction, supervised performance, simulation, etc.), and in many cases a combination of those vehicles. While both training and education consider the learning styles of participants (auditory, visual, etc.), this consideration is much more imperative to successful training. Many times theoretical content will be presented in training, however it is normally minimized and serves the purpose of informing the participants why the training is necessary. Training participants need to understand why the training is necessary because participant buy-in is essential in fulfilling training objectives. This fact is one of the biggest distinctions between training and education. Finally, training is designed and facilitated with the participants' existing knowledge and skill sets in consideration.

Unfortunately and historically, a significant percentage of employers actually provide their employees with safety education rather than safety training – regardless of what they call it. Moreover, it is even worse when this education is poorly delivered. Needless to say, most adult employees do not respond well when their life experiences, knowledge and skill sets are perceived to be irrelevant, or only given cursory acknowledgement. While in most cases employers have not negligently provided safety education when they should have provided training, they are receiving minimum value from their efforts nonetheless. In most cases, employers simply do what they think they're supposed to – mainly because it's what other companies do.

The Necessity of Good Training

In the Chapter titled "Looking for Trouble," you saw that training is frequently the primary control for many hazards. In such instances the actual hazards are unaddressed or have only been mitigated to some extent. Therefore, it only stands to reason that training in any form is better than nothing. While this may be true, one must consider that poor quality training is "just a little better than nothing." Good training, however, can go a long way in preventing loss, even when it's the only control for a given hazard, provided that knowledge or skill deficiency exists.

When training is the only viable hazard control, quality training is critical to avoiding an accident. Business owners must be cognizant of this for two main reasons. Primarily, training is the only thing standing between human life and loss. Secondly, quality training is crucial to legal protection should an accident occur. Trends in litigation and workers' compensation awards reveal an increasing amount of instances where the quality of a company's training has been scrutinized.

What is good training?

As we progress on in defining good training, it is important to note that formality is fundamental and prerequisite. While informal communications and "admonitions" are encouraged as safety coaching activities, they are no substitute for actual training. The safety training system in each small business will vary in needs and complexity. However, here are some fundamental areas that most companies should address:

1. Inventory of Training Needs (list of necessary and routine training courses for all employee classifications)
2. Outline of Training Content and Delivery Methodology
3. Trainer Expectations and Qualifications
4. Training Schedules and Routines (identifying annual, quarterly, hire, etc.)
5. Training Completion Documentation System
6. Training Evaluation Methods

In addition to being part of a systematic process, good training, in the realm of safety and loss control, primarily accomplishes these things:

1. Provides an understanding as to why the training is necessary.
2. Demonstrates application to the participant's work and work environment.
3. Precisely delivers necessary, key knowledge for performing work tasks safely.
4. Imparts and verifies the necessary skills for applying knowledge from the training.
5. Improves safety performance; measurably. (Yes it can be measured)

Now, let's further explore these five areas.

Provides an understanding as to "Why" training is necessary

Adults reference their life and work experiences when they attempt to answer the question, "Why do I need this training?" If employees fully understand the hazards and potential consequences of their work, they are much more likely to utilize the knowledge and skills obtained through the training. This need to understand "why" is tied to a well studied area of safety; risk perception. An employee's risk perception plays a significant role in determining whether or not (or to what extent) the employee will apply the training they are receiving; no matter how good the training itself is. Risk perception deals with how employees regard the consequences and likelihood of an accident. Many times an employee's experiences may lead him to believe that he can be careful in his own way and that training is not necessary. For example, it will be challenging to convince an experienced employee who has lifted boxes of widgets for 15 years in an unsafe manner without incident that he "needs" safe lifting training. However, a newly hired employee that lacks the experience of lifting boxes of widgets will most likely be more open to the necessity of training. Yet, some employees who may acknowledge the possibility of an accident misperceive the consequences of the accident. They may think the worst that could happen to them is a minor injury (i.e., stitches, strain or sprain), when in actuality the consequences may be much more severe (i.e., amputation, paralysis or death). In such cases, there is an issue of risk perception that training must address in order for employees to first take the training to heart. There exists no one recipe to ensuring that safety training adequately addresses risk perception; however diligence in conducting a "needs-assessments" for the training is essential. Employers must carefully consider employee perceptions and norms that exist when designing or having someone else design training.

Only in cases of mental illness or desperate fraud, would anyone want to be hurt. So, it stands to reason that simply telling employees that they could be injured is not a strong motivator. To illustrate this, think about music. Most people like music of one genre or another. Telling someone that you're going to motivate them to "enjoy music" is a pointless statement. Similarly, simply telling employees they should avoid injury by performing work safely is nonspecific and has little to no effect. Information regarding consequences and likelihood must be communicated precisely and credibly to employees. While it will be addressed further in the chapter, this is a good time to point out that the authors do not advocate safety training techniques that employ blood, guts and gore to make employees aware of consequences. With a sound approach, employees can have a good understanding of the consequences of not working safely.

Employees must be able to clearly see the WIIFM principle – What's In It For Me. Training should benefit employees and give them a clear understanding how they benefit from the training. If adults can see personal gain and purpose as a reason to utilize training, they're much more likely to implement training content into their daily work habits. In recent years, the effects of story telling and touching the "heart strings" of employees have proven to be effective methods of communicating personal value. By explaining how injuries may affect a worker's family, we show benefits beyond the workplace. Safety is not the most exciting subject and it many times involves informing employees of further "inconveniences." Therefore, addressing the WIIFM principle is critical to employees receiving the training in a positive manner.

Demonstrate Application to a Particular Work Environment

Have you ever had to endure a generic safety training video where you viewed work environments that didn't resemble reality or your workplace in the slightest? Have you ever had work instructions so generic that they seemed pointless? Too often "canned" safety training materials (i.e., videos, commercially available slides, etc.) make up the majority, if not the entire content of a training program. Employees perceive such training just like you do – boring and obligatory. When adults learn they must see relevance in order to take training seriously.

Good training is not generic, but relates directly to the work environments that employees are expected to apply the skills and knowledge they receive. As eluded earlier, most employees are not at your workplace training session to get an "education" in general safety theory, but to find out how they're supposed to perform their job safely. Generic videos and instructional materials can be used, but they should be employed as supplements to the program to efficiently demonstrate a broad concept or procedure. Employees must see the direct application in order to avoid the perception that training is being conducted simply for compliance purposes and has little true value. The extra effort required to customize training ensures that it will be more efficiently applied, and helps make employees more receptive to future training.

Delivers the necessary, key knowledge for performing work tasks safely

So many well intentioned business owners and safety professionals try to make the "best training ever" by including as much information as possible. While this may be well received by those employees who really appreciate the classroom experience, remember that this is a small percentage of your workforce. Training should provide sufficient ancillary information to aid in the understanding of the material; however such information should be limited to that which is necessary. Employees appreciate conciseness and efficiency in training as much as the business owner.

When developing training, ensure that an inventory of objectives and key competencies is developed. The training should provide complete information and/or hands-on instruction to satisfy these objectives. Content beyond these objectives should be carefully scrutinized for inclusion into the training. If in doubt of the necessity, it is better to include the information rather than to chance that an employee may fail to fully grasp and apply a concept, or miss inclusion of a topic required by a regulation. If you're fairly certain that the content is "fluff", you should err on the side of omitting it. You should always remember that in training, completeness and conciseness must co-exist!

Imparts and verifies the necessary skills for applying knowledge from the training

As illustrated earlier, training differs from education in that training primarily serves to equip employees with a demonstrative or verifiable skill in addition to gaining knowledge. In addition to providing clear instructions and knowledge, training should be a venue where participants demonstrate competency. This element takes the previous accomplishment (number 3 above) a step further.

Using the back safety training example mentioned earlier, we can demonstrate this training accomplishment. If an employee is provided with back safety or lifting training, he should receive formal instruction relative to proper mechanics of lifting objects, holding loads, turning with loads, bringing loads to rest, etc. However, training should not stop at this point – even though in the vast majority of small businesses it does. Participants of the training should then be involved in a structured application of the skills in the training environment or in the work environment. During this "hands on" application of the training, trainers have the opportunity to evaluate how well the information provided in the previous segment was received and the how well the participants are able to apply it. Feedback, reinforcement and correction can be given at this point – the point where the information is freshest in the employees' minds. By detecting deficiencies in the training at this phase, correction and reinforcement can turn what might have been a waste of time into a worthwhile effort. This type of process can be applied, in varying degrees, to other areas of safety training, such as with fall protection, lockout-tagout, erecting scaffolds, etc. By ensuring that a segment of the training is devoted to verifying that information has been transferred and skills have been developed, the value of the training is further established.

Improves Safety Performance Measurably

In a previous chapter titled "Measuring Up," the issue of safety performance was discussed and training was mentioned as an example of a key leading measure of safety performance. Training should produce visible results in the work environment and how employees go about performing their jobs. Employers should make periodic, purposeful observations of work where employees must employ skills they developed in training. During the observations employers should note the number safe and at-risk behaviors. When at-risk behaviors are observed, questions should be asked that help identify why the employee failed to employ the skills obtained in training. Answers to the questions can be used to detect system and culture barriers; and in many cases to see how the training could be improved. When there are few observations of at-risk behaviors (relative to observations of safe behaviors), it could signal accountability issues with a particular employee. Many times though, it can indicate a deficiency with the training that was intended to prevent this behavior from occurring.

To say that training has positively impacted safety performance, the results of the training should be visible long after the training is complete. Effective hazard controls (including training) must sustain safety performance over time, not just for a short period after implementation.

Verifying the Effectiveness of Training

Training, like any other business initiative, should be evaluated for effectiveness. Evaluating the effectiveness of training goes far beyond administering a simple written test upon completion of the training that satisfies regulators. While written exam type evaluations do provide a picture of how much knowledge is retained (or left from previous learning experiences), the true test of training's effectiveness is seen while work is being performed. Companies should continue written evaluations but focus most of their attention on evaluating the work environment and employees. Evaluating employees and work environment involves interviews and observations. Employees should be interviewed long after training is complete and be presented with various scenarios that require them to apply the skills and knowledge from training. Observations deal with both employees and the environment. Employees can be observed, as mentioned earlier, as either acting in a safe or at-risk manner in light of the raining they have received. The work environment can be observed to see if unmitigated hazards exist that training should have remedied (i.e., housekeeping, equipment maintenance, etc.). Positive results indicate success and opportunities for management to reinforce with employees that they have noticed their application of training. Negative results could be due to a variety of factors. In such cases, training should be explored to see if it's one of them. If determined so, the negative results present an opportunity for improvement.

You Don't Have to be Perfect

It's likely that you either feel your training efforts fall short (maybe very short) in many areas, or that a "pie-in-the-sky" approach has been presented. You may also feel that only large corporations can undertake training from the perspective presented. The case of presenting only a "pie-in-the-sky" approach is simply not the case. Countless businesses, both large and small, have successfully addressed training in a progressive fashion and have met great success. If you simply feel you fall short, hang in there! No training system goes to high performance overnight, and small steps in the right direction are very fruitful. There are many aspects of training that affect quality and you can't address them all at the same time. Your training efforts need not be perfect to provide value; however the more quality you build into your training, the greater the return.

Methods of Delivering Training

Before discussing the variety of methods at your disposal for delivering training, it is imperative to have a brief mention of the various learning styles. Learning styles are largely founded upon our natural senses and information perception abilities. For example, some individuals learn best through visual aids and watching demonstrations – visual learners. On the other hand, some learners experience greater success by listening to a lecture about topic – auditory learners. Still yet, some learners face challenges until they can actually interact with the skill – this may represent a more tactile or kinesthetic learner. When considering the various methods of delivering training one must consider those that will appeal to the largest group. When training materials and methods appeal only to a limited adult learning style, training effectiveness is greatly impaired.

As technology and learning research develops, so does the methods in which safety training is delivered to employees. When the VCR became popular, it revolutionized how companies trained employees and created a brand new "safety industry." The VCR has quickly become a rather archaic means of delivering training. Many may read this statement and agree, however they are likely thinking of DVD players, CD-ROMs, and web-based training alternatives to the VCR. In terms of technology, they would be correct. However, it is the contention of this author that our knowledge of how adults learn is the biggest advancement in safety training. Nonetheless, the two contentions actually go hand in hand as they both deal with the ultimate end – delivering training in the most effective manner to the adult learner. Delivery methods certainly must consider the adult learner as much as the content must.

As business owners evaluate whether they will use videos, computer-based learning, lecture, etc., they must always have the majority of their employee population in mind. Furthermore, business owners must be cognizant that sometimes there exists no one best approach to training and a combination of approaches may be necessary. Here are some fundamental considerations to keep in mind when selecting how training will be delivered to participants:

- How familiar and comfortable are my employees with technology?

- Is the method of training appropriate for the aging workforce? (Considering that hearing and vision diminish with age.)

- Do the methods I select only address one type of learner? (i.e., visual, auditory, etc.)

- Does the delivery method engage employees in the learning process and promote skills development?

- Will the delivery method allow for flexibility with customizing content? If not, does it serve to be a value-added supplement?

- After completing the training with this method, will employees be able to demonstrate competency to an outside party such as an OSHA inspector?

Training Supervisors

A common mistake made in small and large businesses alike is the failure to properly train supervisors. For some unknown reason, there's a tendency to subconsciously believe that once an individual becomes a supervisor they have the skills necessary to supervise safety magically bestowed upon them. For example, a new supervisor is frequently given an accident investigation form and told that they must investigate workplace injuries that occur in their department; many times the individual has never performed an investigation of any type in their life. There are several safety skill sets that are unique to supervisors that should be inherent in supervisor training. By purposefully training supervisors how to supervise employees respective of safety, we avoid simply assuming that the supervisor knows the "right thing to do," or will do the right thing when a hazardous situation or accident occurs.

The following represents some fundamental areas that supervisors should receive training on:

- accident investigation skills
- the importance of leading by example
- safety programs and policies directly and peripherally related to their departments
- evaluating employee reports of hazards and near misses
- financial impacts of workers' compensation loss to the company
- conducting work area inspections
- taking corrective actions for safety
- coaching employees for safety improvement

Training Fundamentals

While this chapter has focused on provoking thought on how businesses should strive to maximize the value that they receive from their training efforts, this book would be remiss if some fundamental instructions regarding training were not presented. As the concepts behind the following instructions are thought to be elementary, only the basic instructions are presented.

- Document, Document, Document – not just attendance, but information on the training topic, content outline, trainer, etc.
- Reference all regulatory standards when developing training.
- Ensure that training is given within acceptable time frames and frequencies (again referencing regulatory requirements).
- Document, Document, Document
- Make training concise yet comprehensive.

- Do not limit training to that required by regulatory agencies. Look at hazards and injury trends for training opportunities that may not be "required."

- Ensure that participants gained minimal skills and knowledge.

- Did we say? – Document, Document, Document

CHAPTER 20

Ergonomics

Injuries such as back strains and conditions like carpal tunnel syndrome represent some of the most expensive, prevalent, and difficult to manage claims in the American workers' comp scene. These injuries all stem from hazards commonly referred to as "ergonomic risk factors." Small businesses have just as many ergonomic risk factors as their larger counterparts; and there is no small business "type" that doesn't have at least a few risk factors. Small businesses can't afford to dismiss ergonomics as an issue applicable only to large manufacturers if they hope to take a bite out of their workers' comp.

What is ergonomics?

A very practical definition of ergonomics may be the process of adjusting a work environment (or workstation) to fit the human body rather than making the human body fit the work environment. More specifically, ergonomics is the practice of anticipating, identifying, evaluating and controlling those hazards related to an employee's work environment that may cause illnesses and injuries such as carpal tunnel syndrome, trigger finger syndrome and even back strains. These conditions belong to larger groups of injuries and illnesses called musculoskeletal disorders (MSD) and/or repetitive stress disorders.

When such conditions are considered work-related, they are due either to prolonged (chronic) exposure to an ergonomic risk factor, or from a single, traumatic overexertion event. When man was divinely created, it was an engineering feat beyond comprehension. Even so, the human body was not designed to last forever, nor was the human body designed to be completely adjustable to any task assigned to it. When examining the various tasks within a company that require human interface, potential for ergonomic issues to arise can be found almost anywhere. From data entry personnel, to assembly line workers, to mechanics and countless other roles within a small business – needs exist for ergonomic interventions. Such interventions are necessary to avoid the costly workers' compensation claims the come from unaddressed ergonomic risk factors. Even though ergonomics sounds like a complicated safety engineering issue that applies only to large companies, small businesses must pay close attention to this very real issue that represents one of the largest potentials of workers' comp loss; both from a frequency and severity standpoint.

Given the widespread prevalence of ergonomics hazards, it's no surprise that it has become one of the most important, specialized areas of occupational safety. It is one that has garnered an enormous amount of attention over the last decade and prompted some of the most heated legislative debates associated with OSHA. It remains the only instance where the Congressional Review Act was imposed to overturn an OSHA standard. Maybe most convincing of its importance is the fact that there exists no type of workplace hazard that produces more workers' compensation claims (especially questionable ones) than those related to ergonomics. As such, small business owners must give attention to minimizing ergonomics hazards.

Two Small Business Misconceptions

Thus far, this chapter has not revealed any new, earth-shattering facts about ergonomics considering the vast amount of mainstream media coverage the topic has received. Even with the attention that ergonomics has received, there are still numerous misconceptions that exist. Unfortunately the small business community appears to possess more of these misconceptions than larger companies. Through the authors' extensive interaction with small business owners, two of the most common misconceptions that small business owners verbalize are summed up in the following two statements:

1. We don't have any ergonomic issues.

2. Addressing ergonomic issues is too expensive.

Both of these statements are generalizations that are almost always false. No matter how convinced a small business owner may be that these statements are true for their particular business, they must take a close, very objective look – or face the risks of serious hits to their workers' compensation loss runs.

As previously discussed, ergonomic issues normally exist anywhere employees are involved. As you read through this chapter you'll understand this better. Granted, some ergonomic hazards may present only negligible risk, however when one considers the enormous cost potential, even low probability issues deserve a closer look for possible interventions.

A shift of thinking is required to objectively determine ergonomic exposures within a company. This shift revolves around understanding the subjective nature of workers' compensation claims arising from ergonomic hazards. The associated injuries and illnesses involve soft tissues within the body thus making them difficult, if not impossible, to conclusively diagnose from traditional, more objective medical testing methods such as x-rays. Even with the best, modern diagnostic equipment (i.e., MRIs and nerve conduction analysis) it can be difficult to produce medical evidence supporting the presence of a MSD. For this reason, physicians often make diagnoses based upon the subjective verbal complaints of a patient even when such tests reveal no conclusive findings of a medical problem. Thus, even if a safety professional may conclude that the likelihood of an ergonomic related injury occurring from a particular work task is extremely unlikely, the physician almost always errs on the side of the patient (normally for a host of reasons relating to personal liability – which is somewhat understandable considering the litigious American society). Almost always, if there is only a slight possibility of a causal connection between an employee's work tasks and the symptoms they present, a physician will most likely agree the patient's work "may" have caused the condition and leave it up to administrative law judge in workers' compensation hearing to determine compensability of a claim. If the employer can present no evidence to the contrary; or can present no evidence that a preexisting issue caused the condition, the employer's workers' compensation will many times have to cover the claim – at least to some extent. The odds are not good for the small business owner when claims get to this stage.

There are numerous scientific and highly precise evaluation tools for determining ergonomic exposure thresholds. Many of these tools require the services of a safety professional or even an ergonomist. While many small business owners may not, and understandably so, employ such methods of evaluation, they should be aware of a common pitfall surrounding recommendations from such evaluations. For example, many times a maximum lifting weight may be assigned to particular task. Just because an employee may have been lifting 10 pounds less than the maximum allowed at the time of the injury, it does not mean the claim is any less compensable from a workers' compensation standpoint. Again it is imperative to understand that it is often the subjective perception of physician that ultimately determines the allowable threshold on a case by case basis rather than that of the safety professional or ergonomist. While almost seemingly paradoxical, one must also identify ergonomic risk exposures from a more subjective, qualitative standpoint rather than a quantitative standpoint.

Misconception two may require the most convincing argument to overcome. This is largely due to the fact that the ergonomic interventions of which most people are aware involve enormous process re-engineering efforts (as seen in many of the automotive production industries) or the purchase of specialized equipment to assist humans with tasks (i.e., lifting assists and automation). Surprisingly though, the majority of ergonomic interventions that are implemented often require little to no capital expenditures. Being their own worst enemy, the safety profession many times glamorizes the expensive, large scale interventions because they demonstrate commitment to throw money at a problem. Media sources (speaking of industry trade journals, safety newsletters, etc.) view such interventions as more appealing "success stories" and thus place little emphasis on the inexpensive and less glamorous interventions such as putting adjustable legs on a table, purchasing an anti-fatigue mat, tilting a workstation or buying a new chair. While maybe less glamorous in the trade media's eyes, such interventions are no less effective and no less important. In fact, some ill-thought, improperly researched large scale interventions have proven unsuccessful, and, in-turn caused management to not support any further ergonomic interventions. This "throw the baby out with the bathwater" mentality will not serve these businesses well as their workers' compensation costs will undoubtedly continue to rise. Exposure to the hazards that the failed, "pie-in-the-sky" interventions were intended to control, continue when a less costly, nearly as effective control could have been controlling costs.

What are the risk factors?

Ergonomic risk factors, or hazards, basically fit into a few major categories: force, posture, repetition, contact stress, temperature extremes, and vibration. Ergonomic problems may arise with the presence of only one of the risk factors, or it may be a combination of the risk factors. For example, a certain task may require manipulation of a product with the hands. The manipulation of the product may or may not be of concern in and of itself, however if it has to be performed in a cold environment (as seen in some food preparation operations) it may present a significant ergonomic concern. The small business owner must keep in mind that the presence of one risk factor is enough to warrant further evaluation, and the presence of two or more with one job is a call to action.

Force

Force is an ergonomic risk factor that refers to the amount of physical exertion necessary to perform a work task. One of the most common examples of a force risk factor involves lifting. It is fairly safe to say that all businesses producing or delivering a product have lifting exposures to a certain degree. A large portion of service industries have lifting exposures as well. The other examples of overexertion factors are much more varied across different industries. These examples may involve turning a valve or pulling a lever; events that commonly cause shoulder injuries. Force need not be limited to tasks involving "big" movement of the back or shoulders, but may also apply to the force necessary to twist, squeeze or pinch something with the fingers, frequently causing conditions such as carpal tunnel syndrome.

Posture

Posture risk factors involve the assumed positions necessary, or commonly taken by employees to perform a task. The farther away from a neutral position a body part has to go, the greater the degree of risk that is posed. For example, if an employee's wrists are bent while performing a task, more stress occurs to the carpal tunnel as tendons move through it. (Like taking a string and rubbing it back and forth on the edge of a table). The result of performing even a low force task repetitively with the wrists bent often results in inflammation and swelling of the carpal tunnel and subsequent neurological problems (carpal tunnel syndrome). There are numerous other examples of non-neutral positions associated with various body parts and the injuries and illnesses that occur from poor posture associated with each. Common work tasks that naturally lend themselves to poor posture include computer operators (wrists, shoulders, and neck), electronic or small component repair and assembly, palletizing materials, etc.

There need not be repetition in order for posture to present ergonomic problems. Exerting force in a non-neutral position is frequently a cause for overexertion injuries such as back strains. For example, lifting 10 pounds is not a strenuous task for most employees. However if they have to bend over and lift an object weighing 10 pounds and maneuver it away from the body, the risk of back injury is fairly significant. When weight is held away from the body, the amount of force applied to the spine increases almost exponentially with the increase of distance from the torso.

Repetition

Repetition deals not only with the total amount of times an employee performs a task within a given period, but also the speed at which the tasks is performed. Repetition is a difficult risk factor to quantify. Due to other risk factors playing a part, there's never a clear definition as to "how much is too much" for a particular employee. However, it is safe to say that as the degree and presence of other risk factors increase, the tolerance for repetition decreases.

Contact Stress

Contact stress deals with employees' body parts contacting surfaces or edges while performing tasks. The most common example of this risk factor involves employees resting their forearms on the edge of a table while performing tasks with their hands. The physical contact of the arm against the table while digits and wrists are moving can cause irreversible nerve damage. Contact stress may present a problem by itself, or it may be a risk factor that works in tandem with another.

Vibration and Temperature Extremes

These two risk factors are fairly self explanatory. Since it is assumed that employees will be performing some type of manual task in a cold or hot environment, temperature extremes do not normally exist as a risk factor in and of themselves. Vibration, on the other hand, can cause MSDs without any other risk factors being present in any significant degree. Examples of work presenting vibration risk factors include driving powered industrial trucks, operating pneumatic impact drivers, operating jack hammers, etc. Vibration may be generated by tools or the surrounding work environment.

Listen to Your Employees' Body Language

A method to identify ergonomic risk factors that requires no specialized ergonomic training involves listening to your employees' body language. Mannerisms while performing tasks, workstation and tool modifications and the wearing of athletic or therapeutic devices (i.e., "wrist braces", forearm bands, etc.) often indicate potential ergonomic problems. As these type of actions (or pain reactions) often represent the employee's last resort before filing a claim, failure to recognize these issues and act upon them is inviting a workers' compensation claim.

How to Control Risk Factors

Controlling ergonomic risk factors is not that different than controlling other hazards (see the Chapter entitled "Looking for Trouble"). The three basic controls include engineering, administrative and personal protective equipment. As with controlling other hazards, ergonomics issues frequently warrant a combination of the three hazard control methods. In approaching the control of ergonomic risk factors, engineering controls are preferred with administrative being next and personal protective equipment being the least desirable control.

As previously established, engineering controls are preferred because they actually involve elimination of a hazard. A common example of an ergonomic engineering control is the purchase of materials in smaller, lighter weight or more maneuverable packages. Other examples may involve the purchase of equipment to perform tasks normally performed by employees, or the redesign of a workstation. As many job tasks may have more than one ergonomic risk factor present, a single engineering control may only apply to eliminating one of the risk factors while other types of controls are necessary to address the remaining risk factor(s).

Administrative controls are the most commonly utilized methods as they are almost always chosen to complement other methods of control in addition to being stand alone controls. Common examples of administrative controls include training (e.g., safe lifting, stretching, etc.), tool improvements and work rotations. Work rotations have proven to be one of the most effective and popular administrative controls. The popularity of this control is likely rooted in the fact that work rotations are many times the easiest way to consistently enforce and provide a more definitive lessening of exposure to risk factors.

When controlling ergonomic hazards administratively, care must be taken not to establish "exact thresholds" (i.e., objects weighing more than 50 pounds require a two person lift) and a dogma about their ability to protect employees. So many managers and business owners have a false sense of security with such thresholds. An analogous comparison to this pitfall is when parents restrict teenagers from dating until they reach a certain age. In actuality, a teenager is not any more mature at 16 years and 1 day than they were at 15 years and 360 days. Still yet, parents place stock in a birthday and "feel better" about letting them date. Business owners too many times set ergonomic exposure thresholds and get no benefit other than "feeling better" about the situation.

As with other types of hazards, personal protective equipment (PPE) is considered a last resort. Examples of ergonomic personal protective equipment include anti-vibration gloves, lumbar sacral back supports (back belts), wrist supports (preventative), etc. Unfortunately ergonomic PPE has a lesser degree of effectiveness than other items of personal protective such as safety glasses and cut resistive gloves. In fact, the National Institute of Occupational Safety and Health has published a research report stating there is no conclusive evidence that supports the usage of back supports. Despite the lack of evidence supporting the efficacy of ergonomic PPE, it can be a necessary supplement to the overall ergonomic hazard control effort.

Regulatory Trends

As eluded to earlier in the chapter, the only general ergonomic legislation enacted by OSHA was struck down by the usage of the Congressional Review Act (CRA). Not only did the CRA strike down the ergonomics regulation that had been enacted, it precluded the development of another general ergonomics rule; ever. Thus, unless a state OSHA plan has an ergonomics standard, OSHA continues to cite employers for ergonomic issues the same, unstable way they have in the past – through the general duty clause. OSHA has however started developing industry specific ergonomics guidelines to serve as best practices and guidance for businesses to address ergonomic hazards. These guidelines are being produced on an industry-by-industry basis with those industries demonstrating the highest ergonomic injury rates being developed first. While these guidelines are produced by a regulatory agency, they appear to be providing excellent tools for employers to use in avoiding workers' compensation claims associated with ergonomic risk factors.

CHAPTER 21

Long-Term Health Effects

While most small businesses don't handle "methyl ethyl death", they do sometimes work with solvents, acids, dusts, noise, asbestos, etc. All of these small business exposures pose long term health risks to employees that cannot be ignored. While the exposures may seem harmless now, the price in human life and dollars may not show up for years to come. Act now!

Answering Tough Questions

Inevitably, somewhere in time, most businesses will have one or more employees question, comment or complain about their work with a certain chemical, time spent in a noisy environment, "breathing all that dusty stuff", warnings read from a material safety data sheet, etc. Once brought to attention, managers and business owners are faced with the task of either addressing the matter, or ignoring it with hopes that it will "just go away." You've probably guessed that the latter is not the advised route proposed by this book. Ignoring the issue has many underlying consequences that include jeopardizing employee health; to making employees feel you totally disregard their long term well-being and that you don't have a clue about the situation and don't care to learn. Obviously, the most dreadful consequence of this approach involves overlooking a potentially legitimate concern that leads to an employee developing chronic illnesses such as cancer. It is absolutely imperative to keep in mind that there are legitimate cases involving occupational illnesses and they all stem from either ignoring the employee and exposure, or being ignorant of the effects a certain exposure has (the term "exposure" will ne explained in more detail shortly). Furthermore, all the illegitimate cases were probably made worse and elevated to "class action lawsuit levels" by the same approach. Either way, financial effects can be staggering and can lead to being uninsurable for workers' compensation. In some cases it has resulted in small businesses being bankrupt. Occupational illnesses claims are almost always very expensive!

As someone running a small business you must have a very broad understanding of a vast amount of subjects and most likely are a "jack of all trades". However, it's probably safe to say that you're not an industrial hygienist. Understandably, you may not have a clue about the situation being discussed in this chapter. However, you do not have to be an industrial hygienist to address such a situation and deliver a strategic and ethical response. Responses to employee concerns may include providing information to the employee, contacting an industrial hygienist or simply saying that you are not sure but will find out. This chapter seeks to provide a broad overview of the basis of industrial hygiene. Your goal should be to comfortably provide an initial evaluation, recognize the hazard or potential hazard, and call in trained professionals when necessary. A basic understanding of this specialized area of loss control can help you achieve that.

The tasks being discussed in this chapter deal with a specialized area of occupational safety called industrial hygiene. Industrial hygiene has been defined as a science and art dedicated to anticipating, identifying, evaluating and controlling employee exposure to environmental stresses arising in or from the workplace that may cause illness, impaired health and well-being or significant discomfort. Our discussion here will primarily deal with only the very basics in anticipating and identifying those environmental stresses (or exposures) and the fringe of evaluating those hazards commonly seen in general industry and construction environments. Armed with this basic information, you should be able to determine when someone who specializes in this art and science is needed and call them to take the situation from there. This book sets out to make you a more informed manager, not a safety professional or industrial hygienist.

Understanding Exposure

No doubt you've often heard the statement, "You can never get too much of a good thing." Certainly the person who coined this phrase was not thinking about exposure to chemicals, dust, noise, heat, etc., and the illnesses that accompany such exposures. In almost all cases regarding workplace exposures, and life in general, you most certainly can get too much of a good thing. In fact, too much of anything given over a certain time period can be harmful and sometimes fatal. Water is a good thing. However, you can get too much of it. Ask anyone who has ever nearly drowned or a runner who has suffered from hyponatremia (a condition caused by too much water consumption which leads to a sodium imbalance, and in turn can cause brain damage; even death). The first step, and most pivotal point in determining what to do with an occupational health and hygiene issue, is to determine if a significant exposure exists, or could exist, with a chemical or work environment stress – part of that art and science we spoke of.

Exposure is a term used throughout the world of industrial hygiene to pertain to the hazard itself (i.e., methyl-ethyl-bad -stuff vapors, noise from a grinder, etc.) or to the degree which an employee is subjected to the effects a certain chemical, substance or environmental stress (i.e., 25 parts per million of methyl-ethyl-bad-stuff, 90 decibels of noise, etc.). In evaluating an exposure, the form of the exposure (i.e., dust, fume, vapor, etc.), the method by which it enters or affects the body, and how much is entering the body over a specified time period in comparison to established accepted, or safe, levels must be determined. After reading this chapter you should be able to form a basic conclusion regarding the form of an exposure and its route of entry and then decide whether or not to contact an industrial hygienist to perform the "measurement." However, don't feel bad, and don't hesitate to use their assistance in identifying the form of exposure and route of entry. It is sometimes very difficult.

Time is of the Essence

While understanding the form an exposure takes and its route of entry into the body are the first steps in evaluating an industrial hygiene concern, an equally important consideration involves the amount of time an employee is exposed to a hazard. While there are exposures (i.e., noise at 140 decibels) that may present serious health effects if an employee is subjected to them for a few moments, the majority of times industrial hygiene concerns involve chronic (prolonged) exposures. It is the repeated, work-day long exposures to seemingly tolerable vapors, fumes, dusts, that often cause the most serious illnesses. As implied earlier in the text, many exposures may not necessarily be good, but if they occur over a relatively short amount of time or just occasionally, there may not be any harmful effects to an employee.

Now with the importance of time established, it is time to introduce the concept of Time Weighted Average (TWA). TWA allows us to put into perspective actually how much exposure an employee is experiencing in respect to an entire work day. For example, a maintenance employee may work in a dusty process for one hour each morning; however the rest of their work day presents no dust exposure. If measurements were taken of the concentration of dust irrespective of the length of time the maintenance worker is exposed to the dust, one may draw a conclusion that an employee is exposed beyond "safe limits" and ill advisedly start implementing expensive engineering controls, respiratory protection programs, etc. However, if the dust concentration is measured and then calculated taking into consideration the majority of the work day is dust free, one may likely find that no action is "needed" to protect the employee's health. TWA is a method of calculating an employee's exposure that takes into consideration an entire work day (8 hour basis). The majority of established, safe exposure levels (discussed later on) to certain substances are TWA exposures.

Routes of Exposure

There are essentially four methods by which substances enter the body and cause health problems: inhalation, ingestion, absorption and injection. It is important to remember that substances don't necessarily pose an exposure hazard through only one method, but in many cases have multiple routes that one must protect against. For example, someone performing spray painting operations often has exposure to vapors from the paint but is also involved in mixing the paint and getting it on their hands, thus having an inhalation route and absorption route of entry. Furthermore, the route of entry often determines how a substance will affect the body. In the case with the painter, some of the solvents may cause permanent adverse affects to the lungs and certain "target" organs, while absorption may affect the skin and a different target organ.

Arguably, inhalation is the most commonly encountered route of entry. This is due to several issues, but some are the fact that so many processes produce airborne contaminates, employees generally try to keep materials off their hands and body as much as practical, and hopefully no one is intentionally ingesting or injecting "diphenyl-doo-doo." Breathing however, is an involuntary action that is unavoidable in the presence of an exposure. Therefore much of the established safe exposure limits deal with respiratory protection and the inhalation route of exposure.

Breaking It Down: Key Terminology

Developing a layman's understanding of some basic terminology relating to exposures is a huge step toward being able to make an informed decision regarding exposure. This terminology will serve as a foundation for actually putting some of the technical "mumbo jumbo" contained in an MSDS and safety reference materials to use. Understanding the terminology includes more than simply knowing a definition, but also understanding the basics of application when appropriate. For example, you may know what the common definition of noise is, but a basic understanding of how it is measured and how it affects the body is also important in assessing a noise exposure.

The following presents some of the basic terminology dealing with industrial hygiene matters.

Forms of Respiratory Exposures

- **Vapors** – This term is used to refer to the gaseous phase of a material that is normally in liquid form at room temperature. The term vapor, just like gases and fumes, is frequently misused and often thought to be synonymous with gas and fume. While for many such distinguishing is merely an exercise in semantics, for evaluating an industrial hygiene exposure, it is very important as methods for measuring the three substances are quiet different. Vapor exposures are seen with employees handling open liquid containers, pouring chemicals, spraying paints and solvent, working around liquids that are heated etc. When respiratory protection is needed, knowing whether a substance is a vapor or fume is key to selecting the proper type of equipment.

- **Gases** – This term describe those substances which normally exist in the gas state of matter at normal room temperature. As gases have the most molecular movement they present a challenge for containing and thus many times are encountered as compressed gases. Carbon dioxide, argon, acetylene, nitrogen, etc., are common compressed gases seen in general industry and construction. Employee exposure to these types of gases is rare, and if they are encountered they many times produce acute effects. It is important to remember that gases are often byproducts of reactions involving liquid chemicals, or in the case of carbon monoxide, resultant of a combustion process.

- **Mists** – Similar to vapors in that they are formed from substances that are normally liquid, mists are actually in the liquid form, but are simply droplets suspended in the air either as a result of condensation or being mechanically formed (blower) into a mist. As with vapor exposures, mists can be encountered where employees are spraying solvents, paints, and adhesives and while performing work in environments where condensation of liquids is present.

- **Fumes** – While often mistakenly (either purposefully or ignorantly) called vapors, fumes are quiet different in that they are formed from solid materials. Fumes are actually produced through the heating of a material and producing an airborne particulate. One of the most common processes that produce fume exposures is welding. Welding involves the heating of two metals (an electrode and stock) as well as a flux material – which are all solids. Welding fumes can produce very serious chronic health effects if exposures are sufficient with respect to concentration and time and are uncontrolled. Welding fumes can also produce short-term effects, even though they are not seen as often.

- **Dust** – Dust is the easiest of the respiratory exposures to explain. Dusts are simply smaller sized particles of a solid material that easily become airborne. Dusts are commonly encountered in those environments where employees are sanding and cutting solid materials as well as with the application of materials that come in a powdered form. In many cases, there are permissible dust exposure levels that are specific to the solid substance the dust is generated from. However, one should also know that there are established permissible exposure levels for "general" or "nuisance" dust exposures (i.e., saw dust). While certain nuisance dusts, such as saw dust, are treated this way by OSHA (regulatory perspective), the American Conference of Governmental Industrial Hygienists (ACGIH) may recommend lower exposure levels as a best practice based upon research data which links a specific illness to the dust exposure. (Wood dust has been recognized by the ACGIH as a carcinogen).

Physical Hazards

- **Radiation** – Radiation is simply a form of energy and there are a variety of radiation types and exposures in the work place. Included in the types of radiations are electromagnetic (x-ray), ionizing, infrared, light and others. Sources of radiation vary from medical imaging equipment, radio active materials, metal welding and cutting equipment, technical instruments, etc. Radiation can be in forms that we can see and/or feel such as visible, ultra violet and infrared light radiation. Many times we take measures to control these radiation sources without even measuring the amount of exposure as ability to function, comfort and avoidance of acute injury (not illness) demands such. For example, providing a welding helmet for a welder is a form of control for visible radiation that is harmful to the eyes. Performing a preliminary identification and evaluation of radiation exposures that we cannot see or feel can be a difficult task even for a seasoned safety professional. Thus, if a company has any type of equipment that produces such radiation, professional assistance should be sought.

- **Noise** – Arguably, noise is the most common exposure present in workplaces. Noise refers to sound produced in the workplace that provides no useful or intended purpose. Not to say that playing your stereo too loud will not cause hearing loss, however it would not be referred to as noise as it provides sound intended for a constructive (depending upon the genre of music) purpose. It is important to remember that it is sound pressure waves that cause noise-induced hearing loss, and that noise sound pressure levels are measured in units referred to as decibels (dB). These measures represent a logarithmic progression; meaning they progress exponentially rather than linearly. For example, OSHA considers 90 dB to be twice the amount of noise dosage than 85 dB.

- **Heat Stress** – Heat stress is a rather complex exposure as it is an expression of how temperature and environmental factors affect an employee in a given situation. More than a simple expression of relative temperature and humidity, heat stress deals with how temperature, rate of work, and environmental factors affect the internal working of the body and its ability to maintain homeostasis. Heat stress is not limited to those employees working outdoors in the summer, but may pertain to those working indoors in climate controlled rooms or those housing hot processes, such as ovens. As mentioned, heat stress is always expressed relative to a work rate (light, moderate, heavy, etc., as established by the American Conference for Governmental Industrial Hygienists) and is also a TWA expression. A special instrument called a wet-bulb and globe thermometer (WBGT) is used to determine heat stress. Measurement and detailed analysis of heat stress is something normally best left to professionals.

Knowing How Much Is Too Much

Throughout this chapter there has been mention of "established safe exposure levels", however no details have been provided about such exposure levels. It is now time to develop a basic understanding of what is considered safe and how is it established. First, it is important to understand that such data is not arbitrarily established but is based upon laboratory research, medical findings, toxicology data, etc., produced by researchers and health professionals. Also important is to understand the organizations responsible for establishing safe exposure levels based upon research, findings and recommendations.

There are basically three organizations involved in establishing safe exposure levels. OSHA, National Institute of Occupational Safety and Health (NIOSH), and the American Conference of Governmental Industrial Hygienists (ACGIH) are the three agencies primarily involved in establishing these levels. NIOSH was created as an occupational safety and health research organization as part of the OSH Act of 1970. NIOSH performs some research and also reviews available data to establish recommended exposure limits (RELs) which OSHA considers when making safety legislation. The ACGIH is not a governmental organization (despite its name) that also performs research and reviews available data to recommend safe exposure limits. The ACGIH publishes Threshold Limit Values (TLVs) which serve as a "best practice" or recommended safe exposure level. The ACGIH's TLVs are published periodically and are traditionally accepted as the "best practice" with respect to protecting employee health. Exposure limits recommended by NIOSH and TLV's presented by the ACGIH are published as TWAs.

Understanding what is "permissible" with respect to allowing employees to be exposed without any type of hazard control is most often determined by OSHA's requirements for exposure limits which are referred to as Permissible Exposure Limits (PELs). OSHA PEL's are established after reviewing ACGIH, NIOSH and other information as well as hearing testimony during rulemaking meetings. Final OSHA requirements may be more stringent, less stringent or the same as recommended by NIOSH and/or the ACGIH. The regulatory burden upon an industry affected by such PELs may also be considered when establishing PELs. As with TLVs, PELs are based upon a time weighted average.

Similar to OSHA's PELs are another class of exposure limits that are not necessarily based upon an eight hour work day. Short Term Exposure Limits, STELs, are established to provide guidance on safe levels of exposure to higher concentrations of certain substances on a shorter time exposure. Normally, STELs are based upon a 15 minute exposure and are much greater than the corresponding PEL. For example, an employee may work in an environment known to have noise at 80 dB on a TWA without any ill health effects, however, cannot work any longer than 15 minutes in an environment with noise at 115 dB.

Important to keep in mind is the fact that only a small percentage of the substances and chemicals known to exist actually have established TLVs, and even fewer have PELs. As establishing PELs is a legislative process, it is naturally slow and susceptible to "political assassination". In many states, such as Kentucky, OSHA will use an established TLV in the absence of a PEL to cite and fine employers with respect to an exposure.

Controlling Exposures

As discussed earlier in this book, there are basically three methods of controlling hazards; engineering controls, administrative controls and personal protective equipment. These three methods are employed with occupational health and industrial hygiene exposures in much the same way. Engineering controls is the preferred method of control with administrative controls being next and personal protective equipment being the least desirable. Engineering controls consist of removing hazards or reduce them tremendously through the use of a safer substance, installing dust collection systems, improving ventilation, etc. One of the most common administrative controls for industrial hygiene issues is limiting the amount of time an employee is exposed to a certain hazard through work rotations. Finally, using personal protective equipment such as respirators and ear plugs are the least desirable, but most common because engineering and administrative controls can be cost prohibitive and unfeasible.

Role of the MSDS

This chapter has presented several practical instructions and explanations of the terminology used in understanding if there is a possibility of an exposure hazard, however one important prerequisite to putting this information to use, is understanding exactly what type of substance(s) we're dealing with. As many chemicals used in construction, cleaning, manufacturing, etc., are actually mixtures of other substances, we must look at the various chemical components of a substance in order reference established safe exposure limits. One can only imagine the infinite possibilities of chemical mixtures and different blends/percentages of components that can be mixed together to form one brand name of a substance such as, "John Doe's Miracle Solvent". Therefore, it only stands to reason that one cannot "lookup" the safe exposure limits for John Doe's Miracle Solvent, but one stands a much greater chance of locating such levels for the various chemical components of a brand name substance.

Determining chemical components of a brand name substance is one of the "more useful" purposes of MSDS (material safety data sheet). Manufacturers are required to include a listing of hazardous ingredients and their makeup in an MSDS unless such information is considered to be a trade secret. Almost always, this information is found in section 2 of an MSDS, and manufacturers will commonly publish OSHA PELs and ACGIH TLVs there too. It is always important to look at the date of the MSDS, as PEL's or TLVs may have changed since your copy was written.

Resources

While one may know the chemical ingredients in a brand name substance, one may or may not know the safe exposure limits, recommended controls/personal protective equipment, fire data etc., because many manufacturers produce poor quality MSDS, the substance may be manufactured by your company, or it could be a byproduct of a process. Given these scenarios, it is important to have access to some resources that provide this type of reliable information. Two common sources are NIOSH's Pocket Guide to Chemical Hazards and the ACGIH's published TLVs (a relatively inexpensive booklet). The NIOSH publication is available for free and provides a wealth of safety related information regarding specific substances and recommended controls and PPE. While hard copies of the NIOSH Pocket Guide can still be obtained (at the time of the writing of this book) online access or free CD-ROMs are frequently the most efficient way to access the information. The following web link www.cdc.gov/niosh/npg/npg.html may be followed to the NIOSH pocket guide where you can look up substances by chemical name, CAS #, etc.

Aside from the NIOSH pocket guide, there is a wealth of information, much of it more technical than the small business person would care to reach, available also through the NIOSH website.

Natural Doesn't Necessarily Mean Safe

Often business owners say that a certain product is natural or biodegradable and feel that there are no problems with employees being exposed to the substance. Keep in mind that poison ivy is natural; however, to an allergic person it's a harmful substance. There are many chemicals and substances that occur naturally and are used in the work environment without regard for employee protection because of the assumption that if something is natural and poses no threat to water ways, soil or air it's also safe for employees to work around. As seen with the poison ivy illustration, this simply isn't true. Many natural, and so-called natural substances can cause occupational illnesses and even injuries when employees are exposed to a sufficient amount of them over a specific time. For this reason, it is important to evaluate exposure concerns, even on natural substances.

Obvious Red Flags

While this chapter is intended to provide basic information to assist you in performing a preliminary evaluation of potential hazards, there are certain substances for which is ok to simply assume that the assistance of a safety professional or industrial hygienist is required. Substances such as asbestos, lead, PCBs (poly chlorinated biphenyl) are a few examples of such. These substances can lead to frightening terminal health conditions, and in some states there are specific compensation funds established to provide benefits. If a business owner suspects they have any of these, a knee jerk reaction is understandable, and possibly even encouraged.

Conclusion

Unless you simply remove yourself from any form of current events, you are somewhat aware of the consequences of "unseen" hazards from chemical and environmental exposures. Our current litigious society and modern mass media have most people wondering if a new drug they're taking, workplace chemical or environmental exposure will cause them long term health effects. As this new wave of information infiltrates the American workforce, it requires even small business owners and managers to become somewhat equipped to protect employees and handle questions. This chapter has provided information to make the business owner and manager more informed in order to make an initial response and strategy for fully evaluating a potential exposure. Many times a professional industrial hygienist will be needed to fully evaluate a situation and business owners and managers are encouraged not to make conclusions without first obtaining solid evidence through monitoring data. There exist numerous specialized situations that require professional assistance in the entire process of anticipating and identifying. What is imperative is for the small business owner to realize when he or she needs help and then to be diligent in obtaining that help.

Chapter 22

Fit for Duty

Susceptibility to musculoskeletal injuries, decreased mental concentration, increased fatigue and many other factors contribute to workers' compensation claims. Such factors are influenced – if not controlled by – the health of individual employees. While there is no one best strategy for improving employee wellness, there are some fundamental practices and proven strategies that small businesses can model when setting up their own wellness initiatives.

Fit for Duty

While there may not be a consensus on the best way to promote health and wellness in the workplace, there is a consensus that both are critical factors in preventing injuries, reducing absenteeism, improving quality and boosting productivity. No one will argue the fact that – when a person feels better, they perform better. Probably no other area of business is affected more by health habits than that of occupational safety.

In keeping with the theme of the book, there will be no recital of the mountain of statistics surrounding the health problems in this nation. Besides, if you've been reading the newspapers, watching TV, listening to talk radio or participating in any activity that remotely keeps you "in the loop," you already realize that the health habits of Americans and the rates at which we are becoming ill is alarming. It's not that your authors aren't advocates of research – it's simply that the exact numbers don't matter. Whether heart disease is the number-one or number-two killer matters not. Similarly, it doesn't matter if poor employee health and fitness contributes to 20% of work injuries or 60% of work injuries. What matters is that small business owners realize that poor employee health and wellness is a significant contributor to increased workers' compensation premiums; and that initiatives aimed at improving the health of employees pays off. There are more than ample case studies and valid research showing how companies that have truly committed to promoting health and wellness in their workplace have reaped huge rewards.

Illnesses such heart disease, stroke, hypertension, diabetes, various lung disorders and obesity are legitimate health concerns. Poor dietary choices, lack of physical activity and smoking are unquestionably the biggest factors responsible for such illnesses. Some business owners and managers maintain that such illnesses are the result of personal decisions made by employees and that intervening is "not the company's job." Rest assured that the authors of this book are the biggest proponents of personal responsibility, and are certainly adverse to enabling socialistic systems. However, business owners must realize that while they haven't caused or necessarily contributed to the health habits and status of their employees, it behooves them pay attention and try to help. It simply makes good business sense. The human capital of a small business is worth protecting. Promoting the health and wellbeing of employees, and even making access to the knowledge and resources to achieve it, is truly an investment in your business. Improving productivity, workplace morale, quality, customer service, and company image are just some of the tremendous benefits of employee wellness initiatives. Probably the most compelling of all reasons to promote employee wellness campaigns is the role they can play in taking a BIG bite out of your workers' compensation premiums. Don't let your competition beat you to the punch.

But We're Too Small

Some small businesses may be tempted to once again lean on the "We're so small" crutch when initially considering an employee wellness program. Those who do, most likely have perceptions of onsite workout facilities, company-paid personal trainers, and the like – all initiatives seemingly undertaken only by Fortune 500 companies. Don't let these "big time capital" productions be an illusion of what is necessary – and present the temptation to once again throw the baby out with the bath water. There are numerous things that even the smallest of businesses can do that involve minimal if any expense – things that can make a big impact. This chapter will present an array of ideas for small business owners to evaluate; some involving more expense than others. Since each business' culture and resources have unique limitations, everyone must choose the arsenal that works best for them. It's critical to keep in mind that employee wellness initiatives are always continuous improvement projects. The company doing nothing will benefit by implementing at least one of the ideas. Companies who've already begun their quest to improve employee health will gain insight in going to the next level. We challenge each reader to give an employee wellness initiative a try. We're confident you'll want to do more.

What do the Underwriters Think?

While underwriters will always hone in on loss control consultants' evaluations of "traditional risks" (i.e., falls, machine hazards, trenching, etc.), they are beginning to take extra note of those companies who are demonstrating concern for the overall condition of their employees. As established throughout this book, loss control consultants are normally operating as safety professionals. The safety profession has become inundated with information, seminars and publications about the benefits of employee wellness initiatives. As such, loss control consultants are beginning to ask workers' compensation policyholders about initiatives in this area when they pay them a visit. Companies who are doing something with employee wellness create a very favorable impression about management commitment and efforts to reduce claims – well beyond the wellness initiative itself. This impression shows up on loss control reports that are eventually referenced by underwriters during the policy quotation phase. This impression can affect the underwriter's decisions to offer scheduled credits should they be "on the fence."

Know Your Network

The benefits of having a relationship with a local medical provider have been explained from a claims management standpoint elsewhere in this book, but another very important benefit of having such a relationship lies in the area of health and wellness. Most occupational health clinics – and even some small general practice medical clinics that have a decent-sized contingent of occupational clients – will have some resources, knowledge or both to help with implementing health and wellness initiatives. These clinics will minimally help you plan a health fair at your facility. In many cases where a company has regular business with the medical clinic (i.e., trucking entities needing regular DOT physicals), they may actually plan and conduct the health fair for the company at no charge. The medical professionals with which a company does business are excellent resources for any health and wellness campaign.

The Power to Choose

An overriding principle to keep in mind when selecting and implementing wellness initiatives is that of employee engagement. Different employees will receive different wellness initiatives differently. While some employees may have inhibitions about participating in an aerobics class, they may be very receptive to a smoking cessation class. Most employees have more than one area that needs improvement. Achieving a small success in one area will likely encourage them to participate in another. When employees can have a choice in how they will participate, they are much more likely to participate. Offering options in how employees participate need not be expensive. They simply need to be available for the majority population. For example, different geographic areas of the U.S. have smoking challenges that are greater than others. Companies located in these areas may have smoking cessation as a priority option. The other options would be alternatives for non-smokers, or for furtherance of the smoker's efforts.

Health & Wellness Initiative Ideas

For simplicity sake, these ideas have been condensed into two categories. Passive ideas represent things that companies can enact that are fairly "self- maintaining" (either through an outside source or by nature of the idea). Active ideas are those that require the employer to be involved and at least assist with the maintenance of the initiative.

Passive Ideas

- Ensure vending machines have healthy food choices – or better yet have one dedicated to healthy food choices. (This idea allows for employee choice.)
- Issue pedometers and allow employees to track walking steps per day.
- Measure and mark-off a safe walking area for employees to exercise during breaks or lunch.
- Conduct health fairs. (at least two per year)
- Negotiate a company rate at a local fitness club or YMCA
- Partner with a group health insurance provider or health coaching organization and offer telephonic health coaching.
- Have the health screening company send employees individualized health improvement reports.

Active Ideas

- Track results from company-wide health screenings (often incorporated with health fairs) and compare to posted goals for the company:
    - Blood Pressure Improvements
    - Cholesterol Improvements
    - Diabetes Improvement

    (NOTE: Do not post individual improvements because of privacy laws)

- Sponsor smoking cessation classes
- Host and sponsor periodic brown-bag lunch education opportunities that feature brief, health education. (Ideas for topics include sleep deprivation, exercise techniques, blood pressure improvement, understanding nutrition labels on food, maintaining muscles and bones, osteoporosis, prostate health, breast cancer prevention – the list is endless.)
- Tie performance incentives to health improvement goals.
- Provide traveling employees (i.e. truck drivers) with healthy snacks and beverages.
- Ensure wellness is covered in all safety orientation training.
- Include wellness initiatives in top-of-mind awareness activities.

Making the Ideas Work

If one were to perform an ABC Analysis (an analysis tool that behaviorists use to determine why people do what they do) on most poor health choices, it would be fairly clear that many of the consequences that influence people not to wear personal protective equipment (such as respirators) are the same categorical consequences that promote poor health choices. For example, employees may eat poorly because of such issues as convenience, time savings, self-gratification, and money savings. Many of these consequences are similar to the same reasons employees speed, fail to wear safety glasses, etc. Researchers have found that those consequences that – to the individual doing them – are positive, soon and certain are more powerful than those that are negative. In other words, eating convenient, cheap, fast food of which one enjoys the taste, will always be a more powerful motivator than the consequence of getting heart disease. In order to make wellness efforts work in a small business, the small business owner must try to eliminate the excuses that make the employees make the choices they do (convenience, time etc.).

While health and wellness initiatives can be a challenge to implement, the small business owner must dive in. Research clearly shows that there are real benefits for companies that promote health beyond the workplace. Lower group health insurance and workers' compensation costs are powerful, direct benefits. Indirect benefits such as increased productivity, attendance, safety performance and product or service quality are also present and certainly make having a health and wellness initiative a matter of staying competitive. Small business owners can no longer ignore the need to address the health habits of their workforce or leave wellness to chance.

CHAPTER 23

Legal Pitfalls

As nearly nothing in the legal realm of business is cut and dry, it's important for small business owners to understand the legal premises of workers' compensation. This chapter explores the fundamental legal structure of workers' compensation and offers information for small business owners to consider when making decisions and approaching sensitive claims.

I Thought Workers' Comp Was Legal Protection

Most business owners and managers realize that a central reason they obtain workers' compensation insurance – besides the obvious transfer of financial risk and various states' mandates to have coverage – is to provide legal protection. A basic premise of workers' compensation is that it serves as the exclusive remedy for injured employees to recover "damages." For those not familiar with the legal term "Exclusive remedy," it simply means that employees cannot pursue litigation against their employer before a jury, in a traditional civil court, and that punitive damages do not apply. As with many legal issues, there are some exceptions to that definition, particularly involving willful intent or negligence; and with a few state-specific statutes that permit pursuit of civil litigation in certain circumstances. That having been established, one may wonder why a chapter of this book is devoted to legal pitfalls – if workers' compensation is, in itself, a form of legal protection for the employer.

As each state has its own statutory provisions for workers' compensation, it is nearly impossible to compress into a single chapter of a book all the legal requirements of each state to resolve a workers' compensation claim. Therefore, this chapter will briefly focus on a basic area fairly common to all states with respect to workers' compensation claims themselves – compensability. Since compensability is often a dispute between a claimant and an insurance company (not to imply employers have no role in the dispute) many of the legal pitfalls facing small businesses relate to issues not directly tied to the claim itself. Therefore, the majority of this chapter will address some of these "peripheral" legal pitfalls.

An important point to keep in mind while reading this chapter, is that each state has its own unique workers' compensation system. These systems define benefits differently. They also have varying definitions of workers' compensation terms – which will be presented in this chapter. The information presented in this chapter is a broad and generalized presentation, and chances are your state will have some type of variation with a few, or even several of the terms presented. Each state, employer and workers' compensation claim is unique. As such, you should always default to the counsel of your workers' compensation attorney, employment law attorney, or the attorney working on behalf of your insurance carrier.

Who Made You The Judge?

In nearly all states, an injury or illness is deemed compensable under a state's workers' compensation laws if it is determined that the injury or condition arose out of, and arose in the course of employment. "Arising out of" and "arising in the course of" are two key legal tests that all claims must pass in order for an employee to receive benefits under workers' compensation. In almost all states claims must pass both tests to be considered compensable. "Arising out of employment" deals with a causal connection between the injury or illness and an employee's work. "In the course of" employment involves an injury or illness occurring at a place and time (which is not limited to "being on the clock") consistent with the employment relationship. In understanding these compensability tests, one must keep in mind that workers' compensation is, in most states, "no-fault" – thus meaning it does not matter if an employee's own contributory negligence played a role in the injury or illness (from a compensability standpoint).

These "tests" are not as straight forward as they may seem, in fact both can be rather vague. There are numerous legal doctrines (such as positional risk doctrine, and increased risk doctrine) that are utilized in each state to determine if claims are compensable under that state's workers' compensation laws. Because such doctrines exist, causal connection is not exclusive of the primary work function performed by an employee, but many times encompasses tasks incidental to an employee's main work. For instance, an employee's job may involve travel in a motor vehicle to perform sales calls and warrant overnight stays away from home. If such an employee is injured in a motor vehicle accident while driving to a restaurant for dinner after the work day is done, in most instances this injury would be considered compensable. While the employee's job is performing sales calls, driving to a restaurant is an incidental risk "caused" by the employment. Obviously if another vehicle is involved in the incident and is at-fault, subrogation of the other vehicle's liability insurance may be sought to recover damages incurred through the workers' compensation claim.

Obviously there are exceptions and lines that are drawn (even though legal "lines" are often blurry) to address injuries occurring from certain tasks, such as commuting to a fixed place of work, as not being "causally connected" to employment. One must be mindful that case law precedent and an administrative law judge's interpretation decide questionable claims. Thus, it's not surprising that injuries occurring through things such as horseplay at work can be considered compensable. It is therefore important for business owners to be intimately aware of peripheral tasks employees perform, either with or without permission, and understand that injuries occurring while performing such may be deemed compensable. As a small business owner or manager, this discussion on compensability may serve you best by allowing you to see that each individual claim must be examined from all perspectives and that it is not prudent to prematurely tell employees, "That injury is not covered under workers' compensation."

Paramount Protection

As eluded earlier, some of the biggest legal pitfalls facing small businesses involve management of the injured employee and not management of the claim. The following segments of this chapter address specific legal issues. However, most of them are pitfalls that could be avoided if written employment policies existed and were consistently enforced. Discrimination and wrongful discharge are just two employment legal charges that arise as a result of employment actions taken after a workers' compensation claim occurs. Too often small business owners – or their liability insurers – pay exorbitant amounts in litigation as result of these charges. In some cases they simply go out of business all together. While there's no fool-proof way of preventing accusations and lawsuits, business can help protect themselves from jury judgments in such matters through written policies that are consistently enforced.

There are numerous opportunities for discrimination claims to arise after a work related injury. Just as an employee may contend that they've been treated unfairly because of race, religion, sex, age, labor union affiliation, etc., they may also state that they were treated unfairly because they filed a workers' compensation claim. Most employers are aware of the fact that they cannot blatantly terminate an employee simply for filing a workers' compensation claim. What is not so obvious is that termination, disciplinary actions, penalization (monetary or other incentive) or failure to promote an employee for other legitimate reasons can be – through the aid of a crafty attorney – construed to have occurred because the employee filed a workers' compensation claim. Without the presence of established, written human resources policies that are consistently enforced, it is difficult, at best, to prove that the claim had nothing to do with the action.

Another example of the importance of sound documentation involves occasions when an employee may be off work for an extended period of time and the employer must terminate the injured employee and hire a replacement due to business economic reasons. In many cases, employers are not prohibited by state statutes from terminating an employee who remains off work receiving temporary total disability benefits in order to avoid business hardship. However, employers must be prepared to defend themselves should that employee file a retaliatory discharge lawsuit. As you may expect, the best way to defend yourself in such circumstances is to be able to provide documentation of such a business hardship. Furthermore, the company must have consistently followed this same model for other cases, otherwise the documentation may be worthless when a plaintiff's attorney points out that other employees, whom maybe the business owner "liked better" (and possibly for good reason), were not terminated when similar circumstances were presented.

Knowing When to Keep Your Pie Hole Shut

Many times, small business owners could have avoided legal action and the loss of profit if they would have only known what to say, or (more often) what not to say. One of the biggest mistakes a small business owner can make is to assume the role of a "quasi-physician" or "quasi-attorney" when a questionable claim arises. Many times claimants, legitimate and illegitimate, are further encouraged to take legal action due to the immediate wall of resistance put up by the words and opinions of a business owner or manager who is -- with good intentions – trying to nip a bad situation in the bud. Too often business owners will erroneously label a claim as fraudulent because of circumstances, and prompt the employee to receive legal aid when none is actually need. As most business people know, once legal counsel is obtained, communication walls are erected and an adversarial relationship arises. Business owners must realize that a physician's opinion will be the one that counts regarding the legitimacy of a medical condition, and that an administrative law judge will determine the compensability of a claim if it is contested. Therefore, the energies of business owners and managers should be focused on objectively collecting information to provide that information to the insurance provider or third-party administrator in order to resolve the claim.

Owners and managers must realize that when one employee has a bad experience with an owner or manager following a workers' compensation claim, they will communicate this to other employees in order to prepare them, in case they have a workers' compensation claim. Soon, all employees will be on-guard to obtain legal counsel because they fear that the employer (you) – by default – tries to have all claims denied. Having employees feel they can trust you throughout the claim process is vital to controlling costs and avoiding legal pitfalls.

This segment is not written to contend that small business owners and managers should not be firm and aggressive with claims management, but to say that they should abstain from allowing emotions to take control and rendering opinions they ultimately are not qualified to render. It is the job of experienced claims adjusters to speak to employees about claim compensability and denial. And, it is the job of physicians to diagnose medical conditions. After all, individuals who submit a questionable claim may remain employed by your company after a claim is resolved and their interactions with you during the claim process will determine how awkward it is to see them on a daily basis and how much loyalty they will have toward your business.

Third Party Liability

One of the biggest trends surrounding workers injured on the job involves third party liability. As discussed earlier in this chapter, employers are generally protected from civil litigation because workers' compensation is considered an exclusive remedy. As many states go through workers' compensation reform to stimulate economic growth, injured workers are starting realize that workers' compensation is not the "cash cow" it is commonly and ignorantly thought to be. Many times this realization occurs when the employee sees that, in many states, it is becoming more difficult to find legal counsel due to state-mandated fee caps for attorneys. As to be expected, those injured workers who are really interested in getting rich from a work related injury are not easily deterred. Therefore, filing suit against a party that is not their employer is the most obvious option. Even though judgments in such cases often require the workers' compensation carrier to be reimbursed expenses, the staggering jury awards still make third party lawsuits a worthwhile pursuit for employees who submit fraudulent claims, as well as for personal injury attorneys.

The message to small business owners and managers is to be cognizant of opportunities for employees of other companies to be injured by the products or services provided by your company or while working on your property. For example, "ABC Conveyor" company may manufacture conveyors used by "XYZ Widget Manufacturing". Should an employee of XYZ be injured because of a guarding deficiency (no matter how small), the injured employee may file a civil suit against ABC for the injuries. Indeed, many times product liability insurers may be involved in such a suit, but damage to the company's reputation and insurability may be irreparable. This pitfall not only involves businesses producing products but may be extended to service and construction businesses as well.

Disciplinary Action

While the preceding segment on written policies addressed potential pitfalls surrounding disciplinary action taken after workers' compensation claim has been filed, it is not meant to scare the small business owner or manager from taking action that is warranted. Assuming sound policies that provide a mechanism for delivering disciplinary action are in place, the keys to disciplinary action following a claim are listed below:

1. Ensure that the action is clearly related to the employee misconduct causing the injury.

2. Communicate clearly to the employee that the action is for the specific area of misconduct.

3. Consistently take the same action with other employees who may have violated the policy but did not necessarily have an injury.

An example of a scenario where this would occur would be if an employee sustains a laceration from handling sharp materials with bare hands when cut resistive gloves were provided and were clearly required to be worn, yet the employee deliberately chose not to wear them. Here the employee may receive disciplinary action for not wearing personal protective equipment as required by policy – not for getting cut as a result of not wearing required gloves. In situations such as this, it is prudent for the business to clearly communicate policies, otherwise employees can claim they were unaware or did not fully understand requirements. Moreover if disciplinary action is taken in these types of situations, employees must clearly understand that disciplinary action is due to policy violation – not for getting hurt on the job.

Modified Duty ≠ Immunity

Too many small business employers subconsciously think that employees who are returned to work within the context of modified duty (a.k.a. light duty) are ticking legal time-bombs. They are afraid to hold such employees accountable to general employment standards (i.e., reporting to work on time, being reasonably productive, adhering to dress code, displaying good work ethics, etc.) when their physician-imposed work restrictions do not prohibit them from doing so. This fear often creates frustration, and unfortunately contributes to some companies' reasons for not providing modified duty work assignments. As you have probably become aware, the theme throughout this chapter involves having written policies and consistently enforcing them. Modified duty is no exception to this. While employers must be diligent in doing so, employees who return to work within the context of modified duty can, and should be held accountable for abiding by company policies, to the extent that they are physically able.

Screening Pre Existing Conditions

Post job-offer physicals for employees are excellent tools for preventing workers' compensation claims and controlling costs. Most importantly, such medical screenings can protect those persons offered employment opportunities from being injured by demands of a job they are not physical capable of enduring. As to be expected, these screenings have legal precautions. The American's with Disabilities Act (ADA) wields a dual edged sword to employers using such physicals if they are improperly administered. It is as much of a violation of the ADA to deem an employee to have a disability (as vaguely defined by the Act) when they don't, as it is to discriminate against someone for an actual disability. Here are few key attributes to legally sound post job-offer medical exams:

- They must be administered as "post job-offer." Screening for a disability before a person is offered employment is simply inviting a discrimination charge. It is difficult to prove your reason for not offering an applicant employment was because another candidate was more qualified instead of the medical condition that was discovered during the physical; regardless if the condition is considered to be a "disability" or not. Make an offer of employment contingent upon successfully completing a post job offer physical.

- Allow your company physician to make a "pass" or "fail" determination of the candidate. Business owners and managers should remain removed from the actual physical and "fit for duty" determination. Obviously you must provide the physician with information on job demands in order for him or her to make informed decisions about all candidates, however the less you know about the details of candidates' health, the less that you can be accused of.

- Ensure that detailed job descriptions are available, and that they are tailored to the particular jobs in the company. While many physicians can perform generic physicals, if an employment candidate pursues legal action for not being hired, it's the physical demands of the particular position they were being hired for that will come under the microscope and serve as the standard in a legal action.

- Do not administer a questionnaire yourself and make a determination on whether or not a candidate should be hired. Unless your small business is your own medical practice, you are not a physician and not qualified to make such a decision. Almost always, it's a slam dunk case for a plaintiff's attorney if legal action is sought after someone is denied employment because the owner or a manager saw something on a health questionnaire and made a decision that the applicant was not "fit for duty."

Ensuring Attorney Suitability

All attorneys are not created equal, nor are they all suited for all types of law practice. Many companies have lost crucial employment related lawsuits due to incompetent legal counsel, or counsel that wasn't prepared for the immenseness of employment law. Employment and workers' compensation law is a unique niche that requires experience to effectively litigate claims. Many small businesses retain one general counsel to represent them on a variety of legal matters, and many times this is ok. However, employment law requires attorneys experienced with litigating cases and advising on policy development to avoid big legal no-no's. Hopefully, a company's general counsel will understand the complexity of certain employment cases and refer the business owner to another firm more experienced or specialized in employment law. Nonetheless, there are some attorneys and firms that bite off more than they can chew and do not provide their client with as good of service as they expect. Therefore, it is simply due diligence for a business owner to inquire of a firm's experience with handling employment law issues and then make an informed decision of whether to seek different, or additional legal counsel with a matter.

Disclaimer

This chapter is intended to provide authoritative and reasonably accurate advice on some general legal issues relating to workers' compensation. Readers should also seek the advice of legal counsel to deal with particular issues in their companies as each situation is unique and fact dependant. (We just had to include this!)

CHAPTER 24

There's No Shame in Asking for Help

Although this book provides a wealth of knowledge and tools that you can put to use to take a bite out of your workers' compensation premium, that does not mean that you have to do it all on your own. After all, obtaining competent assistance from outside of your company is not only within your power, it's quite easy, and in many cases – free.

Looking Beyond Yourself

A theme that has been stressed throughout this book is that your company's past workers' compensation claims can impact your future premiums tremendously. If you are effective at preventing injuries and controlling the cost of claims, you will reap the benefits. If you are ineffective, you will pay the piper. Because that point has been made over and over again, you should not need to be convinced that you must do everything in your power to prevent employee injuries and control the cost claims. To that end, this book is packed with the tools you need to take a bite out of your workers' compensation premium.

In several of the preceding chapters, this book provided specific information to help you prevent injuries. More precisely, it explained how to identify hazards before they contribute to injuries. It explained how to conduct safety training with an impact. It explained how to combat ergonomic and industrial hygiene hazards, and much more. In addition to that, the preceding chapters explained how you, as a small business owner or manager, can control the cost of claims through using modified duty, through subrogating claims, through countering the threat of workers' compensation fraud and through other means.

Almost everything presented in this book represents knowledge or tools that you can use to take a bite out of your workers' compensation premium. However, that does not mean that you, the small business owner or manager, must do it all on your own. In fact, if you try to do it on your own, you will be violating the very assertion made at the beginning of this chapter – that you should do "everything in your power" to prevent employee injuries and control the cost of workers' compensation claims. After all, as you will see in this chapter, obtaining competent assistance from outside of your company is not only within your power, it's quite easy, and in many cases – free.

Insurance Loss Control Consultants

It is logical to think of your workers' compensation carrier first when considering the sources of assistance available to you as a small business. After all, you and your insurance carrier are on the same team. Neither of you want employees to become injured. Not only that, but both of you want to minimize the cost of every injury. To that end, virtually every workers' compensation insurance provider makes loss control consultants available to their policyholders. The specific title that these individuals hold differs from one insurance company to the next. Some call these folks risk control specialists, others call them loss prevention representatives, and others refer to them as safety consultants. Regardless of the title on their business card, these are typically safety professionals who have graduated from degree programs in occupational safety and/or have a number of years experience managing the safety function within other companies. They may be directly employed by your insurance carrier or may work for a company that is contracted by the insurance company to provide consultative loss control services. Their job (at least part of it) is to help you prevent injuries and control the cost of your workers' compensation claims.

Although their primary focus is to assist you in your efforts to prevent injuries, they also function as the eyes for the insurance underwriters. While they are at your facility helping you improve upon your existing loss control efforts, they are evaluating your workplace, your employees, your management structure and everything else that helps shape an opinion about your company as an insurance risk. That information is then fed to the insurance underwriters. For that reason, their objective observations and their subjective opinion of your company (and its safety management efforts) can shape your future workers' comp premiums. If their observations and opinions of your company are favorable, it could very well score you a scheduled credit (discount) on your next workers' compensation policy. If their observations are less than favorable, the opposite could occur. In fact their observations and opinions of your risk can even factor into whether your current workers' compensation carrier offers to renew coverage at the end of the current policy period.

Under almost all circumstances, the services provided by your workers' compensation carrier's loss control consultants are free and include things such as onsite consultative visits, periodic assessments of your facility for hazards, help in developing written safety policies and investigation of serious accidents. The services also frequently include free safety posters and signs, safety meeting guides, safety videos, and other helpful safety-related literature. In fact, if most of these things are not available to you free from your current workers' compensation carrier, you may want to question your choice of workers' compensation carrier, as most business owners consider these to be basic services included in the cost of their workers' compensation premium.

Some states require workers' compensation insurance carriers to provide loss control services. In fact, some require that each employer be notified in writing of the availability of loss control services. Other states specify the minimum frequency at which loss control consultants provide assistance. Figure 24.1 depicts states with such requirements, at the writing of this book.

	Insurance Carrier Required to Offer Loss Control Services	Insurance Carrier Required to Notify Policyholder of Loss Control Services	State Defines Minimum Criteria for Loss Control Services
AR	x	x	x
CA	x	x	
CO	x	x	
KS	x	x	
ME	x	x	
MN	x	x	x
MS	x		
MO	x	x	x
MT	x	x	x
NV	x		
NM			x
NY			x
OK	x	x	
OR	x	x	x
PA	x	x	
RI			x
SD	x		x
TX	x	x	x

Figure 24.1

Although most insurance loss control consultants are either direct employees of the insurance carrier or are contracted by the insurance carrier, some large independent insurance agencies have their own loss control consultant(s) who provide the same type of services to their clients. These loss control consultants generally have the same background and qualifications as those employed by the insurance companies. Like the loss control services provided through the insurance companies, the focus of those that are offered by an independent insurance agency is injury prevention and controlling the cost of claims. However, unlike insurance loss control consultants, the loss control consultants who work for an independent insurance agency do not serve as the eyes of the insurance company underwriters. For that reason, their observations and opinions of your business (good or bad) will likely have no impact upon future workers comp premiums. Their only collateral function is to provide you a service (typically for free) that will keep you loyal to that particular insurance agency.

If you have access to loss control consultants through both your insurance company and through your insurance agency, it is perfectly acceptable to use the services of both. In fact, it is quite likely that the two will complement one another, resulting in a high degree of personalized service for your company.

I'm From the Government and I'm Here to Help

Although the above-mentioned loss control consultants are, in many cases, the best first choice for getting the assistance you desire, they are by far not the only option at your disposal. Among the other options are safety professionals made available to you through the state or federal government.

A few states employ safety consultants within the state's department of workers' compensation. Even though they have no vested interest in your success, their goal is to help you prevent work-related injuries and control the cost of claims. In fact, the role of those safety consultants differs very little from the loss control consultants who work for insurance companies or insurance agencies. Like insurance loss control consultants, the safety consultants made available through some state governments' workers' compensation departments generally offer free on-site consultations, provide free safety-related publications, maintain a free safety video lending library, and will evaluate (or assist in developing) written injury prevention and cost-containment policies. Although they are government employees, they are not compliance officers. Their role is not to make a determination whether or not your company is in compliance with safety-related laws and standards. They are not secret agents for OSHA, and will not report deficiencies they observe to OSHA or any other enforcement body. They are merely safety consultants for which you have paid in advance, through your tax dollars. Use them whenever you can.

OSHA Consultation Programs

Separate from the safety consultants that some states provide to assist employers with workers' compensation issues are the consultative services that all states have to help employers comply with applicable OSHA requirements. Some states use Federal OSHA to enforce occupational safety standards and others (called state-plan states) use their own state government agency. Regardless of whether it is the federal government or the state government that enforces OSHA standards, an OSHA consultation program has been established in your state. Much of the funding for these consultative services comes from the federal government. But each state has its own unique OSHA consultative service. Depending upon the state, these consultative services may be a part of the state government, or may be offered through a state university or other entity.

Irrespective of who provides the consultative service, there are some common characteristics of each state's OSHA consultation program. First, the consultative services are free. Second, the OSHA consultation programs in each state are completely voluntary. If you want the services that are offered, you must request them. Third, the OSHA consultation programs have been established primarily to provide a service to small businesses – because even the government understands that small businesses simply do not have the resources that large businesses have. Fourth, consultative services through the OSHA consultation programs do not generate citations or fines. Even if there are numerous violations of OSHA standards evidenced through these visits, the individuals conducting the consultative service will not issue a citation. Fifth, the consultative services are confidential. Your company name and any information you provide about your workplace, as well as any unsafe condition that is uncovered as a result of the consultation (under normal circumstances) will not be reported to the OSHA enforcement office. The goal of these consultative services is to assist employers improve upon their occupational safety efforts, not to punish employers for their shortfalls. Because of that, the only time that a representative from the state OSHA consultation program will refer a situation to the OSHA enforcement office is when the employer fails to control or eliminate a serious hazard that was identified during the consultative visit. In fact in some instances, employers who solicit consultative services through the state OSHA consultation program may be exempt from routine OSHA compliance inspections for a year following the consultation.

Although the consultation programs are administered by individual states, the manner in which the services are provided is fairly uniform. If you request a comprehensive consultation, you can expect to first meet briefly with the consultant in an opening conference. During the opening conference the consultant will explain his role and your obligation as an employer to address the hazards evidenced as a result of the consultation. Following his assessment of your facility; an observation of your employees performing their duties; and an evaluation of your written safety programs, there will be a closing conference between you and the consultant. During that closing conference the findings will be discussed with you. At that time you and the consultant can discuss problems, possible solutions and abatement periods to eliminate or control any serious hazards identified from the consultation. Following the on-site consultation, you will receive a written report of recommendations and agreements.

Contact information for each state's OSHA consultation program is provided on www.chompcompbook.com. Also provided is the Internet address for each state's OSHA consultation program, where you can generally find helpful literature, sample policies, and more

College Interns

Yet another source of assistance that you can use to strengthen your company's safety efforts is college internships. Many students pursuing degrees in the occupational safety and health (OSH) field have the option of earning college credits for participating in an internship program. In fact some schools, particularly those with programs accredited through the Accreditation Board for Engineering and Technology (ABET), require students to intern for 1 semester prior to graduation.

An OSH internship works much like any other college internship. The employer contacts the internship program within a college (or OSH degree program coordinator/chair) and makes known the desire to participate in the program. After discussing the work-related tasks that an intern would perform, the internship coordinator explains what is required of the employer, which will include having projects defined and ready, and providing honest feedback and evaluation regarding the intern's performance. Although not essential, it is common for these internships to occur over the summer semester. In many cases the intern will temporarily relocate to the area for the period of the internship and then return to the college campus to complete the final year of his degree program.

This is one of the most overlooked sources of assistance available to businesses today. Although the overwhelming majority of businesses in the United States are small businesses, it is generally the largest companies that tap into the college intern pool the most. Generally, small business owners are simply unaware and unfamiliar with OSH internships.

If you have been encouraged by an insurance loss control consultant or someone else to develop a safety management system, but you have little or nothing upon which to build, an OSH college intern may be a great place to get the help you need. They have learned in the classroom how to craft safety-related policies; how to conduct employee training; how to identify and control hazards; and how to fit all of that into a workable safety management system. Furthermore, they are eager to apply their classroom knowledge to a real workplace. You can provide that opportunity to them while at the same time benefit from the knowledge and enthusiasm that interns will bring to your small business.

A list of colleges and universities with certificate or degree programs in occupational safety and health fields is provided at www.chompcompbook.com. Many of these (including all of the ones marked as being ABET accredited) will have existing internship programs through which you may be able to secure an intern for your company. However, even those that do not have a formal internship program may permit students to earn college credit for work that allows them to apply the principals of safety and health management in a nonacademic setting.

Private Sector Safety Consultants

It is possible that the amount or the type of assistance that you need is more than you can get from your insurance company, from the OSHA consultation program or from other free sources of assistance. If so, you may consider turning to an independent safety consultant for assistance. For small businesses, independent safety consultants are often used to help develop written safety programs; to conduct industrial hygiene monitoring; or to conduct employee safety training. There are of course, large safety consulting firms. However, as a small business owner or manager yourself, you may appreciate that many safety consultants are either self-employed entrepreneurs, or work in a small businesses that provides safety consulting and training.

Perhaps the biggest benefit of using a safety consultant instead of (or in addition to) the other sources of assistance presented in this chapter, is that you get to choose with whom you will be working. This means that you get to select an individual who understands your needs and who can meet those needs to your satisfaction. You get to choose someone that will give you the amount of time and attention you desire. You get to pick someone that understands your business. Plus you get to choose someone that you trust. The biggest drawback to using an independent safety consultant is the cost. Whereas there are a number of sources available to small businesses that are free, you will be hard-pressed to find an independent safety consultant to provide his services without charging a fee. However, depending upon the business in which you are engaged, you may consider bartering the goods and services that your company has to offer in exchange for the services of an independent safety consultant.

If you choose to look to the private sector for a safety consultant, you certainly want to get the best and most competent consultant for your money. Most reputable safety consultants have a college degree in the discipline of Occupational Safety, Industrial Hygiene or a related field. Many also have earned a professional designation such as CSP (Certified Safety Professional) or CIH (Certified Industrial Hygienist). By hiring a safety consultant with these qualifications, you can be more confident that you have someone with knowledge and experience in the areas of safety and/or industrial hygiene.

Although college degrees and professional designations are indicators of a safety consultant's education, experience and commitment to the field of safety, in choosing safety consultants the greatest weight should be given to their past performance as a consultant. Examine their work history. Look for evidence that they have successfully done what you want them to do. Then call some of the companies for which they have provided consultative services.

Lastly, consider how well the safety consultant interacts with you and your employees. Does he speak plain English or does he frequently use safety jargon? If you cannot understand what he is saying, what good is his advice?

You Gotta Ask

Certainly there is no shame in asking for help. In fact there is wisdom in humbling yourself and having someone from outside of your company look at your operation and your loss control efforts from a perspective other than your own.

Even though there are a variety of professional sources for this assistance, you will not reap the benefit of these resources unless you take the initiative to ask for help. The time to do that is now – before you have a string of injuries – before you suspect one of your employees of workers' compensation fraud – and before your workers' compensation premiums get out of hand.

CHAPTER 25

Help is at Your Fingertips

The Internet should be viewed as an invaluable resource for every small business concerned with preventing injuries and controlling the cost of workers compensation. This chapter directs you to specific websites where you can find information that will aid in your efforts, and eliminate countless hours of searching.

Help is at Your Fingertips

Chapter 1, "The Small Business Dilemma," highlighted that in some ways small businesses are at a distinct disadvantage to larger businesses when it comes to workers' compensation. One of the realities that contributes to the inequity is that the owners and managers within small businesses often wear many hats. In a small business, few managers have a single defined job. Because there are more business management tasks than there are managers, they become a jack-of-all-trades. Unlike larger companies, small businesses simply do not have the advantage of being able to hire a seasoned safety professional to guide and administer their injury prevention efforts. For the same reason they cannot hire a person with a strong background in workers' compensation insurance simply to control the cost of claims. By necessity, these and other functions of management get thrust upon whoever seems to be best suited for the responsibility, without regard for those individuals' knowledge and experience. For that reason alone, the Internet should be viewed as an invaluable resource for every small business concerned with preventing injuries and controlling the cost of workers' compensation.

For those who are thrust into the management role of preventing injuries and controlling the cost of claims, the Internet does more than any other resource to level the playing field between large companies and small businesses. The wealth of information simply sitting out there waiting for you to view it is simply beyond human comprehension. However, the irony is that this wealth of information is not only an indispensable resource for small business; the sheer volume of information can be a source of futility. After all, most people who use the Internet will admit that they have seen huge blocks of time disappear while searching for some specific information, and have had little of value to show for their time and effort.

This chapter is intended to introduce you to some valuable Internet resources. With very few exceptions, commercial web-sites have been intentionally excluded from the Internet resources presented in this chapter. Those web-sites are easy enough to find through the use of any Internet search engine.

Your Insurance Company's Website

It is very likely that the insurance company that your small business uses for workers' compensation coverage has its own web-site. That should be the very first stop for the individuals in your company who are charged with reporting injuries, managing workers' compensation claims and guiding injury prevention efforts. When your company paid its workers' compensation premium, you paid for the services that the insurance company has to offer to all of its policyholders. Many of those services are able to be accessed through the insurance companies' web-sites. These services may include on-line reporting, access to claims information, information pertaining to medical provider networks and much more. The websites of workers' compensation carriers also frequently contain a host of information to help policyholders prevent employee injuries. These often include training aids, such as PowerPoint presentations, safety videos, and guides for conducting safety meeting. In the same vein, these web-sites also frequently contain sample safety policies, sample OSHA compliance programs, safety inspection checklists and more.

Your State's Workers' Compensation Website

After becoming familiar with what is available on your insurance carrier's web-site, visit your states' workers' compensation website. These sites frequently contain a guide (normally in the form of a handbook) providing an overview of the workers' compensation laws in the respective state. The state workers' compensation web-site generally provides the forms needed to report claims, the text of the state's workers' compensation statutes, contact information for reporting suspected fraud and more. Furthermore, in states that offer statutory discounts for implementing a drug-free workplace program or other safety management initiatives, the requirements and procedures for acquiring those discounts are explained on the state's workers' compensation web-site. (See "Appendix A" for a list of state workers' compensation agencies and their respective web-site addresses.)

OSHA's Website

Another excellent source of information is the federal OSHA website (www.osha.gov). This site includes an alphabetized subject index that lists various chemical, physical and other hazards. If you cannot find what you are looking for there, use the website's search option. In addition to information about specific hazards, the OSHA website contains federal health and safety regulations, a wide variety of publications, and news about governmental safety and health policy.

Of particular interest to small business employers is OSHA's small business web-page to which there is a link from OSHA's home page. This page offers many resources designed specifically for smaller employers and provides access to the most popular materials for small businesses, from free on-site consultation to interactive computer software, technical information and easy-to-follow guides addressing specific OSHA standards.

The website's Quick Start program is an Internet-based resource intended specifically for small business employers. This is a step-by-step guide to help small businesses identify many of the major OSHA requirements and guidance materials to help them comply with those requirements.

Also of interest to small business employers and managers is the Safety and Health Achievement Recognition Program (SHARP) that is available on the federal OSHA website. This is a program through which OSHA recognizes small business employers who operate an exemplary safety and health management system. Acceptance into SHARP by OSHA is an achievement of status that will single you out among your business peers as a model for worksite safety and health management. Upon receiving SHARP recognition, your worksite will be exempt from programmed OSHA inspections during the period that your SHARP certification is valid.

Other Beneficial Web Resources

Although the resources listed above will provide you with a wealth of information, they barely scratch the surface of the beneficial information available on the Internet to assist small businesses take a bite out of their workers' compensation premium. The following are a few select resources.

e-Law Advisors

e-Laws Advisors are interactive Internet-based tools that provide easy-to-understand information about a number of federal laws. They include a Confined Spaces Advisor, a Fire Safety Advisor, a Hazard Awareness Advisor, a Lead in Construction Advisor, and more. Each Advisor is intended to simulate the interaction you might have with an employment law expert. The e-law advisors ask questions and provide answers based upon the responses that you provide.

Of particular interest to virtually all small businesses is the Drug-Free Workplace Advisor. This e-Law Advisor helps you learn more about creating substance abuse prevention programs that promote a safe and productive workplace. If you are a Federal contractor or grantee, the Drug-Free Workplace Advisor also helps you learn about the Drug-Free Workplace Act of 1988 and which of its requirements, if any, apply to you.

NIOSH

Beyond OSHA and the Department of Labor's Internet resources, there is a wealth of information on the website of the National Institute of Occupational Safety and Health (NIOSH). Specifically, the NIOSH web-site has a Small Business web-page that includes a document entitled, "Safety and Health Resource Guide for Small Businesses" as well as links to numerous additional resources helpful to small businesses on the NIOSH website. The site's small business web-page is located at www.cdc.gov/niosh/topics/smbus

National Ag Safety Database

For small businesses employers involved in the agriculture industry, the National Ag Safety Database (NASD) is a valuable Internet Resource. The NASD (www.cdc.gov/NASD) was developed to educate workers and managers about hazards associated with agriculture-related injuries and illnesses, and to provide injury prevention information to the agriculture industry. The information contained in the NASD is contributed by safety professionals and organizations from across the nation.

eLCOSH

For small business employers in the construction trades, this is your resource. The Electronic Library of Construction Occupational Safety and Health (eLCOSH) was developed and is maintained by the Center to Protect Workers' Rights and is intended to provide accurate, user-friendly information about safety and health for construction workers from a wide range of sources worldwide. The eLCOSH website (www.cdc.gov/elcosh) allows searches of the documents contained on the website by trade, by hazard and by the type of job-site, and has a separate listing of materials intended specifically for safety training. This site even includes many resources in Spanish.

OR-OSHA

If you want to get your supervisors trained to prevent and respond to work-related injuries more effectively, you may want to consider some of the free on-line training programs maintained on Oregon OSHA's (OR-OSHA) website (www.cbs.state.or.us/external/osha). These can be accessed from the OR-OSHA Small Business Resources web-page. The small business page also includes materials used in Oregon OSHA small business training as well as more than 100 Oregon OSHA publications. It is notable that Oregon is a state plan state for OSHA compliance and as such, has some state-specific rules that are more stringent than Federal OSHA standards.

Washington's Department of Labor and Industries

Washington (another state plan state for OSHA compliance) maintains a website that has quite a few resources for employers to aid in the training of employees, supervisors and managers. These are accessible from the "Training Tools" section of the website. These include on-line training programs ranging from general safety topics such as accident investigations, to much more specific training, such as band-saw safety. This site also includes safety videos that are viewable or downloadable from the web-site, as well as materials to assist in meeting safety and health training requirements. Visit the website at www.lni.wa.gov/Safety/TrainTools.

free-training.com

www.free-training.com hosts free-online training programs. Courses currently available include Forklift Operation and Safety, Hazard Communication, Personal Protection Equipment, Back Safety, plus links to free training programs hosted on other websites.

National Workzone Safety Information Clearinghouse

A safety resource for construction trades that involve working in highway workzones is the National Workzone Safety Information Clearinghouse. The website for this clearinghouse includes information on courses, programs, workshops, and videos that are related to work zone safety. Links to the websites of agencies that provide work zone safety training are also provided. This website can be located at http://wzsafety.tamu.edu

Toolbox Topics

www.toolboxtopic.com is another web-site that will be of interest to construction and general industry small business employers alike. It contains hundreds of pre-written guides for conducting safety toolbox talks. The content is separated into three primary categories – construction industry, general industry, and fleet safety. It also includes industry-specific safety manuals, checklists, and PowerPoint presentations. Although this is a commercial site on which safety-related items are marketed, all of the above-mentioned resources are made available free, with no strings attached.

Safety & Health Management Systems for Small Businesses

The Safety & Health Management Systems for Small Businesses is a web-based training program designed to assist small businesses develop and implement an effective safety and health management system. It is a free on-line training course created by North Carolina State University and funded by an OSHA-sponsored grant. Find it at www.ies.ncsu.edu/safetyhealthmgmt. This free on-line training program is comprised of 6 modules.
- Introduction to Safety & Health Management Systems
- Management Leadership
- Worksite Analysis
- Hazard Prevention and Control
- Safety and Health Training
- Post-Assessment

CCOHS

Although the Canadian Centre for Occupational Health and Safety (CCOHS) is a Canadian government agency, you will find their website quite useful and will find the information presented in an easy-to-find and easy-to understand format. Their Internet address is www.ccohs.com

Oklahoma State University

The Environmental, Safety and Health Department of Oklahoma State University has a very user-friendly on-line safety library at www.pp.okstate.edu/ehs/LINKS.

Vermont Safety Information Resources

The website of Vermont Safety Information Resources (SIRI) is found at www.hazard.com and has a host of resources to include an on-line library of safety-related PowerPoint presentations, graphics and text documents, as well as a list of safety consultants and trainers.

ezFacts

ezFacts is a web-based resource maintained by Lab Safety Supply and is another source for accurate safety information. ezFacts can be accessed through the Info Library link on www.labsafety.com. Much of the information contained in this side is intended to provide you with knowledge for choosing proper safety-related products. However, the material is also beneficial for conducting safety training.

Find a Safety Trainer

If you want a safety professional to conduct some of your employee safety training, you may be interested in looking at the website www.findasafetytrainer.com. It is maintained by National Safety Compliance, Inc. (a company that markets safety videos and other safety training materials) and provides a searchable index of safety trainers by geographical location and by training topic.

National Safety Council's Safety and Health Buyers Guide

Once you have decided the type of safety devise that you want to buy, find-out who sells it by accessing the National Safety Council's Safety and Health Buyers guide. This on-line guide is continuously updated and serves as a comprehensive source for safety product and services information. It includes links to supplier websites, as well as multiple categories listed by geographic location.

Texas Division of Workers' Compensation

The web-sites maintained by most state workers' compensation agencies are generally limited to information such as statutes, forms and other material that are applicable only to businesses in that state. That cannot be said about the website maintained by the Texas Division of Workers' Compensation. In addition to the obligatory state-specific information, you will find free safety and health publications – from "Avoiding Falls in Sawmills" to "Waitstaff Health & Safety Training Program"). Their website (www.tdi.state.tx.us/wc/indexwc) is a must see.

www.ChompCompBook.com

The above are just a sample of the beneficial resources at your fingertips. You are encouraged to frequently check our web resource links at www.ChompCompBook.com. As we become aware of helpful websites to help small business owners and managers like you take a bite out of their workers' compensation premiums, we will add them to our web resources links. If you would like to recommend any to be included, contact the authors through www.ChompCompBook.com.

CHAPTER 26

The Secret Weapon

Certainly, you are encouraged to implement each of the measures presented in earlier chapters. However, the significance and impact of employing "The Secret Weapon" is unparalleled and should be afforded highest priority within your business.

Unveiling the Secret Weapon

In the preceding chapters, this book presented quite a few measures that were aimed at helping you take a bite out of your workers' compensation premium. Some of these were intended to help you catch and correct administrative errors that inflate your premium. Others were intended to help prevent employees from being injured at work. Still others were directed at helping minimize claims-related costs. Implemented individually, any of the measures presented in the preceding chapters have the potential to reduce expenses for your small business. Implemented collectively, they are virtually guaranteed to take a bite out of your workers' compensation premium.

However, there is one last measure to be presented before you jump head first into the fray – a measure that the authors passionately call "the secret weapon." It is a measure that not only has the power to impact your workers' compensation premiums, it will also equip you to confront virtually all of the challenges that you may face as a small business owner or manager. Beyond that, this secret weapon even has the power to divert problems that might otherwise devastate a small business.

To be succinct, the "secret weapon" is the power and the providence of the Almighty God. It is acknowledging His sovereignty and turning to Him for help. More specifically, it involves maintaining the proper perspective of God's role in your small business, regardless of the personal sacrifices that you made to get where you are. It involves praying to God in faith and trusting in Him to answer your prayers. And, it involves seeking God's guidance and relying on his direction, even when His ways differ from your own. In other words, the secret weapon espoused in this final chapter is to accept God as your business partner – your "senior" business partner.

The fact that this is the final chapter in this book is not meant to imply that leaning on the power and providence of God is the least important or least effective means of achieving your goal of lower workers' compensation costs. Nor is it meant to imply that faith, prayer and submission to God should be relegated to a last resort. In fact, quite the opposite is true. Earnestly and persistently seeking God's will, and faithfully trusting in Him is more reliable and more effective than any of the self-directed measures presented in the preceding chapters.

Proper Perspective

You might be thinking that the subject-matter of this chapter has no place in a book aimed at helping employers minimize the cost of their workers' compensation insurance. After all, God doesn't care about your insurance premiums – right? Granted, insurance premiums are probably not going to be the topic of a Sunday morning sermon, but God most certainly does care about how you, as a small business owner or manager, handle your company's finances.

Business finances were much simpler during the Biblical era. There were few large employers, aside from the Roman government. So individual entrepreneurs and small businesses were very prevalent. But the small business owners during the time of Jesus' brief ministry did not have credit cards or checkbooks. There was not a bank on every corner offering small business loans at exorbitant interest rates. Employers were not faced with the financial challenge of complying with OSHA, EPA, FMLA, ADA and other government mandates. Furthermore, employers were not required to purchase and maintain an injury insurance policy for employees (a.k.a. workers' compensation insurance). Despite the simpler financial system, the recorded words of Jesus address issues relating to money and possessions more than just about any other subject. Why Jesus said so much about that topic is likely rooted in the power of money and possessions to take our focus off of God.

Perhaps the most important truth to grasp with respect to both personal and business finances is that God is the true owner of everything. The Bible indicates that "The earth is the Lord's, and everything in it, the world and all who live in it." (Psalm 24:1, NIV) Even if you toiled years to establish and grow your small business with great personal sacrifice, the fact remains that it ultimately belongs to God. You are merely called to manage what he has entrusted to you.

However, even if you acknowledge that God is concerned about how you handle your business finances (the big picture), you may question if He is really concerned about something as trivial as how much you pay for workers' compensation insurance. He most certainly is. With the proper perspective of ownership, every effort to properly manage your business expenses (including how much you pay for workers' compensation) is an act of worship. And it is our worship that God desires and deserves.

A Helping Hand

Certainly, God is honored by those who maintain a proper perspective of ownership and who properly manage what has been entrusted to them. But attempting to manage your small business finances to His honor is not a burden that is placed solely upon your shoulders. God Himself offers a helping hand.

God's ability to interact with the world is what is referenced earlier as His providence. He is not a detached being, merely observing the events of today. Instead, He is actively involved, intervening to bring about good. The Bible speaks to that reality in stating that "...God causes everything to work together for the good of those who love God and are called according to His purpose for them." (Romans 8:28, NLT).

He has the ability to protect your employees; to heal them if they become injured; to counter the lures of insurance fraud; to guide your company's injury prevention efforts; and so much more. He is a much welcome helping hand – and His hand has the power to accomplish much more than you could ever imagine.

Tapping into Unlimited Power

Despite the knowledge of God's power, far too many people fail to tap into that power. Collectively, small business owners are likely no different – seeking God's intervention when a calamity arises, but keeping Him uninvolved and in the background when things are functioning well.

If that describes your approach, you are challenged to evaluate your rationale. If you are convinced of God's power and providence, why would you fail to actively seek His involvement to avert problems rather than merely rely on Him to intervene when problems surface?

Tapping into the power of God requires prayer. Quite simply, "prayer" is communicating with God. There is no magic formula and no requirement to speak eloquently. God simply desires our heartfelt and sincere communication. Naturally, business partners expect one another to communicate openly and honestly. Without that communication, their relationship and their business would quickly deteriorate. If you expect God to be an active partner in your small business, the expectation for communication is the same.

Despite the simplicity of prayer, the power of prayer should not be underestimated. God has the power to answer prayers and He uses that power to answer prayers that are in agreement with His will. Although His answers will not always be the answers you are seeking – and they may not always fit your timetable, His answers to prayer are always in your best interest. We can be assured that when we pray according to God's will, He will respond powerfully. The Bible tells us "This is the confidence we have in approaching God: that if we ask anything according to His will, He hears us. And if we know that He hears us – whatever we ask – we know that we have what we asked of Him." (1 John 5:14-15, NIV)

If you are wandering what you should pray about, the answer is quite simple. Pray for everything. The Bible says, "Do not be anxious about anything, but in everything, by prayer and petition, with thanksgiving, present your requests to God." (Philippians 4:6, NIV) However, within the context of the topic being presented in this book, there are some very specific things that you can begin praying for daily.

Pray for Wisdom

The Bible says, "If any of you lacks wisdom, he should ask God, who gives generously to all without finding fault, and it will be given to him" (James 1:5, NIV). This is a comforting truth for small business owners and managers who are faced with an endless list of responsibilities, and whose employees' personal safety and careers are greatly influenced by the decisions they make. Pray that God will give you wisdom to make the right hiring decisions and the right decisions in strengthening your company's injury prevention efforts.

On the topic of wisdom, the Bible reveals that there is safety in a multitude of counselors (Proverbs 11:14, NKJ). With that in-mind, pray that God will place unbiased wise counsel in your path and that He will give you the humility to seek their advice.

Pray for Effectiveness

Many times small business owners or managers employ safety initiatives in the hope that those measures will have a positive impact. You are encouraged to do more than merely hope for your injury-prevention measures to be effective. Pray for God to bless your efforts and cause them to be effective. Pray for Him to reveal to you weaknesses in those initiatives and for Him to instill in you the humility to make the necessary changes.

Pray for Protection

Certainly, as a small business owner or manager, you want to do everything in your power to protect your employees from physical harm. Much of the content of this book is directed at helping you attain that objective. But your efforts to protect your employees should not end there. Throughout the Bible there are countless examples of individuals and entire nations who have been protected from physical harm through the intervening power of God. As such, you are encouraged to pray earnestly and persistently that God will protect your employees and keep them from being injured.

Pray for Healing

If an employee is injured or becomes sick, rest in the confidence that Jesus Christ is also known as "The Great Physician." His role as physician and healer is so pervasive in His recorded life that it would impossible to understand His mission apart from it. During his ministry on earth, His time was consumed by encounters with people who were sick, blind, lame, deaf, leprous, paralyzed or mentally ill.

In complete confidence in His ability, pray that God will bring physical healing to employees who are injured at work. Pray that God will relieve their pain and restore them to their former measure of health.

Pray for God to Direct your Words and Actions

When employees are injured at work, emotions can run high. The injured employee may be concerned that his injury claim may cause you or his coworkers to question his integrity. He may be worried about a potential loss of income during the recovery period and how that will impact his personal finances. The injured employee may even question his job security if the injury causes a prolonged absence from work. As the employer, your words and actions can either exasperate or quell those emotions. For that reason, you are encouraged to pray for God to guide your words and actions. Ask Him to reveal the ways in which you might effectively provide reassurance and express compassion for injured employees.

Pray for Godly Employees

Certainly small business employers are aware of the potential infectious influence of poor hiring choices. Hiring the wrong employee can decrease employee morale, increase the potential for workers' compensation fraud, or dismantle your company's overall injury prevention efforts. Exercising wisdom and proceeding with caution when selecting new employees is certainly advisable. However, you are additionally encouraged to pray for God's intervention. Pray that He will staff your company with Godly employees and that He will daily draw them each into a closer walk with Him. Pray specifically that God will protect your employees from the lures of insurance fraud. Furthermore, pray that God will protect your employees from illicit drugs, greed, laziness and other negative influences that threaten to corrupt them.

Pray for a Proper Perspective

As mentioned earlier in this chapter, as a small business owner or manager you have been entrusted with resources and charged with managing them properly. God is ultimately the owner of your business. Since it is not always easy to maintain an awareness of that reality, pray that God will help you filter daily business decisions through that paradigm.

Seeking and Submitting to Authority

Relying upon the power and providence of God not only requires a proper perspective of His ownership of your business – it not only requires communicating with God through prayer, it requires actively seeking His guidance and direction, and submitting to His authority.

Seeking God's guidance and direction requires turning to the inerrant and inspired word of God, the Holy Bible. Although it is much more than an "instruction manual," the Bible provides reliable insight into God's will, including His will for how you manage your small business. Despite being a couple thousand years old, it is timeless and relevant, even today. And through studying the bible, your eyes will be opened to countless insights.

- Certainly your business will have both good times and bad. Through the person of Joseph you will learn how to respond to both adversity and prosperity.

- If you are a typical small business owner or manager, you have more responsibilities than you can handle. Through the person of Moses you will learn that delegating responsibilities is a Biblical concept.

- As a small business employer, you will likely employ a few people who raise your blood-pressure. Through the Biblical story of Rehoboam you will learn not to treat them harshly.

- Although you may be the head decision-maker within your small business, through the person of Ahasuerus you will learn to consult with others before making a major decision.

- You will undoubtedly have employees that have problems that impact them deeply, to include problems relating to workers' compensation claims. Through the person of Jesus himself you will see the wisdom in actively caring for others.

Hundreds of other insights relevant to managing your small business can be learned through an intentional study of God's word. Applying those insights will have a positive impact upon your small business, to include your efforts at preventing employee injuries and managing workers' compensation costs. If you do not routinely study the Bible to seek God's direction for managing your small business, consider beginning with the books of Proverbs and Ecclesiastics, as therein is contained an abundance of insight that can be directly related to business management.

Necessarily, seeking God's guidance and direction must be accompanied by submission to His will. In fact the Bible warns against listening to God's words of wisdom and failing to apply them in your life. (James 1:22)

Conclusion

It is the intent of the authors that reserving this important topic for the end of this book will leave a profound and lasting impact upon each reader. God is, and will always be the ultimate business partner. You are encouraged to seek His guidance and rely on His direction.

Furthermore, know that the "secret weapon" was never intended to be a secret. You are encouraged to share with other small business owners and managers how you have leaned upon the power and providence of God and how He has had a positive impact on your business.

Although it is certainly within God's power and providence to impact any area of your business, it is His forgiveness of your sins and the sacrifice which that forgiveness required, that is immeasurably more significant. If you cannot say with absolute certainty that your sins have been forgiven and that you will spend eternity in Heaven, please turn to the following pages, labeled "The Most Important Decision." It will provide a brief explanation of Gospel (Good News) of Jesus Christ and will point you to some invaluable resources.

Comments and Questions

Lighted Path Publishers, LLC and the authors of "Chomp Comp" welcome comments, questions, success stories and additional insights. All correspondence will be provided directly to the authors, who will make every attempt to respond personally to each. For contact information, see www.chompcompbook.com.

The Most Important Decision

All scriptures in this section are from the King James Version.

Have you ever considered life's most important decision? This decision doesn't involve workers' compensation, real estate, your business, your retirement plan or even the spouse you choose (although that's certainly a big one). Actually the most important decision anyone can ever make is where they choose to spend eternity. Death is certain; however the time, place and circumstances are highly uncertain. Every individual makes a personal choice, whether they know it or not, about their destiny beyond this very fragile and temporary life. It is our sincere desire and prayer that you've considered this question and have already chosen eternal life in Heaven through Jesus Christ. But, if you haven't, please read further with an open mind and heart to learn how you can.

Some may wonder if choosing Jesus is necessary to go to Heaven, or if there is some other way. The Bible says in Acts 4:12, "Neither is there salvation in any other: for there is none other name under heaven given among men, whereby we must be saved." The Bible records an event where Jesus encountered a man named Nicodemus, who was certainly a "religious person"; in fact, he was a ruler of the Jews. Nicodemus acknowledged that there was something very special and very powerful about Jesus because of the miracles he performed; however he was reluctant to put his trust in him as Lord and Savior. Jesus detected Nicodemus' skepticism and responded by saying: "Verily, verily, I say unto thee, except a man be born again, he cannot see the kingdom of

God." (John 3:3) The concept of being "born again" perplexed Nicodemus. Jesus' used this encounter with Nicodemus to speak directly to the world and explain this rebirth as one of spiritual nature. Jesus is the only way to Heaven, and life's most important decision is whether we put our trust in him and accept him as our personal Lord and Savior.

> "Jesus saith unto him, I am the way, the truth, and the life: no man cometh unto the father, but by me."
> (John 14:6)

So How Do I Choose Jesus?

Acknowledge your Condition

First, understand your need for savior. The Bible plainly tells us that we have all sinned and that we don't measure up to God's standard holiness.

> "For all have sinned and come short of the glory of God"
> (Romans 3:23)
>
> "As it is written, there are none righteous, no not one."
> (Romans 3:10)

Understand the Cost

We must understand that there is a penalty for our sin; death.

> "For the wages of sin is death..."
> (Romans 6:23a)

The Bible explains this death as eternal separation from God in a place called Hell. We owe a debt for our sin and the only way any person can pay that debt is to spend eternity there.

> "But the fearful, and unbelieving, and the abominable, and murderers, and whoremongers, and sorcerers, and idolaters, and all liars, shall have their part in the lake which burneth with fire and brimstone: which is the second death."
>
> (Revelation 21:8)

Notice the list of people deserving of the second death; a list ranging from those who simply chose not to believe to liars to murderers. This is a sobering list of people owing the same debt for a variety of different sin; sins that may not appear to be equally deserving from our human perspective. Many times when compare ourselves to others we may appear to be a "good person". However, God's standard of comparison is not other people, but his son Jesus Christ who lived a perfect, sinless life. We'll never measure up - no matter how many "good deeds" one does.

Acknowledge the saving power of Jesus Christ

> "But God commendeth his love toward us, in that while we were yet sinners, Christ died for us."
>
> (Romans 5:8)
>
> "The wages of sin is death, but the gift of God is eternal life through Jesus Christ our Lord."
>
> (Romans 6:23)
>
> "For God so loved the world that he gave his only begotten son that whosoever believeth in him should not perish, but have everlasting life."
>
> (John 3:16)

Jesus Christ, God's only son, came to earth, lived a perfect, sinless life and died a cruel death on the cross to pay our sin debt. Christ sacrificially took our punishment by giving his life and enduring the shame of our sin. Christ served as the ultimate, final, and only acceptable sacrifice for all mankind through the shedding of his blood. Christ's blood was shed so that we might, through his sacrifice have remission of our sins. When Christ saves us, His blood is applied to our account in heaven, and in God's eyes, he sees as clean.

> "And almost all things are by the law purged with blood; and without shedding blood is no remission."
> (Hebrews 9:22)

Showing that he was indeed the Messiah, Christ rose from the grave on the third day and is alive and at the right hand of God to serve as advocate for those who would trust him as Savior.

> "Blessed be the God and Father of our Lord Jesus Christ, which according to his abundant mercy hath begotten us again unto a lively hope by the resurrection of Jesus Christ from the dead."
> (I Peter 1:3)

Accept and Repent

Through faith accept Christ as your personal Savior and repent of sin.

To accept Christ as personal savior, we must through sincere prayer ask Him to forgive us and save us from our sin, and invite him into our heart. In doing so, we by faith acknowledge and put our trust in His shed blood, death, burial and resurrection.

> "The Lord is nigh unto them that are of a broken heart; and saveth such as be of a contrite [crushed / broken] spirit."
>
> (Psalms 34:18)
>
> "The Lord is nigh unto them that are of a broken heart; and saveth such as be of a contrite [crushed / broken] spirit."
>
> (Psalms 34:18)
>
> "That if thou shalt confess with thy mouth the Lord Jesus, and shalt believe in thine heart that God hath raised him from the dead, thou shalt be saved."
>
> (Romans 10:9)
>
> "For whosoever shall call upon the name of the Lord shall be saved."
>
> (Romans 10:13)
>
> "For by grace, are you saved through Faith; and that not of yourselves: it is the gift of God: Not of works lest any man should boast."
>
> (Ephesians 2:8)

Many say that this is simply too easy. Indeed it is easy for us, but keep in mind that Christ, through his love, did the hard part for us. Salvation is a gift to us, but Christ had to pay for it through his sacrifice. God's grace is truly amazing.

Confession and Baptism

Let others know of your decision to accept Christ through confession and baptism.

As part of our salvation, God requires us to confess him to others as our Lord and Savior.

> "Whosoever therefore shall confess me before men, him will I confess also before my Father which is in heaven. But whosoever shall deny me before men, him will I also deny before my Father which is in heaven."
>
> (Matthew 10:32-33)

> "That if thou shalt confess with thy mouth the Lord Jesus, and shalt believe in thine heart that God hath raised him from the dead, thou shalt be saved."
>
> (Romans 10:9)

Christ commands us to be baptized. Biblical, full immersion baptism fulfills a commandment from God and is a public testimony of our salvation. We demonstrate that as Christ was buried and rose again, we are also buried to our old selves, and we are rising as a new creature in Christ.

> "And he commanded them to be baptized in the name of the Lord..."
>
> (Acts 10:48)
>
> "Buried with him in baptism, wherein also ye are risen with him through the faith of the operation of God, who hath raised him from the dead."
>
> (Colossians 2:12)
>
> "Know ye not, that so many of us as were baptized into Jesus Christ were baptized into his death? Therefore we are buried with him by baptism into death: that like as Christ was raised up from the dead by the glory of the Father, even so we also should walk in the newness of life. For if we have been planted together in the likeness of his death, we shall be also in the likeness of his resurrection."
>
> (Romans 6:3-5)

> "Then Peter said unto them, Repent, and be baptized every one of you in the name of Jesus Christ for the remission of sins, and ye shall receive the gift of the Holy Ghost."
>
> (Acts 2:38)

What's next?

After accepting Christ and being baptized, the Holy Spirit dwells within us and becomes our guiding compass. We should start striving to be more and more like Christ, as we have turned from our sins [repentance], forsaking our old nature. The Holy Spirit helps us and comforts us through this process of sanctification (getting more and more like Christ and less like the world).

Read your Bible faithfully

The Holy Bible is God's inspired and infallible word; God's love letter to us and our instruction manual for life.

> "So then faith cometh by hearing, and hearing by the word of God."
>
> (Romans 10:17).
>
> "Study to shew thyself approved unto God, a workman that needeth not to be ashamed, rightfully dividing the word of truth."
>
> (II Timothy 2:15)

Pray

God wants to hear from us and wants to help us with our Christian walk.

> "Seek the Lord and his strength, seek his face continually."
> (I Chronicles 16:11)
>
> "Ask, and it shall be given you: seek and ye shall find; knock, and it shall be opened unto you:"
> (Matthew 7:7)
>
> "And he spake a parable unto them to this end, that men ought always to pray, and not to faint;"
> (Luke 18:1)

Get Involved

Get involved with a local, Bible teaching church.

> "And let us consider one another to provoke unto love and to good works: Not forsaking the assembling of ourselves together ... exhorting one another: and so much the more, as ye see the day [Christ's returning] approaching."
> (Hebrews 10:25)

Keep short accounts with God

When we get saved we are indeed new creatures in Christ, we do not magically lose the ability to be tempted, nor do we become perfect. If after being saved, we sin, the Holy Spirit will reveal it to us and we should repent, ask forgiveness and ask for God's help in forsaking that sin. When writing to Christians, John the beloved said:

> "If we confess our sins, he is faithful and just to forgive us our sins, and to cleanse us from all unrighteousness."
> (I John 1:9)

In Conclusion

As a business person, you'll probably have the chance to build wealth; in some cases great wealth. It's certainly our hope and prayer that you are blessed with wealth and prosperity. Moreover, it's our sincere prayer that everyone reading this book will first and foremost develop spiritual wealth. As we close, we ask that you seriously consider what the Bible says,

> "For what shall it profit a man, if he shall gain the whole world, and lose his own soul?"
>
> (Mark 8:36)

Would you this moment sincerely pray this simple prayer from your heart to God and accept Christ as your personal savior?

> Dear Lord Jesus, I know I am a sinner. I believe you died and rose again for me. Please forgive me of my sins. I accept your free gift of salvation. Come into my heart and save me. I trust you and you alone to take me to heaven when I die. Thank you for saving me. Amen.

If you've prayed this prayer and accepted Christ as your personal savior, we want to congratulate you on making the wisest decision you'll ever make. We rejoice with you in your new life would love to hear from you. If you would be so kind as to write or email your decision, we'd certainly love to hear from you. If you'd like more information on your new walk with Christ, we'd be glad to provide that as well.

Address:

Lighted Path Publishers, LLC
9606 Marceitta Way
Louisville, KY 40291

Email via www.ChompCompBook.com

APPENDIX A

State Government Agencies

Because the topic of workers' compensation is a political football, most state workers' compensation systems are in a relatively constant state of flux. For that reason, the authors of Chomp Comp have intentionally strayed from discussing the attributes of different states workers' compensation systems. Instead, the authors have elected to direct you (the small business owner) to authoritative sources for up-to-date information about the workers' compensation system within specific states.

Alabama
Workers' Compensation Division
http://dir.alabama.gov/wc/

Alaska
Workers' Compensation Division
http://www.labor.state.ak.us/wc/wc.htm
(907) 465-2790

Arizona
Industrial Commission of Arizona
http://www.ica.state.az.us/
(602) 542-4411

State Compensation Fund
http://www.statefund.com/
(602) 631-2000

Arkansas
Workers' Compensation Commission
http://www.awcc.state.ar.us/
(800) 622-4472

California
Commission on Health and Safety and Workers' Compensation
http://www.dir.ca.gov/CHSWC/
(510) 622-3959

Division of Workers' Compensation
http://www.dir.ca.gov/dwc/
(800) 736-7401, (510) 286-7100

Division of Workers' Compensation Medical Unit
http://www.dir.ca.gov/IMC/imchp.html
(800) 794-6900
Complaint Line: (800) 999-1041

Workers' Compensation Appeals Board
http://www.dir.ca.gov/WCAB/
(800) 736-7401, (415) 703-5020

Self-Insurance Plans
http://www.dir.ca.gov/SIP/
(916) 483-3392

State Compensation Insurance Fund
http://www.scif.com/
(888) 222-3211
Fraud Hotline: (888) 786-7372

Colorado
Division of Workers' Compensation
http://www.coworkforce.com/dwc/
(888) 390-7936

Industrial Claims Appeals Office
http://www.coworkforce.com/icao/
(303) 318-8131

Connecticut
Workers' Compensation Commission
http://wcc.state.ct.us/
(860) 493-1500
Compensation Review Board (CRB)
http://wcc.state.ct.us/index2.htm
(203) 493-1500

Delaware
Office of Workers' Compensation
www.delawareworks.com/industrialaffairs/services/WorkersComp
(302) 761-8200 (Wilmington)
(302) 422-1134 (Milford)

District of Columbia
Office of Workers' Compensation
www.does.dc.gov/does/cwp/view.asp?a=1232&Q=537428
(202) 671-1000
Office of Hearings and Adjudication
www.does.dc.gov/does/cwp/view.asp?a=1232&Q=537904
(202) 671-2233

Florida
Division of Workers' Compensation
www.fldfs.com/WC/
(850) 921-6966
Workers' Compensation Oversight Board
www.doi.state.fl.us/wc/pdf/2kAR_OversightBoard.PDF
(850) 487-2613

Georgia
Georgia State Board of Workers' Compensation
http://sbwc.georgia.gov/
(800) 533-0682, (404) 656-3875
Enforcement Division: (404) 657-1391
Safety Library: (404) 656-9057
Georgia Subsequent Injury Trust Fund
http://sitf.georgia.gov/
(404) 206-6360

Hawaii

Disability Compensation Division
http://hawaii.gov/labor/dcd/index.shtml
(808) 586-9151

Labor & Industrial Relations Appeals Board
http://hawaii.gov/labor/hlirab/index.shtml
(808) 586-8600

Idaho

Idaho Industrial Commission
http://www.iic.idaho.gov/
(800) 950-2110, (208) 334-6000

State Insurance Fund
http://www.idahosif.org/
(800) 334-2370

Illinois

Illinois Workers' Compensation Commission
http://www.iwcc.il.gov/
(866) 352-3033

Indiana

Workers' Compensation Board of Indiana
http://www.in.gov/workcomp/
(317) 232-3808

Iowa

Iowa Division of Workers' Compensation
http://www.iowaworkforce.org/wc/
(800) 562-4692

Kansas

Division of Workers' Compensation
http://www.dol.ks.gov/WC/HTML/wc_ALL.html
(800) 332-0353

Kentucky

Office of Workers' Claims
http://www.labor.ky.gov/workersclaims/
(502) 564-5550

Division of Workers' Compensation Funds
http://www.labor.ky.gov/ows/workerscompensationfunds/
(502) 564-3070
Workers' Compensation Funding Commission
http://www.kwcfc.ky.gov/
(502) 573-3505
Kentucky Workers' Compensation Law (via CompEd, Inc.)
http://www.comped.net/

Louisiana

Office of Workers' Compensation Administration
http://www.laworks.net/wrk_owca.asp
(225) 342-7555,
Fraud: (800) 201-3362
Safety: (800) 201-2497

Maine

Workers' Compensation Board
http://www.maine.gov/wcb/
(207) 287-3751

Maryland

Maryland Workers' Compensation Commission
http://www.wcc.state.md.us/
(800) 492-0479, (410) 864-5100
Fraud: (800) 846-4069
Insured Workers' Insurance Fund
http://www.iwif.com/
(800) 264-IWIF (4943), (410) 494-2000
Injury Reporting Hotline: (888) 410-1400
Fraud: (888) ANTI-FRAUD (268-4372)

Massachusetts

Department of Industrial Accidents
http://www.mass.gov/dia/
(800) 323-3249
Massachusetts Workers' Compensation Advisory Council
http://www.mass.gov/wcac/
(617) 727-4900, ext. 378
Workers' Compensation Rating & Inspection Bureau
https://www.wcribma.org/mass/
(617) 439-9030

Michigan

Workers' Compensation Agency
http://www.michigan.gov/wca
(888) 396-5041, (313) 456-2400
Michigan Economic Development Corporation
http://medc.michigan.org/
(888) 522-0103, (517) 373-9808
Michigan Business Guide to Workers' Compensation
http://medc.michigan.org/services/workerscomp/
Compensation Cost Control Service
http://www.michigan.gov/wca/0,1607,7-191-26925-41305--,00.html
Compensation Advisory Organization of Michigan (CAOM)
http://www.caom.com/

Minnesota

Workers' Compensation Division
http://www.doli.state.mn.us/workcomp.html
(800) 365-4584
Workers' Compensation Court of Appeals
http://www.workerscomp.state.mn.us/
(651) 296-6526

Mississippi

Mississippi Workers' Compensation Commission
http://www.mwcc.state.ms.us/
(601) 987-4200,
Fraud: (601) 359-4250

Missouri

Division of Workers' Compensation
http://www.dolir.missouri.gov/wc/
(573) 751-4231
Employer Hotline: (888) 837-6069,
Fraud and Noncompliance: (800)-592-6003, (573)-526-6630,
Workers' Safety Program: (573) 526-3504
Labor and Industrial Relations Commission
http://www.dolir.state.mo.us/lirc/index.htm
(573) 751-2461

Montana

Employment Relations Division
http://erd.dli.mt.gov
Workers' Compensation Claims Assistance Bureau
http://erd.dli.mt.gov/wcclaims/wcchome.asp

(406) 444-6543
Workers' Compensation Regulation Bureau
http://erd.dli.mt.gov/wcregs/wcrhome.asp
(406) 444-6541
Workers' Compensation Court
http://wcc.dli.mt.gov/
(406) 444-7794
Montana State Fund
http://www.montanastatefund.com/
(406) 444-6500
Claim Reporting/ Customer Service: (800) 332-6102
Fraud Reporting: (888) 682-7463
Self Insurers' Guaranty Fund
(406) 549-8849

Nebraska

Workers' Compensation Court
http://www.wcc.ne.gov/
(402) 471-6468 (Lincoln and out of state)

Nevada

Department of Business & Industry
http://dbi.state.nv.us/
(775) 687-4250
Division of Industrial Relations
http://dirweb.state.nv.us/
(775) 684-7260
Industrial Insurance Regulation Section
http://dirweb.state.nv.us/iirs.htm
(775) 684-7270
Workers' Compensation Section
http://dirweb.state.nv.us/WCS/wcs.htm
(702) 486-9080
Employers Insurance Company of Nevada
http://www.employersinsco.com/
(888) 682-6671
Claim Reporting: (888) 900-1455
Underwriting/Insurance Services: (888) 682-6671

New Hampshire

Workers' Compensation Division
http://www.labor.state.nh.us/workers_compensation.asp
(603) 271-3174 (claims)
(603) 271-2042 (coverage)

New Jersey

Division of Workers' Compensation
http://www.nj.gov/labor/wc/wcindex.html
(609) 292-2515

N.J. Compensation Rating and Inspection Bureau
http://www.njcrib.com/
(973) 622-6014

New Mexico

Workers' Compensation Administration
http://www.state.nm.us/wca/
(800) 255-7965
Help Line/Hot Line: (866) WORKOMP (967-5667)

New York

New York State Workers' Compensation Board
http://www.wcb.state.ny.us/
(518) 474-6670

New York State Insurance Fund
http://www.nysif.com/
(212) 312-9000

North Carolina

North Carolina Industrial Commission
http://www.comp.state.nc.us/
(919) 807-2500
Fraud Investigations Section: (888) 891-4895
http://www.comp.state.nc.us/ncic/pages/fraud.htm
Ombudsman Section: (800) 688-8349
http://www.comp.state.nc.us/ncic/pages/ombudsmn.htm
Safety Education Section: (919) 807-2603
http://www.comp.state.nc.us/ncic/pages/safety.htm

North Dakota

Workforce Safety & Insurance
http://www.WorkforceSafety.com/
(800) 777-5033
Fraud: (800) 243-3331
Safety and Loss Prevention: (701) 328-3886

Ohio

Ohio Bureau of Workers' Compensation
http://www.ohiobwc.com/
(800) OHIOBWC (800-644-6292)
Ombudsman: (800) 335-0996
Industrial Commission of Ohio
http://www.ohioic.com/index.jsp
(800) 521-2691, (614) 466-6136

Oklahoma

Department of Labor
http://www.okdol.state.ok.us/
(888) 269-5353, (405) 528-1500
Workers' Enforcement Compensation Division
http://www.okdol.state.ok.us/workcomp/index.htm
Oklahoma Workers' Compensation Court
http://www.owcc.state.ok.us/
(800) 522-8210
CompSource Oklahoma
http://www.compsourceok.com/
(800) 347-3863, (405) 232-7663
Fraud Hotline: (800) 899-1847

Oregon

Department of Consumer & Business Services
http://egov.oregon.gov/DCBS/
(503) 378-4100
Workers' Compensation Division
http://wcd.oregon.gov/
(800) 452-0288
Fraud Hotline: (800) 422-8778
Small Business Ombudsman: (503) 378-4209
Ombudsman for Injured Workers: (800) 927-1271, (503) 378-3351
Workers' Compensation Board
http://www.cbs.state.or.us/external/wcb/index.html
(503) 378-3308
Workers' Compensation Management-Labor Advisory Committee
http://www.oregon.gov/DCBS/MLAC/
(503) 947-7867
Ombudsman for Injured Workers
http://egov.oregon.gov/DCBS/OIW/index.shtml
(800) 927-1271, (503) 378-3351
Ombudsman for Small Business
http://egov.oregon.gov/DCBS/SBO/index.shtml
(503) 378-4209

SAIF Corporation
http://www.saif.com/
(800) 285-8525, (503) 373-8000

Pennsylvania

Bureau of Workers' Compensation
www.dli.state.pa.us/landi/cwp/view.asp?a=138&Q=58929&landiPNav=|#1026
(800) 482-2383, (717) 772-4447
State Workers' Insurance Fund
www.dli.state.pa.us/landi/cwp/view.asp?a=151&Q=58236&landiNavDLTEST=|852|1065|2548|
(570) 963-4635

Rhode Island

Workers' Compensation Court
http://www.courts.state.ri.us/workers/defaultnew-workers.htm
(401) 458-5000
Medical Advisory Board
http://www.courts.ri.gov/workers/medical/medical-advisory.htm
(401) 458-3460
Department of Labor and Training
http://www.dlt.ri.gov/
(401) 462-8000
Workers' Compensation Division
http://www.dlt.ri.gov/wc/
(401) 462-8100

South Carolina

Workers' Compensation Commission
http://www.wcc.state.sc.us/
(803) 737-5700
South Carolina State Accident Fund
http://www.myscgov.com/scoa/
(800) 521-6576, (803) 896-5800

South Dakota

Division of Labor and Management
http://www.state.sd.us/dol/dlm/dlm-home.htm
(605) 773-3681

Tennessee
Workers' Compensation Division
http://www.state.tn.us/labor-wfd/wcomp.html
(800) 332-2667 (within Tennessee), (615) 532-4812

Texas
Division of Workers' Compensation
http://www.tdi.state.tx.us/wc/indexwc.html
(512) 804-4000, Fax: (512) 804-4431,
Customer Relations/Services: (512) 804-4100 or 804-4636
Fraud Hotline: (888) 327-8818 or (512) 804-4703
Safety Violations Hotline: (800) 452-9595

Utah
Industrial Accidents Division
http://www.ind-com.state.ut.us/indacc/indacc.htm
(801) 530-6800
Workers' Compensation Fund of Utah
http://www.wcf-utah.com/
(800) 446-2667

Vermont
Workers' Compensation Division
http://159.105.83.167/WorkersCompensation/tabid/114/default.aspx
(802) 828-2286

Virginia
Virginia Workers' Compensation Commission
http://www.vwc.state.va.us
(877) 664-2566

Washington
Department of Labor and Industries
http://www.lni.wa.gov/
(800) 547-8367, (360) 902-4200
Workers' Comp Claims
http://www.lni.wa.gov/ClaimsIns/Claims/default.asp
Board of Industrial Insurance Appeals
http://www.biia.wa.gov/
(800) 442-0447, (360) 753-9646

West Virginia

BrickStreet Mutual Insurance Company
http://ww w.brickstreet.com/
Administrative Services: (888) 4-WV-COMP and (304) 926-3400
Insurance: (866) 45BRICK (452-7425) and (304) 926-3470
Workers' Compensation Industrial Council
http://www.wvinsurance.gov/wc/industrialcouncil/index.htm

Wisconsin

Workers' Compensation Division
http://www.dwd.state.wi.us/wc/default.htm
(608) 266-1340
Fraud (608) 261-8486
Workers' Compensation Advisory Council
http://www.dwd.state.wi.us/wc/councils/wcac/default.htm
(608) 266-6841
Wisconsin Labor and Industry Review Commission
http://www.dwd.state.wi.us/lirc/
(608) 266-9850

Wyoming

Workers' Safety and Compensation Division
http://wydoe.state.wy.us/doe.asp?ID=9
(307) 777-7159
To Report an Injury: (800) 870-8883 or (307) 777-7441
To Report Fraud: (888) 996-9226 or (307) 777-6552